365 French Fries Recipes

(365 French Fries Recipes - Volume 1)

Mary Correa

Copyright: Published in the United States by Mary Correa/ © MARY CORREA

Published on November, 24 2020

All rights reserved. No part of this publication may be reproduced, stored in retrieval system, copied in any form or by any means, electronic, mechanical, photocopying, recording or otherwise transmitted without written permission from the publisher. Please do not participate in or encourage piracy of this material in any way. You must not circulate this book in any format. MARY CORREA does not control or direct users' actions and is not responsible for the information or content shared, harm and/or actions of the book readers.

In accordance with the U.S. Copyright Act of 1976, the scanning, uploading and electronic sharing of any part of this book without the permission of the publisher constitute unlawful piracy and theft of the author's intellectual property. If you would like to use material from the book (other than just simply for reviewing the book), prior permission must be obtained by contacting the author at author@fetarecipes.com

Thank you for your support of the author's rights.

Content

CHAPTER 1: SWEET POTATO FRIES RECIPES 9

1. Baked Sweet & Spicy Sweet Potato Fries Recipe 9
2. Crispy Baked Sweet Potato Fries Recipe 9
3. Deep Fried Garden Vegetables Recipe 10
4. Fried Apples And Yams Recipe 10
5. Fried Sweet Potatoes Golden Hills Way Recipe 10
6. Fried Sweet Potatoes Recipe 11
7. Grilled Chicken Tikka Recipe Recipe 11
8. Lanas Accidental Healthy Vegan Ginger Stir Fry 12
9. Savory Baked Sweet Potato Fries Recipe .. 13
10. Simple Fried Sweet Potatoes Recipe 13
11. Southern Fried Sweet Potatoes Recipe 14
12. Special Fried Potatoes Recipe 14
13. Sweet And Spicy Pan Fried Pumpkin Recipe 15
14. Sweet Hot BBQ Potato Fries Recipe 15
15. Sweet Potato Chips (fries) Recipe 15
16. Sweet Potato Dip Recipe 16
17. Yummeh! Spiced Yam Fries Recipe 16

CHAPTER 2: BAKED FRIES RECIPES 16

18. American Steak Fries With Coriander Seeds Recipe 17
19. Avocado Fries With Sweet Chipotle Dip Recipe 17
20. BAKED VEGETABLE FRY Recipe 17
21. Bacon Cheese Fries Recipe 18
22. Baked Carrot Fries Recipe 18
23. Baked French Fries Recipe 18
24. Baked Homemade Chips Recipe 19
25. Baked Lemon Fries Recipe 19
26. Baked Sweet Potato Fries Recipe 19
27. Baked Yam And Purple Potato Fries Recipe 20
28. Baked Zucchini Fries Recipe 20
29. Breaded And Baked Fries Recipe 20
30. COWBOY FRIES Recipe 21
31. Cheese Fries With Taco Ranch Dipping Sauce Recipe 21
32. Chili Cheese Fries Recipe 21
33. Chipotle Fried Onion Rings Recipe 22
34. Crispy Oven Fries Recipe 22
35. Crispy Ranch Fries With Fry Sauce Recipe 22
36. Crispy Seasoned Oven Fries Recipe 23
37. Croque Madame Fried Egg Ham And Cheese Sandwich Recipe 23
38. Deen Family Fried Baked Potato Recipe .. 24
39. Easy No Fry Eggplant Parmesean Recipe 24
40. Easy Rosemary Fries Recipe 24
41. French Fried Onion Cornbread Recipe 25
42. French Fried Onions 25
43. French Fries With Cumin Ketchup Recipe 26
44. Fried Green Tomatoes Recipe 26
45. Fried Onion Potato Dish Recipe 26
46. Fried Zucchini Recipe 27
47. GARLIC DILL FRIES Recipe 27
48. GEMS FREEDOM FRIES Recipe 28
49. Garlic And Parmesan Fries Recipe 28
50. Garlicky Baked Fries Recipe 28
51. Greek Style Oven Fries Recipe 29
52. Green Bean Fries Recipe 29
53. Guiltless Steak Fries Recipe 29
54. Healthy Oven Fried Vegetables Recipe 30
55. Healthy Sweet Potato Fries W/ Dipping Sauce Recipe 30
56. Home Made French Fries Recipe 31
57. Homemade French Fries Recipe 31
58. Hooters Fries Recipe 31
59. Italian Veggie Cheese Burger Wsweet Potato Fries Recipe 32
60. Masala Chips Recipe 32
61. No Fry Eggplant Parmesean Recipe 32
62. No Guilt Oven Fries Recipe 33
63. OVEN BAKED CARROT FRIES Recipe 33
64. Onion And Cheese Crusted French Fries Recipe 34
65. Oven "fries" Recipe 34
66. Oven Baked Carrot Fries Recipe 34
67. Oven Baked Sweet Potato Fries Recipe 35
68. Oven Fried Cauliflower Recipe 35
69. Oven Fried Eggplant Recipe 35
70. Oven Fried Garlic Fries Recipe 36
71. Oven Fried Green Tomatoes Recipe 36

72. Oven Fried Parmesan Chicken Strips Recipe 36
73. Oven Fried Potatoes Recipe 37
74. Oven Fried Sweet Potatoes Recipe 37
75. Oven Fried Tex Mex Onion Rings Recipe 37
76. Oven Fried Zucchini Sticks Recipe 38
77. Oven Fries Recipe 38
78. Oven Home Fries With Peppers Onions Recipe 38
79. Oven Roasted Chili Cumin Fries Recipe .. 39
80. Oven Roasted Sweet Potato Fries Recipe 39
81. Oven Fried French Fries Recipe 39
82. Oven Fried Vegetables Recipe 40
83. Oven Fried Zucchini Sticks Recipe 40
84. Oven Fried Zucchini In A Crunchy Parmesan Crust Recipe 40
85. Parmesan Oven Fries Recipe 41
86. Pizza Fries Recipe 41
87. Ranch Tastic Butternut Fries With Bacon Recipe 41
88. Roasted Sweet Potato Fries Recipe 42
89. Rosemary Oven Fried Potatoes Recipe 43
90. Rumbledethumps Scottish Fried Veggies Recipe 43
91. Smash Fries Recipe 43
92. Spiced Country Fries Recipe 44
93. Spicy Baked Sweet Potato Fries Recipe 44
94. Spicy Buffalo Wing Style Fries Recipe 44
95. Spicy Steak Fries Recipe 44
96. Sweet Garlic Butternut Fries Recipe 45
97. Sweet Potato Fries Recipe 45
98. Sweet Potato Fries With Banana Ketchup Recipe 46
99. Sweet Potato Fries With Spicy Mayo Recipe 46
100. Sweet Potatoe Fries Recipe 46
101. Toaster Oven Fried Potatoes Recipe 47
102. Wet Fries Recipe 47
103. Whacky Baked Carrot And Turnip Fries Recipe 47
104. Yuppie Fries Recipe 48
105. Zucchini Oven Fries Recipe 48
106. Hot Jacky Yam Fries Recipe 49
107. Zucchini Fries Recipe 49

CHAPTER 3: HOME FRIES RECIPES 49

108. Best Home Fried Potatoes Recipe 49

109. Breakfast Home Fries Recipe 50
110. Chicago Style Home Fries Recipe 50
111. Deep Fried Home Made Potato Chips Recipe 50
112. Elaines Home Fries With A Plus Recipe ... 51
113. Home Fried New Potatoes Recipe 51
114. Home Fried Potatoes Recipe 51
115. Home Fries 1 Recipe 52
116. Home Fries Made Easy Recipe 52
117. Indian Home Fries Recipe 52
118. JKs Home Fries Recipe 53
119. Light Breakfast Potatoes Recipe 53
120. Potato Frittata From Mrs. Dash Recipe ... 53
121. Smokey Saucy Homefries Recipe 54
122. Spicy Diner Style Home Fries Recipe 54
123. Sweet Potato Home Fries Recipe 55
124. Truffled Home Fries Recipe 55

CHAPTER 4: AWESOME FRENCH FRIES RECIPES 56

125. A And W Sauce For Coney Syle Fries Recipe 56
126. Air Fryer French Fries Recipe 56
127. Almanzo Wilders Fried Apples N Onions Recipe 57
128. Antique Recipe For Fried Potatoes Recipe 57
129. Asian Crisp Fried Noodles And Chili Vegetables Recipe 57
130. Asian Stir Fried Broccoli Recipe 58
131. Asparagus And Mushroom Stir Fry Recipe 58
132. Authentic Chinese Fried Rice Recipe 58
133. Baby Bok Choy Stir Fry Recipe 59
134. Bacon Fried Green Beans Recipe 59
135. Bacon Fried Rice Recipe 60
136. Bacon And Cheddar Fries Recipe 60
137. Batter Fried Zucchini Flowers Recipe 60
138. Bea Coles French Fried Onion Rings Recipe 61
139. Bears Fried Asparagus Recipe 61
140. Beer Battered French Fries Recipe 61
141. Best Fried Egg Sandwich Recipe 62
142. Blue Cheese Fried Potatoes Recipe 62
143. Bok Choy And Crimini Stir Fry Recipe 63
144. Broccoli And Cauliflower Stir Fry Recipe . 63
145. Buttermilk Fried Corn Recipe 63

146. Buttermilk Fried Green Beans Recipe 64
147. CAMPFIRE FRENCH FRIES Recipe 64
148. Cajun Fried Okra With Bacon Recipe 65
149. Caribbean Stir Fried Shrimp Recipe 65
150. Cauliflower Potato Fry Recipe 66
151. Chicken Fried Rice Recipe 66
152. Chicken And Sausage Sandwiches With Fried Bell Peppers Recipe 66
153. Chili Fried Potatoes Recipe 67
154. Chili Fried Onion Rings Recipe 67
155. Chinese Style Fried Rice Recipe 68
156. Coconut Fried Rice Recipe 68
157. Copycat Kentucky Fried Chicken Potato Wedges Recipe 69
158. Country Store Fried Apples Recipe 69
159. Creamy Cheesey Confetti Fried Corn With Bacon Recipe 70
160. Creamy Fried Corn Recipe 70
161. Crispy Cajun Fries Recipe 71
162. Crispy Coated Cajun Fries Recipe 71
163. Crispy Fried Eggplant Recipe 71
164. Cumin Ketchup And Chili Salted French Fries Recipe 72
165. Dads Fried Cabbage Recipe 72
166. Dal Fry Recipe 72
167. Dans Fried Green Tomatoes Recipe 73
168. Deep Fried Asparagus Or Okra Recipe 73
169. Deep Fried Chicken Drumlets Recipe 74
170. Deep Fried Corn On The Cob Recipe 74
171. Deep Fried Mac And Cheese Recipe 75
172. Deep Fried Mars Bar Recipe 75
173. Deep Fried Okra Recipe 75
174. Deep Fried Vegetables Recipe 76
175. Deep Fried Oyster Po Boy Sandwiches With Spicy Remoulade Sauce Recipe 76
176. Definitive Fries Recipe 77
177. Delightful Tofu Fried Rice Recipe 77
178. Easy Stir Fried Spinach Ci Recipe 78
179. Elaines BBQ Stir Fry Recipe 78
180. Elaines Chinese Fried Rice Recipe 79
181. Elaines Pepper Stir Fry Recipe 79
182. Elaines Stir Fried Vegetable Medley With Port Wine Sauce Recipe 80
183. FRENCH FRIED SKUNK Recipe 80
184. FRIED CUCUMBERS Recipe 80
185. FRIED FANTAIL SHRIMP IN BEER BATTER Recipe 81
186. FRIED GREEN TOMATOES Recipe 81
187. FRIED TOMATO SANDWICHES Recipe 81
188. Fabulous Fried Cabbage Recipe 82
189. Faux Fried Chicken Nuggets Vegetarianvegan Recipe 82
190. Franks Low Fat French Fries Recipe 83
191. French Fried Cauliflower Recipe 83
192. French Fried Onion Rings Recipe 83
193. French Fried Potatoes Recipe 83
194. French Fried Zuchini Recipe 84
195. French Fry Eggplant Recipe 84
196. French Fry Poboy Recipe 85
197. French Fried Potato Skewers Recipe 85
198. Fresh Corn And Veggie Summer Stir Fry Recipe 85
199. Fried Apple Jacks Recipe 86
200. Fried Apples And Onions Recipe 86
201. Fried Apples Recipe 86
202. Fried Apples With Bacon Recipe 87
203. Fried Apples Classic And Deluxe Recipe .. 87
204. Fried Artichokes Recipe 87
205. Fried Asparagus Recipe 88
206. Fried Baby Artichokes Recipe 88
207. Fried Bananas Kluay Tod Thailand Recipe 89
208. Fried Bell Pepper Rings With Horseradish Dip Recipe 89
209. Fried Bologna Sandwich Recipe 90
210. Fried Cabbage Recipe 90
211. Fried Cabbage With Bacon Onion And Garlic Recipe 91
212. Fried Catfish Sandwiches With Spicy Mayonnaise Recipe 91
213. Fried Cauliflower Recipe 91
214. Fried Chocolate Tofu Recipe 92
215. Fried Corn From Texas Recipe 92
216. Fried Corn Off The Cob Recipe 92
217. Fried Corn On The Cob Recipe 93
218. Fried Corn Recipe 93
219. Fried Corn Tennessee Style Recipe 94
220. Fried Dill Pickles Recipe 94
221. Fried Dogs And Sausages In BBQ Sauce Recipe 94
222. Fried Fish In A Pocket Recipe 95
223. Fried Fish Sandwich Recipe 95
224. Fried Fish Tacos Recipe 96

225. Fried Green Beans Recipe 96
226. Fried Green Beans Dry Recipe 96
227. Fried Green Tomato Slices Recipe 97
228. Fried Green Tomatoes N More Recipe 97
229. Fried Green Tomatoes With Crabmeat Remoulade Recipe 97
230. Fried Haloumi Lemon Dressing Recipe ... 98
231. Fried Hot Dog Sandwich Recipe 98
232. Fried Okra Recipe 99
233. Fried Peanut Butter And Banana Sandwich Recipe 99
234. Fried Peanut Butter And Banana Sandwiches Recipe 99
235. Fried Pickles Recipe 100
236. Fried Plantains Recipe 100
237. Fried Potato Patties With Dry Shrimp Recipe 100
238. Fried Potato Salad Recipe 101
239. Fried Potatoes With Hoisin Sauce Recipe 101
240. Fried Potatoes With Onions Recipe 102
241. Fried Potatoes With Tartar Sauce Recipe 102
242. Fried Shrimp PoBoy Recipe 102
243. Fried Spinach Patties Recipe 103
244. Fried Squid Po Boy With Avocado And Black Chile Oil Recipe 103
245. Fried Sweet And Sour Potatoes Recipe ... 104
246. Fried Tofu With Peanut Recipe 104
247. Fried Tofu With A Special Dipping Sauce Recipe 104
248. Fried Whole Okra Recipe 105
249. Fried Yellow Squash Recipe 105
250. Fried Yucca And Mojo Recipe 106
251. Fried Cucumbers Recipe 106
252. Fried Peanut Butter And Bannan Sandwich Recipe 106
253. Fry Free Samosas Recipe 107
254. Fry Bread Tacos Recipe 107
255. Fryed Cabbage Recipe 108
256. Garlic Fried Asparagus Recipe................. 108
257. Garlic Fried Potatoes Recipe 108
258. Garlic And Pepper Stir Fry Recipe 109
259. Garlicky Stir Fried Shanghai Bok Choy Recipe 109
260. Ginger Fried Rice Recipe 109
261. Glazed Teriyaki Chicken Stir Fry Sub Recipe 110
262. Gluten Free Fried Eggplant Recipe 110
263. Grandmas Fried Potatoes Recipe 111
264. Greek Fries Recipe 111
265. Green Banana Fries Recipe 112
266. Green Beans With Almonds And Fried Onions Recipe 112
267. Grilled Fiesta Fries Recipe 113
268. Grilled Steak Fries Recipe 113
269. Harvest Cider Poutine Recipe 113
270. Herbfarm Roasted Asparagus Salad With Fried Sage Recipe 114
271. Iron Skillet Fried Squash Recipe 115
272. KFC Original Fried Chicken Recipe 115
273. Kai Lan Stir Fry Recipe 115
274. Lanas Country Cream Gravy For Fried Chicken More Recipe 116
275. Leahs French Fried Onion Circles Recipe 116
276. Lemony Chickpea Stir Fry Recipe 117
277. Lone Star Bacon And Cheddar Fries Recipe 117
278. MIMMIES FRIED APPLE PIES Recipe 117
279. Maple Fried Apples Recipe 118
280. Maw Maws Fried Green Tomatoes Recipe 118
281. Mexican Fried Rice Recipe 119
282. Mexican Stir Fry Recipe............................. 119
283. Moms Winter FryUp Recipe 120
284. Mountain Country Fried Green Onions Recipe 120
285. Multi Flavored Thai Fried Rice Recipe ... 121
286. Mushroom Chili Fry Recipe 121
287. Not Really Fried Potatoes Recipe 122
288. OVEN BAKED COTTAGE FRIES Recipe 122
289. Oil Boiled Potato Planks Recipe 123
290. Okie Fried Okra Recipe 123
291. Okra With Onions And Tomatoes Fried Bhindi Recipe 123
292. Oriental Veggie TVP Fried Rice Recipe. 124
293. Outbacks Aussie Fries And Dip Recipe . 124
294. Pad Thai Fried Noodles Recipe 125
295. Pan Fried Cabbage Recipe 125
296. Pan Fried Tofu With Yoghurt Sauce And Soy Puffs Recipe 126
297. Panisses Chickpea Flour Fries Recipe 126

298. Paula Deens Fried Onion Rings With Chili Sauce Recipe 127
299. Portobello Fries Recipe 127
300. Quick And Easy Fried Rice Recipe 127
301. Quick Vegie Stir Fry With Hokkien Noodles Recipe 128
302. Raw Broccoli And Sprout Stir Fry Recipe 128
303. Rosemary Roasted Oven Fries Recipe 129
304. SO CAL FRIED CORN Recipe 129
305. Savory Fried Polenta Recipe 129
306. Scrambled Egg And Potato Fry Recipe .. 130
307. Sesame Asparagus And Carrots Stir Fry Recipe 130
308. Sesame Tofu Stir Fry Recipe 130
309. Shanghai Pan Fried Noodles With Cabbage And Pork Recipe 131
310. Southern Fried Corn Recipe 131
311. Southern Fried Cream And Butter Corn Recipe 132
312. Southern Fried Okra Recipe 132
313. Southwestern Fried Corn Recipe 132
314. SoyaBean Fry Recipe 133
315. Spiced Fried Potatoes Recipe 133
316. Spicy Fried Green Tomatoes Recipe 134
317. Spicy Fried Spinach Recipe 134
318. Spicy Stir Fried Eggplant Recipe 134
319. Stir Fried Asparagus Recipe 135
320. Stir Fried Asparagus With Ginger Garlic And Basil Recipe 135
321. Stir Fried Asparagus With Sesame Seeds Recipe 136
322. Stir Fried Broccoli Red Onion And Red Pepper Recipe 136
323. Stir Fried Cabbage Recipe 136
324. Stir Fried Carrots With Cumin And Lime Recipe 137
325. Stir Fried Green Beans With Coconut Recipe 137
326. Stir Fried Rice Recipe 137
327. Stir Fried Sesame Asparagus Recipe 138
328. Stir Fry Garlic Spinach With Anchovies Recipe 138
329. Stir Fryed Cabbage With Italian Sausage Recipe 139
330. Stir Fry Chive Recipe 139
331. Stir Fry Broccoli Florets With Garlic And Roasted Red Peppers Recipe 140
332. Stir Fried Tofu In Black Bean Sauce Recipe 140
333. Stir Fried Bok Choy Recipe 140
334. Stir Fried Broccoli Raab Recipe Broccoli Rapa Strascinati Recipe 141
335. Stir Fried Cabbage Recipe 141
336. Stir Fried Eggplant Recipe 142
337. Stir Fried Rice And Dal Recipe 142
338. Stir Fry Bean Spout Recipe 143
339. Sugar Snap Peas And Salami Stir Fry Recipe 143
340. Summer Stir Fry Recipe 143
341. Sweet And Sour Stir Fry Vegetables Recipe 144
342. TWISTED STIR FRY Recipe 145
343. Teriyaki Vegtable Fried Rice Recipe 145
344. Tofu Cashew Stir Fry Recipe 145
345. Tofu Veggie And Almond Stir Fry Recipe 146
346. Tofu Veggie Stir Fry Recipe 146
347. Toor Dal Fry Recipe 147
348. Turkish Style Fried Mussels Midye Tava Recipe 147
349. Tyler Florences Fried Green Tomatoes Recipe 147
350. Ultimate Comfort Food Fried Potatoes With Eggs Recipe 148
351. Vegetable Fried Rice Recipe 148
352. Vegetable Mushroom Fried Rice Recipe 149
353. Vegetable Stir Fry Recipe 149
354. Vegetables Stir Fry Vegetarian Recipe 149
355. Vegetables Stir Fry Recipe 150
356. Vegetarian Fried Rice Recipe 150
357. Vegetarian Rice Vermicelly Stir Fry Recipe 151
358. Veggie Fried Rice Recipe 151
359. Veggie Sun Fry Recipe 152
360. Chinese Deep Fried Green Beans Recipe 152
361. Fried Pies Recipe 152
362. Maori Fried Bread Recipe 153
363. Pan Fried Green Beans Recipe 153
364. Sweet Fried Chicken Recipe 153
365. Vegetarian Fried Rice Recipe 154

INDEX **155**

CONCLUSION..158

Chapter 1: Sweet Potato Fries Recipes

***

1. Baked Sweet & Spicy Sweet Potato Fries Recipe

Serving: 4 | Prep: | Cook: 30mins | Ready in:

Ingredients

- 3 sweet potatoes- washed & scrubbed
- 3 tbsp dark brown sugar
- 1 tbsp cayenne pepper
- 1/2-1 tbsp smokey paprika
- 1/2 tbsp extra virgin olive oil
- coarse black pepper- few grinds
- salt- to taste
- 1 tbsp dark brown sugar (for garnishing)
- few sprigs of chive- finely chopped
- PAM olive oil flavor

Direction

- 1. Preheat oven to 425. In a small bowl whisk together oil, pepper, cayenne pepper and paprika.
- 2. Cut the potatoes into strips (french-fries size) and lay them on a baking sheet. Pour oil mixture over potatoes and toss until evenly coated. Spray with some pam and make sure each strip is hitting the baking sheet. Sprinkle with brown sugar evenly over potatoes.
- 3. Bake for 30-35 minutes until darker and crispy, tossing every 10 minutes. Remove and cool. While cooling, sprinkle with remaining brown sugar and garnish with chives. Serve with your favourite dipping sauce- I recommend Honey Mustard YUM

2. Crispy Baked Sweet Potato Fries Recipe

Serving: 0 | Prep: | Cook: 25mins | Ready in:

Ingredients

- 1 small sweet potato per serving
- cornstarch
- olive oil
- seasonings of choice - I used salt & pepper

Direction

- Peel sweet potatoes and cut into uniform pieces about the size of medium fries (not thick steak fries or shoestrings). Let soak in a bowl of water for 1-4 hours (not mandatory but recommended).
- Preheat oven to 425F.
- Put about 1 tsp. of cornstarch in a plastic bag and add pieces equaling about 1 potato. Twist the top of the bag so it forms a sort of balloon and shake around to distribute cornstarch. The potato pieces should be lightly dusted with cornstarch all over. Add more if needed.
- Place dusted potato pieces onto a non-stick baking sheet in one layer, leaving a bit of room between. Repeat with remaining sweet potato.
- Drizzle olive oil over potatoes - starting with about 1 tbsp. Season as desired. Use your hands to distribute oil & make sure they're well coated. Add more oil as needed.
- Rearrange on baking sheet, making sure to leave room between each one. The more space they have the crispier they'll get.
- Place in oven and bake for 15 minutes, or until desired crispness is reached.
- These are delicious served with a variety of dipping sauces, from something as simple as honey to a Sriracha mayo or Horseradish Dipping Sauce.

3. Deep Fried Garden Vegetables Recipe

Serving: 6 | Prep: | Cook: | Ready in:

Ingredients

- Batter
- 1-1/2 cups Pillsbury BEST® All Purpose flour, divided
- 2 tablespoons cornstarch
- 3/4 teaspoon baking powder
- 1/2 teaspoon salt
- 1/4 teaspoon pepper
- 1 cup milk
- 1 egg, lightly beaten
- Crisco® All-vegetable shortening, for deep frying
- vegetables
- Choose any combination of the following:
- 1/4 inch slices zucchini
- 1/4 inch trimmed green beans
- large mushrooms
- 1/8 inch slices carrot
- 1/8 inch slices sweet potato
- 1/2 inch strips green or red bell pepper

Direction

- 1. Combine 1 cup flour, cornstarch, baking powder, salt, pepper, milk, and egg in medium bowl. Stir until smooth. Refrigerate 30 minutes.
- 2. Heat 2 or 3 inches Crisco to 365°F in deep fryer or deep saucepan. Heat oven to 200°F.
- 3. Place 1/2 cup flour in paper or plastic bag. Add vegetables a few at a time. Shake to coat. Shake off excess flour.
- 4. Dip vegetables, a few at a time, in batter. Let excess drip off. Fry in shortening heated to 365°F. Fry 3 or 4 minutes or until golden brown. Turn as needed for even browning. Drain on paper towels.
- 5. Place fried vegetables on heatproof plate, or pan in 200°F oven to keep warm until all vegetables are fried. Sprinkle lightly with salt. Serve immediately.

4. Fried Apples And Yams Recipe

Serving: 4 | Prep: | Cook: 25mins | Ready in:

Ingredients

- 1 – 29 oz. can yams
- 2 med. Fugi apples
- ½ cup dark brown sugar
- ½ stick butter or margarine

Direction

- Prep:
- Core and chop apples. You want the apples to be bite size, but not too small.
- Cook:
- In a 4 qt. saucepan or an iron skillet (I find that the dish tastes better if cooked in an iron skillet), melt butter and sauté apples, don't let them get too mushy. Add yams, breaking into bite size pieces. Add brown sugar and let the mixture cook until the yams have softened and mashed together, don't mash them yourself, they will do this on their own. Stir mixture often. Cook for about 20 - 25 minutes on medium heat.

5. Fried Sweet Potatoes Golden Hills Way Recipe

Serving: 8 | Prep: | Cook: 10mins | Ready in:

Ingredients

- Fresh sweet potatoes, peeled and sliced (uncooked)
- At least 1 stick butter or margarine
- salt
- sugar

Direction

- Melt butter or margarine in a large skillet. Add sweet potatoes. Fry potatoes, stirring as necessary. Cover and continue cooking stirring occasionally. When about half done, add ½ to 1 cup sugar and ½ t. salt (for a full skillet).

6. Fried Sweet Potatoes Recipe

Serving: 8 | Prep: | Cook: 20mins | Ready in:

Ingredients

- 6 sweet potatoes, peeled
- 1/2 cup butter
- 2 cups packed light brown sugar

Direction

- Bring a large pot of water to a boil. Add peeled sweet potatoes and boil for about 4 mins. Remove from water and cut into 1/2 inch slices.
- Melt butter in a large frying pan over medium heat. Stir in brown sugar until dissolved, adding more butter if necessary. Add sweet potatoes, fry until golden brown and fork tender, turning occasionally. Serve hot and ENJOY!

7. Grilled Chicken Tikka Recipe Recipe

Serving: 1 | Prep: | Cook: 1mins | Ready in:

Ingredients

- The word tikka means bits, pieces or chunks in Indian. chicken Tikka is an easy-to-cook dish in which chicken chunks are marinated in special spices and then grilled on skewers. This is one of India's most popular dishes. chicken Tikka can also be made into chicken Tikka Masala, where the grilled chicken pieces are added to a tasty gravy.
- Traditionally, chicken tikka is baked in a clay oven called a tandoor, which basically makes this recipe a boneless chicken version of the Indian dish tandoori chicken. Since most of us don't have a tandoor, using a grill or the oven is a good alternative.
- You need to plan ahead when making this dish as the chicken should sit in the yogurt and spice marinade overnight. Also, if using wooden skewers, make sure to soak them for 10 minutes in water before threading the chicken (this keeps the wood from burning). Enjoy this chicken tikka with warm naan, or use to make chicken tikka masala.
- What You'll Need
- 1 cup finely chopped fresh coriander (cilantro) leaves
- 2 tbsp. ginger paste
- 3 tbsp. garlic paste
- 3 to 4 tbsp. garam masala
- 6 peppercorns or 2 dry red chilies
- 1/2 tsp. orange food coloring
- 1 cup fresh unsweetened yogurt (should not be sour)
- 2 1/4 lbs. (1 kg.) skinless and boneless chicken breast or thigh, cut into 2-inch chunks
- 1 large onion, cut into very thin rings
- 3 tbsp. freshly squeezed lime or lemon juice
- Lime or lemon wedges for garnish
- 1 tsp. chaat masala (available at most Indian groceries)
- How to Make It
- Grind the chopped coriander (keep some aside for garnishing) and all other marinade ingredients (except yogurt) into a smooth paste in a food processor.
- Pour the spice mix into a large bowl and add yogurt. Mix well. Add the chicken pieces and mix well. Cover the bowl and refrigerate. Allow to marinate overnight.
- Thread the chicken onto skewers and keep ready.

- Preheat your oven or grill to medium-high (400 F/200 C).
- Place the skewers on the grill or in your oven with a tray underneath to catch drippings. Roast open until the chicken is browned on all sides and tender, about 12 to 15 minutes.
- Remove from skewers and put the chicken on a plate.
- Put the onion rings in a separate bowl and squeeze lime juice over them. Sprinkle the chaat masala over and mix well so the onions are fully coated.
- Garnish the chicken Tikka with these onion rings and serve with naa

Direction

- The word tikka means bits, pieces or chunks in Indian. Chicken Tikka is an easy-to-cook dish in which chicken chunks are marinated in special spices and then grilled on skewers. This is one of India's most popular dishes. Chicken Tikka can also be made into Chicken Tikka Masala, where the grilled chicken pieces are added to a tasty gravy.
- Traditionally, chicken tikka is baked in a clay oven called a tandoor, which basically makes this recipe a boneless chicken version of the Indian dish tandoori chicken. Since most of us don't have a tandoor, using a grill or the oven is a good alternative.
- You need to plan ahead when making this dish as the chicken should sit in the yogurt and spice marinade overnight. Also, if using wooden skewers, make sure to soak them for 10 minutes in water before threading the chicken (this keeps the wood from burning). Enjoy this chicken tikka with warm naan, or use to make chicken tikka masala.
- What You'll Need
- 1 cup finely chopped fresh coriander (cilantro) leaves
- 2 tbsp. ginger paste
- 3 tbsp. garlic paste
- 3 to 4 tbsp. garam masala
- 6 peppercorns or 2 dry red chilies
- 1/2 tsp. orange food colouring

- 1 cup fresh unsweetened yogurt (should not be sour)
- 2 1/4 lbs. (1 kg.) skinless and boneless chicken breast or thigh, cut into 2-inch chunks
- 1 large onion, cut into very thin rings
- 3 tbsp. freshly squeezed lime or lemon juice
- Lime or lemon wedges for garnish
- 1 tsp. chaat masala (available at most Indian groceries)
- How to Make It
- Grind the chopped coriander (keep some aside for garnishing) and all other marinade ingredients (except yogurt) into a smooth paste in a food processor.
- Pour the spice mix into a large bowl and add yogurt. Mix well. Add the chicken pieces and mix well. Cover the bowl and refrigerate. Allow to marinate overnight.
- Thread the chicken onto skewers and keep ready.
- Preheat your oven or grill to medium-high (400 F/200 C).
- Place the skewers on the grill or in your oven with a tray underneath to catch drippings. Roast open until the chicken is browned on all sides and tender, about 12 to 15 minutes.
- Remove from skewers and put the chicken on a plate.
- Put the onion rings in a separate bowl and squeeze lime juice over them. Sprinkle the chaat masala over and mix well so the onions are fully coated.
- Garnish the Chicken Tikka with these onion rings and serve with naan

8. Lanas Accidental Healthy Vegan Ginger Stir Fry

Serving: 4 | Prep: | Cook: 10mins | Ready in:

Ingredients

- 1 tablespoon cornstarch
- 1 clove garlic, crushed

- 1 teaspoons chopped fresh ginger root
- 3-4 Tbs. EVOO divided =EVOO is extra virgin olive oil
- 1 1/2 cups cut white or other sweet potato
- (I had white and they were incredible)
- 1/2 cup chopped carrots
- 1 cup yellow or other squash rounds
- 3/4 cup red bell pepper
- 1 to 2 tablespoons low sodium soy sauce
- 4 tablespoons water
- 1 cup chopped onions
- salt and fresh pepper to taste (if desired)

Direction

- In a bowl, blend cornstarch, garlic, and 2 tablespoons EVOO until cornstarch is dissolved.
- Add 1 teaspoon ginger; mix.
- To heated skillet or wok (with EVOO), add carrots, sweet potatoes, peppers, squash, (onions last).
- Add water as needed.
- Cook vegetables in EVOO (to your desired crispness level), stirring constantly to prevent burning.
- Stir in soy sauce and water.
- Add sauce (mixed) and cook for a couple more minutes.
- Cook in medium heat, stirring very often, until vegetables are tender but still crisp.

9. Savory Baked Sweet Potato Fries Recipe

Serving: 0 | Prep: | Cook: 45mins | Ready in:

Ingredients

- 4 medium sweet potatoes, cut in thin sticks
- 2 Tblsps olive oil
- 1/2 tsp paprika
- 1/2 tsp lemon pepper
- salt to taste

Direction

- Preheat oven to 400°. Peel and cut the sweet potatoes into thin sticks resembling French fries. Cover with water and boil for 4 minutes or until slightly tender.
- Mix the olive oil and seasonings in a medium bowl and add the potato sticks, tossing to coat.
- Spray a baking sheet lightly with non-stick cooking spray. Spread potato sticks evenly on the baking sheet and bake for 30 minutes, turning once or twice during baking.

10. Simple Fried Sweet Potatoes Recipe

Serving: 68 | Prep: | Cook: 15mins | Ready in:

Ingredients

- This is a recipe for simple pan fried sweet potatoes with butter.
- Ingredients
- 2 pounds large sweet potatoes, sliced 1/8-inch thick
- 5 tablespoons un-salted butter

Direction

- Preparation:
- Heat butter in a large heavy skillet. When butter is melted, add the sliced sweet potatoes. Cover and lower heat. After about 5 minutes, uncover and turn the sweet potatoes with a spatula. Cover and continue to cook until tender, another 5 minutes. Check frequently to make sure the potatoes don't burn. Uncover and continue to cook for a few minutes, to glaze the potatoes. Serve hot.
- You can also peel the potatoes and boil for about 5 min. then slice 1/4 to 1/2 inch thick and sauté in a melted brown sugar and butter mixture till done.

- The butter would work better for higher heat if it was clarified (heated and all particles that don't melt removed, just pure liquid left).
- You can add cinnamon, brown sugar or any number of spices. I am going to top mine with candied pecans, but my wife likes marshmallows and cashews on her sweet potatoes. I also like a little maple syrup or Molasses added.
- I made these for thanksgiving and I made a simple syrup(1 to 1 sugar and water) added a small amount of cinnamon and a little maple syrup and about a tsp. of vanilla extract with about half a stick of un-salted butter. I let syrup thicken and covered the yams about half way up. I used 4 large yams I sliced them about 1/2 thick and layered them standing on the edge in a large baking dish. I let them cook awhile and then put on the glazed pecans this was a very much talked about dish at the meal. I did boil yams about 5 min. before slicing.

11. Southern Fried Sweet Potatoes Recipe

Serving: 4 | Prep: | Cook: 15mins | Ready in:

Ingredients

- 3 good sized sweet potatoes
- 3 tbs. butter

Direction

- Peel and slice the potatoes from end to end about 1/3 inch thick.
- Wash the potatoes.
- Melt the butter in a large skillet, I prefer an iron skillet.
- Put the potatoes in the hot butter and fry, stirring occasionally.
- They will be done when tender, about 15 minutes.

12. Special Fried Potatoes Recipe

Serving: 4 | Prep: | Cook: 25mins | Ready in:

Ingredients

- Four med red or regular potatoes
- two med sweet potatoes
- small onion (1/3 cup chopped)
- 4-5 cloves of garlic
- 2-3 tsp. dillweed
- salt and pepper to taste
- olive oil (enough to coat pan well but not drench the potatoes) or cooking oil of your choice

Direction

- Peel (or don't) the red potatoes, peel (recommended) sweet potatoes. Cut into quarters, then into smaller chunks.
- *Also, keep in mind that sweet potato cooks quicker than regular russets or reds, they may tend to get mushy. To prevent this from happening if you like, you may add the sweet potato about 5 to 7 minutes after the other ingredients start cooking. I like them mushy myself and I just throw them all in at once.
- Chop garlic and onion (I like to use my food processor for speed)
- Add potatoes, garlic, and onion to preheated, oiled skillet.
- Toss around the vegetables to coat it in the oil.
- Sprinkle half the dill weed, salt, and pepper on top and mix the spices in the potatoes.
- Then add rest of spices and toss again.
- Let the potatoes cook in the skillet with a lid, turning occasionally to prevent burning.
- Cook with lid on for about 10-15 minutes then remove lid and allow potatoes to brown and cook until finished

13. Sweet And Spicy Pan Fried Pumpkin Recipe

Serving: 2 | Prep: | Cook: 10mins | Ready in:

Ingredients

- 2 cups pumpkin, in 2" cubes (can substitute butternut squash, or sweet potato!)
- 2 tbsp sweet chili sauce
- salt

Direction

- Peel and cube fresh, raw pumpkin and place in a microwave-safe dish.
- Cover with plastic wrap, or moist tea towel and steam until just tender (1-2 minutes)
- Spray a large skillet with non-stick or oil spray and warm over medium heat.
- Place steamed pumpkin cubes in an even layer across the bottom of the skillet and allow to pan-fry until lightly browned on the underside.
- Flip cubes over and scatter sweet chili sauce over top, gently pushing around the cubes until decently coated.
- Continue to fry until underside is browned.
- Serve hot!
- Note: A few folks have asked about Sweet Chili Sauce--It's a sugary/spicy red chili sauce from Thailand. You can find it most American/Canadian stores in the Asian aisle under the brand names "Thai Kitchen" or "Taste of Thai." Aussies and Brits should be familiar with this sauce.
- Nutrition: 60 Calories; Fat Free; 412mg Sodium; 13.5g Carbs; .6g Dietary Fibre; 7.6g Sugars; 1.2g Protein; 171% Vitamin A; 2% Calcium; 17% Vitamin C; 5% Iron

14. Sweet Hot BBQ Potato Fries Recipe

Serving: 4 | Prep: | Cook: 10mins | Ready in:

Ingredients

- • 2 pounds sweet potatoes or yams, peeled, cut lengthwise into 1/2-inch-thick slices, each slice cut lengthwise into 1/2-inch-wide strips
- • 1/4 cup extra-virgin olive oil
- • 1 tablespoon chopped fresh rosemary
- • 1 tablespoon (packed) golden brown sugar
- • 1 teaspoon garlic powder
- • 1/4 teaspoon cayenne pepper
- • Additional olive oil

Direction

- Prepare barbecue (medium heat).
- Place potatoes in 13x9x2-inch baking dish. Add 1/4 cup oil, chopped fresh rosemary, brown sugar, garlic powder, and cayenne pepper to potatoes. Sprinkle potatoes with salt and pepper; toss to coat.
- Brush grill lightly with oil. Place potatoes on grill, spacing about 1 inch apart. Grill until potatoes are tender and slightly charred, turning occasionally, about 10 minutes total.
- Transfer potatoes to bowl, season to taste with salt and pepper, and serve.

15. Sweet Potato Chips (fries) Recipe

Serving: 4 | Prep: | Cook: 30mins | Ready in:

Ingredients

- 2 lb. sweet potatoes, peeled, cut into wedges
- 1/4 C. olive oil
- 1 tbsp. Jamaican jerk seasoning
- 1/2 tsp. crushed red pepper flakes
- 1 clove garlic, crushes
- Coarse sea salt and black pepper to taste

- 4 sheets of heavy duty foil, approx 18x20

Direction

- Place your peeled, wedged potatoes in a large bowl.
- In a smaller bowl add olive oil, seasoning, pepper flakes and garlic, whisk well and pour over potatoes, turning them to coat evenly.
- Place an even amount of potatoes in each packet, and seal each packet tightly.
- The best part about this dish is you can cook it three different ways, in the camp fire directly, on your camp stove or in your oven of your camp trailer, I have done all three and they all turn out great. If using an oven cook at 400' F and bake 25-30 minutes until tender. If using camp stove or fire, keep turning packets for even cooking, you want to cook it at the hottest spot possible for maximum crispness.
- Serve with BBQ chicken packets and enjoy!

16. Sweet Potato Dip Recipe

Serving: 0 | Prep: | Cook: 2mins |Ready in:

Ingredients

- mayo
- jelly
- onion, finely chopped

Direction

- I can only eat those oh-so-filling sweet potato fries with this dip: mayo, onion and jelly. I have used different ones. Today it is guava. Red onion or white- important. I wonder if the kids will eat it...

17. Yummeh! Spiced Yam Fries Recipe

Serving: 4 | Prep: | Cook: 1hours |Ready in:

Ingredients

- 1 yam (Or sweet potato, whichever, I can never tell them apart)
- 2 Tbsp extra virgin olive oil, separated
- 2 Tbsp dark brown sugar
- sea salt, cinnamon, onion and chili powder, smoked paprika and some parsley for garnish.

Direction

- Preheat the oven for 400 F
- Wash the yam, then with a sharp knife, cut the yam into shoestring fries. You can cut them into steak fries too but I like the shoestring ones better. Put 1 Tbsp. of the oil into the bottom of an oven-safe roasting pan, spreading it around a little. Pile all your cut fries in there and drizzle the other Tbsp. all over the top of the fries. Put the brown sugar and however much spices you want over it too. With your hand or a pair of tongs, mix it all around until the fries are evenly coated with everything.
- Roast at 400 F for a half hour, take them out and mix them all up again. Not with your hands this time, unless you want to make a trip to the emergency burn ward. Once they're mixed up again, put them back into the oven to continue roasting for another half hour.
- Ding! After that, they'll be done and you'll have the most awesome side dish ever!!!

Chapter 2: Baked Fries Recipes

***

18. American Steak Fries With Coriander Seeds Recipe

Serving: 6 | Prep: | Cook: 40mins | Ready in:

Ingredients

- 2 pounds unpeeled russet potatoes, scrubbed, cut lengthwise into 1/2-inch thick sticks
- 2 tablespoons olive oil
- 1 1/2 teaspoons coriander seeds, cracked
- 1 teaspoon dried thyme
- kosher salt

Direction

- Preheat oven to 450F degrees.
- Spray large rimmed baking sheet with non-stick spray.
- Toss potatoes with olive oil, coriander seeds and thyme in large bowl.
- Transfer to prepared sheet and spread in single layer.
- Sprinkle with salt and pepper.
- Place in top third of oven and bake until golden, occasionally turning with spatula (about 40 minutes).
- Season to taste with kosher salt and serve.

19. Avocado Fries With Sweet Chipotle Dip Recipe

Serving: 2 | Prep: | Cook: 35mins | Ready in:

Ingredients

- 3 Firm Avocados
- 2 Eggs
- 1/2 Cup Oat Flour (Or – almond Meal)
- Salt and Pepper
- ~~~~~~~~~~~~~~~~~~~~~
- Skinny Chipotle Dip

- 1/4 Cup Non-Fat Greek Yogurt (I like Fage 0%)
- 2 Tbsp Low-Fat Cottage cheese
- 1 Tsp Chipotle chili powder
- 2 Tsp raw honey
- Blend all ingredients in a food processor or blender until smooth.
- Serve in a dipping bowl. Enjoy!

Direction

- Pre-heat oven to 425 F.
- Cut avocados into "fry-sized" wedges.
- In one bowl add 1/2 cup of oat flour or almond meal.
- In a separate bowl beat two eggs, until blended.
- Add salt and pepper to the eggs.
- Dip Avocado slices in eggs (one slice at a time) then directly place them in the flour. Make sure they're completely covered in flour.
- Place avocado fries on a parchment covered baking sheet evenly spaced.
- Bake for 25 minutes (or until brown) flipping them once.
- Serve hot.

20. BAKED VEGETABLE FRY Recipe

Serving: 8 | Prep: | Cook: 30mins | Ready in:

Ingredients

- 2 TEACUPS CHOPPED MIXED BOILED
- vegetables (French beans, carrots, cauliflower, green peas)
- 2 CHOPPED onion
- 4 TABLESPOONS CHOPPED capsicum
- 2 chopped tomatoes
- 1/2 TO 1 TEASPOON CHILLI POWDER
- A PINCH garam masala
- 2 TABLESPOONS CHOPPED coriander

- 4 TABLESPOONS GRATED PANEER, PLUS A LITTLE EXTRA FOR TOPPING(cottage cheese)
- 1 1/2 TEACUPS TOMATO gravy
- 4 TEASPOONS oil
- salt TO TASTE

Direction

- Heat the oil and fry the onions for 1/2 minute. Add the capsicum and tomatoes and fry again for 2 minutes. Add the vegetables, chilli powder, garam masala, coriander and salt and cook for a few minutes. Spread the tomato gravy on top and sprinkle a little grated paneer over it. Bake in a hot oven at 200c for 10 minutes. `

21. Bacon Cheese Fries Recipe

Serving: 6 | Prep: | Cook: 25mins |Ready in:

Ingredients

- 1 pkg (32oz) frozen french fries
- 1 cup (4oz) shredded cheddar cheese
- 1/2 cup thinly sliced green onions
- 1/4 cup cooked crumbled bacon
- ranch salad dressing

Direction

- Cook french-fries according to package directions.
- Place fries on a broiler-proof dish or platter.
- Sprinkle with cheese, onions and bacon.
- Broil for 1-2 minutes or until cheese is melted.
- Serve with ranch dressing.

22. Baked Carrot Fries Recipe

Serving: 4 | Prep: | Cook: 25mins |Ready in:

Ingredients

- 1 lb peeled, skinny baby carrots (or regular carrots, peeled and cut into sticks)
- 1 tbsp olive oil
- salt and pepper, to taste

Direction

- Preheat oven to 400 F.
- If baby carrots are on the thick side, slice them lengthwise in halves or quarters. Toss carrots with olive oil and season w/ salt and pepper.
- Place carrots in a single layer on a baking sheet lined w/ parchment paper.
- Bake for 20-25 minutes or until they start to crisp.
- Serve as is or with your favourite dip. Garlic aioli is great w/ these!

23. Baked French Fries Recipe

Serving: 4 | Prep: | Cook: 45mins |Ready in:

Ingredients

- 4 large potatoes
- 4 Tbsp olive oil
- 2 tsp paprika
- 2 tsp garlic powder
- 2 tsp chili powder
- 2 tsp onion powder

Direction

- Preheat oven to 400.
- Cut potatoes into wedges.
- Mix oil and seasonings together in bowl.
- Add potatoes and make sure all are coated well with mixture.
- Place on baking sheet.
- Bake for 40-45 minutes turning once.
- ** I have used different seasonings such as minced garlic, red pepper flakes, cayenne pepper, if you experiment you'll find the right flavour for you and your family. :o)

- I serve these with crumbled bacon and melted shredded cheese sometimes with ranch, and sometimes with no toppings and just ketchup, they are delicious anyway you decide.
- ENJOY!

24. Baked Homemade Chips Recipe

Serving: 0 | Prep: | Cook: 45mins | Ready in:

Ingredients

- 1 beets
- 1 Taro
- 1 yam
- 1 Purple potato
- oil spray
- salt

Direction

- Peel all of the roots; slice each one using a mandolin slicer; I used 1/8-inch thickness for the roots other than the taro, where 1/16-inch is better.
- Arrange them in a baking pan (one layer only), slightly spray with olive oil and sprinkle with some salt; turn them around and do the same on the other side.
- Roast in the oven for about 30 minutes on 325 degrees, and they are ready (watch them closely, they need to be perfectly crispy but shouldn't be burned). Allow them to get to room temperature and enjoy the sound of crunchiness . You can eat them as is (my preferred version), dip them, and add to a salad or in a sandwich. Enjoy.

25. Baked Lemon Fries Recipe

Serving: 4 | Prep: | Cook: 40mins | Ready in:

Ingredients

- 6 idaho potatoes
- 1/4 cup extra-virgin olive oil
- 1 tablespoon salt
- 1/2 teaspoon freshly ground black pepper
- 3 lemons, zested
- 2 tablespoons freshly chopped Italian parsley leaves
- 2 tablespoons minced garlic

Direction

- Preheat the oven to 450 degrees F.
- Peel potatoes and cut into 3/8-inch thick slices (lengthwise) cut again into 3/8-inch thick fries. Place the potatoes into a bowl with cold water; this will help keep the fries crisp and white. Just before cooking, drain water and place on paper towel, pat dry completely. Put in a bowl; add olive oil, 1 tablespoon salt, 1/2 teaspoon black pepper. Toss well and lay out in 1 layer on non-stick baking sheets. Bake until light brown. Cook for approximately 30 to 40 minutes, turning frequently until golden brown.
- Remove from oven. Add lemon zest, parsley, garlic, salt and pepper. Toss well and serve.

26. Baked Sweet Potato Fries Recipe

Serving: 4 | Prep: | Cook: 30mins | Ready in:

Ingredients

- Non stick cooking spray
- 1 lb medium sweet potatoes
- 1 Tbsp butter, melted
- 1/4 tsp seasoned salt
- Dash ground nutmeg

Direction

- Lightly coat 15 x 10 x 1 inch baking pan with cooking spray. Scrub potatoes; cut lengthwise into quarters. Cut each quarter into two wedges. Arrange potatoes in a single layer in pan. Combine margarine or butter, salt, and nutmeg. Brush onto potatoes. Bake at 425 degrees for 20-30 minutes or until brown and tender.

27. Baked Yam And Purple Potato Fries Recipe

Serving: 5 | Prep: | Cook: 30mins | Ready in:

Ingredients

- 2 large garnet yams
- 3 large purple potatoes
- olive oil spray
- season with Braggs and cayenne pepper or
- salt and pepper or
- soy sauce or
- I tried shredded ginger and minced garlic too mmmm or
- anything

Direction

- Slice potatoes into steak fry sized pieces
- Arrange in glass baking dish
- Spray with olive oil
- Turn in pan until coated with oil
- Add seasoning
- Bake at 400 until done about 30 min longer if you want them to be crispy

28. Baked Zucchini Fries Recipe

Serving: 16 | Prep: | Cook: 20mins | Ready in:

Ingredients

- 2 cups unseasoned bread crumbs
- 1/2 cup grated parmesan cheese
- 1 t kosher salt
- 1/2 t ground black pepper
- 2 cups flour
- 4 large eggs, beaten
- 6 medium zucchini, unpeeled, but lengthwise into 2" long and 1/4" thick strips

Direction

- Combine bread crumbs, Parmesan cheese, salt and pepper in a bowl or zipper top plastic bag. Place flour in a separate bowl and beaten eggs in another bowl. Dip zucchini sticks first in the flour until lightly coated, then in the beaten eggs. Toss them in the bread crumb mixture until covered. Transfer zucchini to a non-stick baking sheet and bake until coating is crisp, about 20 minutes. Cool slightly before eating. Serve w/ ketchup or tomato coulis.

29. Breaded And Baked Fries Recipe

Serving: 2 | Prep: | Cook: 40mins | Ready in:

Ingredients

- 2 potatoes
- 1/2 cup Italian-seasoned dry bread crumbs
- 2 tsp grated parmesan
- 1/4 teaspoon salt
- 1/8 teaspoon cayenne powder
- milk or egg
- olive oil, for drizzling

Direction

- Preheat the oven to 400°F. Peel the potatoes and Cut into sticks. Partially boil the potato sticks in water for 5 min. Remove and pat dry.
- In a shallow dish, combine the bread crumbs, cheese, 1/4 teaspoon salt, and cayenne.
- Take milk in a bowl, dip potato in milk and roll in bread mixture. Place it on greased baking tray. Drizzle olive oil.

- Bake for about 30 minutes, until golden on the underside. Flip and bake for about 5 minutes more. Sprinkle with additional salt and serve

30. COWBOY FRIES Recipe

Serving: 4 | Prep: | Cook: 15mins | Ready in:

Ingredients

- 6 potatoes, cut into French fries
- ¼ c. butter
- 4 TB honey garlic barbecue sauce or ketchup
- 1 tsp brown sugar
- 1 tsp chili powder
- ¼ tsp garlic salt or powder

Direction

- Peel potatoes; slicing into French fries.
- Meanwhile; in a small saucepan; melt margarine. Add barbecue sauce, brown sugar, chili powder and garlic salt.
- Pour sauce over potatoes and stir until coated. Place fries on baking sheet. Bake in preheated 400 F oven for approximately 45 minutes.

31. Cheese Fries With Taco Ranch Dipping Sauce Recipe

Serving: 4 | Prep: | Cook: 30mins | Ready in:

Ingredients

- 1 cup ranch salad dressing
- 1 envelope taco seasoning
- 1 pkg. frozen spicy French fries, prepare as directed
- 4 strips bacon, cooked and crumbled
- 1/2 cup jack cheese, shredded

Direction

- Prepare fries according to directions
- Take out of oven
- Sprinkle cheese and bacon over fries
- Return to hot oven until cheese is melted
- Combine ranch dressing and taco seasoning
- Serve fries with dipping sauce

32. Chili Cheese Fries Recipe

Serving: 4 | Prep: | Cook: 35mins | Ready in:

Ingredients

- 1 (24-ounce) bag frozen French fries
- For the Chili
- 2 pounds ground beef
- 3 garlic cloves
- 1 (8-ounce) can tomato sauce
- 1 tablespoon ground cumin
- 2 tablespoons chili powder
- 1 teaspoon salt
- 1 teaspoon ground oregano
- 1/4 teaspoon cayenne powder
- For the Nacho Cheese
- 1 1/2 cups milk
- 4 ounces cream cheese
- 1/2 pound Velveeta cheese
- 1/2 teaspoon cayenne
- 1/2 teaspoon garlic powder
- 1 1/2 cups shredded cheddar
- 1 tablespoon taco sauce
- 1 teaspoon hot sauce

Direction

- Gather the ingredients.
- Brown the ground beef and garlic in a large pot.
- Add the tomato sauce and spices to the ground beef mixture. Stir to combine, then simmer on low for at least 20 minutes or up to 2 hours.
- For Cheese Sauce and Fries
- Gather the ingredients.

- Spread out the French fries on a parchment paper-lined baking sheet so that they are in an even layer. Bake in a preheated 425 F oven for 25 minutes.
- Heat the milk, spices, cream cheese, and Velveeta in a small saucepan on very low heat, stirring frequently.
- Slowly whisk in the shredded cheddar cheese.
- Whisk in the hot sauce and taco sauce.
- Stir the French fries halfway through baking to ensure they are crispy on all sides.
- Pile the French fries onto the centre of the baking sheet and top them with the remaining shredded cheddar.
- Broil the baking sheet until the cheese is just melted, but not browned.
- Top the cheesy fries with about half of the chili.
- Top the chili fries with the homemade nacho cheese.
- Add chopped scallions and extra taco sauce if you wish.
- Serve and enjoy!

33. Chipotle Fried Onion Rings Recipe

Serving: 2 | Prep: | Cook: 10mins | Ready in:

Ingredients

- 1 md white onion
- corn oil for deep-frying
- 1/2 c all-purpose flour
- 2 ts Chipotle rub
- 2 tablespoon red pepper flakes

Direction

- Preheat oven to 250F and line a large baking sheet with paper towels. With a mandoline or other manual slicer, slice onion paper thin and separate into rings. In a deep kettle or deep fryer heat 2 inches oil to 375F. While oil is heating, in a large bowl stir together flour and chipotle rub and pepper flakes. Dredge onions in flour mixture; shake off excess flour & deep fry until onions are crispy. Serve Hot.

34. Crispy Oven Fries Recipe

Serving: 4 | Prep: | Cook: 45mins | Ready in:

Ingredients

- 4 russet potatoes (6 to 8 oz. each), peeled and cut into 1/2" slices
- 6 Tbs vegetable oil
- 1 Tbs cornstarch
- 1 tsp salt

Direction

- Microwave potatoes: Adjust oven rack to lowest position and heat oven to 450 degrees. Place potatoes in a bowl, wrap tightly with plastic, and microwave until translucent around edges, 3 to 5 mins, shaking bowl half-way through to redistribute potatoes. Transfer potatoes to cooling rack and thoroughly blot dry with paper towels.
- Heat oil: Coat rimmed baking sheet with 5 Tbsp. of oil. Transfer to oven and heat until just smoking, 5 to 7 mins. Meanwhile, whisk remaining oil, cornstarch and salt in large bowl. Add potatoes and toss to coat.
- Bake potatoes: Arrange in single layer on hot baking sheet and bake till deep, golden brown and crisp, 25 to 35 mins, flipping potatoes half-way through cooking time. Transfer to paper towel-lined plate and blot with additional paper towels. Serve.

35. Crispy Ranch Fries With Fry Sauce Recipe

Serving: 4 | Prep: | Cook: 15mins | Ready in:

Ingredients

- 1 (26 oz.) bag frozen extra crispy fast food fries (I used shoestring fries)
- 1 pkg. dry ranch dressing mix, divided
- 1/2 cup ketchup
- 1/2 cup salad dressing

Direction

- Measure out 1 Tbsp. ranch dressing mix and set aside.
- In a small bowl, mix salad dressing until nice and smooth. Then mix in ketchup and remaining ranch dressing. Put sauce in refrigerator.
- Preheat oven to 450 degrees. Spray a rimmed baking sheet with non-stick spray.
- Place fries in a single layer on you baking sheet and sprinkle evenly with the 1 Tbsp. ranch dressing mix you set aside earlier.
- Bake for 11 to 15 minutes (or until you think they are nice and crispy). Serve fries with sauce.

36. Crispy Seasoned Oven Fries Recipe

Serving: 4 | Prep: | Cook: 20mins | Ready in:

Ingredients

- 2 large baking potatoes
- 4 teaspoons plain breadcrumbs
- 1/2 teaspoon garlic powder
- 1/2 teaspoon dried oregano
- 1/2 teaspoon chili powder
- 1/4 teaspoon sea salt
- 1/4 teaspoon freshly ground black pepper
- 2 egg whites
- olive oil cooking spray

Direction

- Heat oven to 400°F. Slice potatoes in half lengthwise; cut each half into 1/4- to 1/2-inch-thick fries; pat dry with a paper towel. In a bowl, combine breadcrumbs with spices. In another bowl, whisk egg whites until foamy, about 1 minute; add fries to coat. Toss fries in spice mixture until evenly coated. Coat a baking sheet with cooking spray; arrange fries on sheet with space in between; spritz fries with cooking spray. Bake, turning once, until fries are golden and crispy, about 20 minutes.

37. Croque Madame Fried Egg Ham And Cheese Sandwich Recipe

Serving: 4 | Prep: | Cook: 17mins | Ready in:

Ingredients

- 2 tbsp butter
- 2 tbsp flour
- 1 1/2 c milk
- A pinch each of salt, freshly ground pepper, and nutmeg
- 1 1/2 c Gruyère cheese, grated
- 1/4 c grated parmesan cheese
- 8 slices of French bread
- 12 ounces ham, sliced
- Dijon mustard
- 4 eggs (chicken or quail)
- oil

Direction

- Preheat oven to 400°F.
- Melt butter in a small saucepan on medium heat until it just starts to bubble.
- Add the flour and cook, stirring until smooth and golden in colour. Slowly whisk in milk and cook until thick. Remove from heat.
- Add the salt, pepper, and nutmeg.
- Stir in the Parmesan and 1/4 cup of the grated Gruyère. Set aside.

- Lay out the bread slices on a baking sheet and toast them in the oven.
- Spread some butter on the bread slices before you toast them if you want.
- Lightly brush half of the toasted slices with mustard. Add the ham slices and about 1 cup of the remaining Gruyère cheese. Top with the other toasted bread slices.
- Spoon on the béchamel sauce to the tops of the sandwiches. Sprinkle with the remaining Gruyère cheese.
- Place on a broiling pan. Bake in the oven for 4 minutes, then turn on the broiler and broil for an additional 3 minutes, until the cheese topping is bubbly and lightly browned. Set aside.
- Heat oil in pan and fried eggs, sunny side up.
- Top a fried egg on each sandwich and serve.

38. Deen Family Fried Baked Potato Recipe

Serving: 1 | Prep: | Cook: 20mins | Ready in:

Ingredients

- large baked potato
- 1 pork chop, thinly sliced
- 1/2 cup all-purpose flour
- 1/2 cup jack cheddar cheese
- 1/4 cup bacon bits
- 2-3 tablespoon cream cheese
- 1/2 teaspoon Paula Deen's House seasoning
- 1/2 teaspoon seasoned salt

Direction

- With a meat mallet, beat pork chop until tender and thin.
- Coat with flour and place in deep fryer, allowing it to cook for 5-10 minutes.
- Cut into strips and add to scooped out baked potato.
- Add cheddar, cream cheese, and bacon to taste.
- Bake potato once more for about 5-10 minutes.
- Add The Lady's House Seasonings and seasoning salt to taste.
- Add melted butter as topping

39. Easy No Fry Eggplant Parmesean Recipe

Serving: 8 | Prep: | Cook: 45mins | Ready in:

Ingredients

- 3 med. eggplants
- 2 c. seasoned breadcrumbs
- sale
- 1 c. parmesean or romano grated cheese
- 1 ball sliced or grated mozzerella cheese
- olive oil
- 2 jars seasoned pasta sauce or homemade

Direction

- Preheat oven to 350 deg.
- After slicing eggplant, salt and place on paper towels for 25 min.
- Pat dry and place slices on 2 cookie sheets
- Drizzle olive oil over slices - Bake for 35 min. turning once
- Layer in 9X13 pan - pasta sauce, eggplant, mozzarella cheese, bread crumbs.
- Layer until all eggplant is gone, ending with cheese on top.
- Cover with aluminum foil and bake 35-40 min. or until bubbly
- Take foil off 10 minutes before done to brown.
- Enjoy...............

40. Easy Rosemary Fries Recipe

Serving: 6 | Prep: | Cook: | Ready in:

Ingredients

- 4 baking potatoes (about 3 pounds)
- 1/4 cup vegetable oil
- 1 Tbsp. kosher salt
- 2 Tbsp. chopped rosemary
- 1 tsp. crushed red pepper flakes
- 1 tsp. paprika

Direction

- 1) Preheat oven to 450*F. Coat roasting pan with non-stick cooking spray. Cut each baking potato lengthwise into 8 wedges. Place wedges in prepared pan.
- 2) Drizzle potatoes with oil. Sprinkle with salt, rosemary and pepper flakes, tossing well to coat. Spread potatoes for even roasting and sprinkle with paprika.
- 3) Bake 30 to 40 minutes or until potatoes are golden brown, stirring occasionally. Serve with your favourite low fat/no fat dipping sauce.

41. French Fried Onion Cornbread Recipe

Serving: 4 | Prep: | Cook: 60mins | Ready in:

Ingredients

- 1 cup Martha white cornmeal
- 1 cup Martha white flour
- 1 Tablespoon sugar
- 4 teaspoons baking powder
- 1/2 teaspoon salt
- 1 egg
- 1 cup milk
- 1/2 cup oil
- 1/2 cup finely crushed French fried onions
- 1 Tablespoon parmesan cheese
- 1 cup sour cream

Direction

- Combine first five ingredients in bowl. Add egg, milk, sour cream, and oil beating until smooth. Coat a greased cast iron skillet with onion crumbs and cheese, reserving excess crumbs. Pour batter into prepared pan. Sprinkle with reserved crumbs. Cook at 400 degrees for 1 hour. Invert onto a wire rack to cool.

42. French Fried Onions

Serving: 0 | Prep: | Cook: | Ready in:

Ingredients

- 3 large onions, sliced into thin rings
- 2 cups milk
- 2 cups all-purpose flour
- 1 pinch garlic powder, or to taste
- 1 pinch onion powder, or to taste
- 1 pinch ground white pepper, or to taste
- salt to taste
- vegetable oil for frying

Direction

- Soak onions in milk for 5 minutes.
- Combine flour, garlic powder, onion powder, white pepper, and salt. Add a handful of onions and toss to coat. Remove and repeat with remaining onions, one handful at a time.
- Heat oil in a large skillet or deep fryer. Fry onion in batches, stirring as needed, until evenly browned, 2 to 3 minutes each. Drain on paper towels and season with more salt. Store in an airtight container.
- Cook's Note:
- Use any seasonings you prefer.
- Editor's Notes:
- We have determined the nutritional value of oil for frying based on a retention value of 10% after cooking. Amount will vary depending on cooking time and temperature, ingredient density, and specific type of oil used.
- Nutrition data for this recipe includes the full amount of milk and flour. The actual amount consumed will vary.

- Nutrition Facts
- Per Serving:
- 38.5 calories; protein 1.2g 2% DV; carbohydrates 6.4g 2% DV; fat 0.9g 1% DV; cholesterol 1mg; sodium 9.5mg.

43. French Fries With Cumin Ketchup Recipe

Serving: 4 | Prep: | Cook: 20mins | Ready in:

Ingredients

- 1/2 cup ketchup
- 1 teaspoon ground cumin
- 1 teaspoon balsamic vinegar
- 2 teaspoons salt
- 2 teaspoons chili powder
- 1 package frozen french fries

Direction

- Combine ketchup, cumin and vinegar in bowl.
- Combine salt and chili powder in another dish.
- Cover both and let stand at room temperature while preparing French fries.
- Place potatoes on cookie sheet and bake at 350 for 30 minutes.
- Place fries in basket lined with paper towels.
- Sprinkle with chili and salt then serve with cumin ketchup.

44. Fried Green Tomatoes Recipe

Serving: 8 | Prep: | Cook: 20mins | Ready in:

Ingredients

- 24 slices fresh green tomatoes, 1/4-inch thick each (about 6 large green tomatoes)
- Freshly ground black pepper
- 1 2/3 cups all-purpose flour
- 2 tablespoons cornstarch
- 4 large eggs
- 2 tablespoons milk
- 1 1/2 cups yellow cornmeal
- 3 tablespoons chopped green onions, green part only, for garnish

Direction

- Season the tomatoes with salt and freshly ground black pepper, to taste. Place the 1 cup of the flour in a small bowl with the cornstarch and mix well. In a separate bowl, whisk together the eggs and milk. In a third bowl, combine the remaining 2/3 cup flour, the cornmeal, and the remaining 2 tablespoons of Essence. Dredge each slice of tomato in the flour mixture. Dip each slice in the egg wash, letting the excess drip off. Finally, dredge each slice in the cornmeal mixture, coating completely.
- Heat 1/2 cup of oil in a large sauté pan over medium-low heat. When the oil is hot, pan-fry the tomatoes, in batches, until golden and crispy on both sides, about 1 1/2 to 2 minutes per side. Add the remaining 1/2 cup of oil to the sauté pan as needed, preheating the oil before frying the tomatoes. Remove the browned tomatoes and drain on paper towels. Season lightly with salt, to taste.

45. Fried Onion Potato Dish Recipe

Serving: 8 | Prep: | Cook: 55mins | Ready in:

Ingredients

- 4 cups frozen hash browns
- 1 package butter and herb mashed potato mix
- 1 stick butter softened
- 4 ounces cream cheese softened
- 1 cup shredded monterey jack cheese
- 1/2 cup sour cream
- 1/2 teaspoon garlic salt
- 1/2 teaspoon salt

- 1/2 teaspoon freshly-ground black pepper
- 2 cups boiling water
- 2 cups prepared French fried onion rings

Direction

- Preheat oven to 350.
- Bring a pot of water to boiling then add hash browns and cook 5 minutes then drain well.
- In a large bowl mix together the cooked hash browns, mashed potato mix, butter, cream cheese, jack cheese, sour cream, garlic salt, salt and pepper.
- Stir in the boiling water and place in a greased casserole dish.
- Bake for 45 minutes then sprinkle onion rings over casserole and bake 8 minutes longer.

46. Fried Zucchini Recipe

Serving: 2 | Prep: | Cook: 13mins | Ready in:

Ingredients

- olive oil spray (real olive oil, not Pam)
- 1 1/2 teaspoons unbleached all-purpose flour
- 2 tablespoons plain dried bread crumbs
- 1 1/2 teaspoons grated reduced-fat parmesan cheese
- 1 teaspoon finely chopped fresh parsley
- 1/2 teaspoon garlic powder
- 1/4 teaspoon dried oregano
- 1/8 teaspoon salt
- 1/8 teaspoon pepper
- 1 large egg white
- 2 small zuchhinis, cut into 3/4-inch rounds (about 12 rounds)
- 1/3 cup low-fat marinara sauce

Direction

- Preheat the oven to 425.
- Mist a medium non-stick baking sheet with spray.
- Spoon the flour into a medium shallow bowl. Put the bread crumbs, Parmesan, parsley, garlic powder, oregano, salt and pepper in a medium resealable plastic bag.
- Use a fork to beat the egg white in a small bowl until bubbly.
- Dip both sides of one zucchini round in the flour, and then roll it to coat it completely. Shake off any excess and dip it in the egg to cover it. Let any excess drip off, and then drop the round into the crumb bag and shake gently to coat it. Repeat with each round, and then place them in a single layer, not touching, on the prepared baking sheet.
- Lightly mist the tops with spray. Bake for 7 minutes, and then carefully flip them and bake for another 4 to 6 minutes, or until the outsides are golden brown and the insides are tender. Lightly mist the tops with spray.
- Meanwhile, just before the zucchini is done, put the marinara sauce in a small microwave-safe bowl. Microwave on low in 30-second intervals until warm.
- Serve the zucchini immediately with the marina sauce on the side for dipping.

47. GARLIC DILL FRIES Recipe

Serving: 4 | Prep: | Cook: 30mins | Ready in:

Ingredients

- 1 sack 16-to-18-oz crispy-style frozen french fries
- 3 Tbsp unsalted butter
- 4 Tbsp fresh dill, chopped
- 1 clove garlic, minced
- salt & pepper to taste

Direction

- Preheat oven according to package directions for fries.
- Spread the fries out in a single layer on a rimmed cookie sheet.

- Place in the oven when it reaches the desired temperature.
- A minute or two before the fries are done, combine in a small bowl the remaining ingredients.
- Melt over low heat or in the microwave.
- Once the fries are done and very crisp, transfer to a large shallow bowl, drizzle with the melted garlic-dill butter and toss to coat the fries evenly.
- Have a taste to check if they need more salt or pepper.

48. GEMS FREEDOM FRIES Recipe

Serving: 4 | Prep: | Cook: 35mins | Ready in:

Ingredients

- 3 large potatoes
- 1 1/2 Tbs. oil

Direction

- Preheat oven to 475°.
- Peel potatoes, and cut into long strips about 1/2 inch wide.
- Wash and dry strips thoroughly on paper towels.
- Toss in a bowl with oil as if making a salad.
- When strips are thoroughly coated with the oil, spread them in a single layer on a cookie sheet and place in preheated oven for 35 minutes.
- Turn strips periodically to brown on all sides.
- If a crispier, browner potato is desired, run under broiler for a minute or two.
- Sprinkle with salt before serving.

49. Garlic And Parmesan Fries Recipe

Serving: 4 | Prep: | Cook: 20mins | Ready in:

Ingredients

- garlic and parmesan cheese Fries
- Ingredients:
- 1 bag of frozen fries (your favorite kind)
- 5 or more cloves of minced garlic
- 1 stick of butter
- salt
- 1/4 - 1 cup of parmesan cheese

Direction

- Bake fries according to directions.
- In a small pan, melt one stick butter.
- Turn heat to medium and add at least five cloves (or more, if you wish) minced garlic.
- Add salt to your taste.
- Cook garlic in butter on low heat (garlic burns quickly, so you'll need to watch it).
- Once fries are done, transfer to a dish and spoon the garlic/salt/butter mixture over the top. Sprinkle with parmesan cheese.
- Enjoy!

50. Garlicky Baked Fries Recipe

Serving: 2 | Prep: | Cook: 40mins | Ready in:

Ingredients

- 2 garlic cloves, chopped
- 4 tbsp olive oil
- 2 potatoes peeled and cut in wedges
- 2 tsp cornstarch
- 1/2 tsp salt
- ground black pepper
- 1/2 tsp cayenne pepper

Direction

- Preheat the oven at 200°C-400°F.
- Partially boil wedges in water for 5 min.
- Put the garlic and the oil in a pan, heat until fragrant.
- In a plastic bag (or else a bowl with plastic wrap covering it), add the potatoes and the Garlic oil. Let it stand for 10 min.
- Combine the cornstarch, salt, black and cayenne pepper in a small bowl. Sprinkle over the potatoes and toss to coat. (Do not remove garlic)
- Arrange the potatoes on a single layer in the baking pan and bake, turning them every now and then, until golden brown and crisp (it took 30 minutes in my oven).

51. Greek Style Oven Fries Recipe

Serving: 6 | Prep: | Cook: 50mins | Ready in:

Ingredients

- 3 MEDIUM UNPEELED baking potatoes (ABOUT 1 1/2 POUNDS)
- 2 TBS lemon juice
- 2 TSP olive oil
- 1 TSP DRIED oregano
- 1/4 TSP pepper
- 1/4 TSP salt
- 2 cloves garlic, MINCED
- vegetable oil cooking spray

Direction

- Cut each potato lengthwise into 8 wedges
- Combine lemon juice, olive oil, oregano, pepper, salt and garlic in a large bowl
- Add potatoes and toss well to coat
- Place potatoes skin side down on a baking sheet that has been coated with cooking spray
- Bake at 400 degrees for 45mins or until potatoes are tender and lightly browned

52. Green Bean Fries Recipe

Serving: 4 | Prep: | Cook: 45mins | Ready in:

Ingredients

- 1 bag of pre-washed green beans
- 1 small red onion, diced
- 1 tbsp olive oil
- garlic powder
- onion powder
- salt
- your choice of spices

Direction

- Preheat oven to 350 degrees.
- Place green beans and onion in small bowl.
- Add olive oil and turn until all are evenly coated in a light coating.
- Sprinkle desired amount of spices on green beans. Don't be shy with seasonings, and don't be afraid to try different combinations. Sometimes I like it simple and I just add garlic, onion powder and salt, other times I want it spicy and I add lots of cumin and chili pepper.
- Mix spices evenly on green beans and then spread evenly on baking sheet.
- Bake for 30-45 minutes, flipping occasionally. Feel free to taste when testing and to add any spices desired while it cooks. The green beans will the tips of the green beans are crunchy and the onions are browned.

53. Guiltless Steak Fries Recipe

Serving: 2 | Prep: | Cook: 35mins | Ready in:

Ingredients

- 1 large baking potato
- oil or spray to coat pan
- oil to lightly coat potatoes (optional)
- Your choice of table seasoning, such as Mrs. Dash.

Direction

- Wash potato well. Do not peel. Slice the potato in half, lengthwise. Then slice each half into 3 or 4 thick lengths. Coat a baking sheet with oil. Place the potatoes on the pan. At this point, you can drizzle the potatoes lightly with oil if you choose - it is not necessary, especially if you are watching your fat intake. Then sprinkle liberally with your seasoning of choice. Bake at 400 degrees for approximately 35 minutes. Serve with ketchup or my favourite, steak sauce.

54. Healthy Oven Fried Vegetables Recipe

Serving: 4 | Prep: | Cook: 12mins | Ready in:

Ingredients

- 1/4 c. fine dry bread crumbs
- 1 T. parmesan cheese
- 1/8 t. paprika
- 2/3 c. 1/4" sliced mushrooms
- 2 T. Italian salad dressing
- 2/3 c. 1/4" thick sliced onion rings
- 2/3 c. 1/4" thick sliced cauliflower

Direction

- Preheat oven to 450 degrees.
- Spray a baking sheet with cooking oil spray.
- Set aside.
- Stir together breadcrumbs, parmesan cheese and paprika in a 9" pie plate until well mixed.
- Place vegetables in a medium bowl.
- Drizzle salad dressing over vegetables and toss till coated.
- Roll vegetables in crumb mixture till coated.
- Place the coated vegetables in a single layer on the baking sheet. Bake for 10-12 minutes or until golden.
- NUTRITION FACTS:
- Serving Size: 1

- Servings per Recipe: 4
- Calories 101
- Calories from Fat 58
- Total Fat 6g
- Saturated Fat 1g
- Mono Fat 0g
- Cholesterol 1mg 0%
- Sodium 340mg 14%
- Total Carbs 9g 3%
- Dietary Fibre 1g 5%
- Sugars 1g

55. Healthy Sweet Potato Fries W/ Dipping Sauce Recipe

Serving: 2 | Prep: | Cook: 45mins | Ready in:

Ingredients

- 1 large yam or sweet potato --well washed and cut into french fry pieces
- 7-spices   middle eastern (cinnamon, black pepper, cardamon, feenugreek, cloves , allspice, ginger, nutmeg) I get it at a Lebanese bakery/store.
- 2 tsp. olive oil
- non-stick spray
- SAUCE :
- 2 Tablespoons orange marmalade
- 2 Tablespoons sour cream (or Better than sour cream by tofutti)
- 1 tsp. finely chopped red onion
- Mix these three ingredients together and adjust amounts to taste. Serve with finished healthy sweet potato fries.

Direction

- In a deep narrow bowl, drip the oil. Next throw in your spices-I used about 2 teaspoons, and sprinkled more when the fries were spread on the baking pan + tin foil.   But now, with the oil and the spices in the bowl, dump in the raw potatoes, and toss them with a wooden spoon or spatula, or big hand around and around and over and under until ~equally covered. If the 2 tsp. oil isn't enough, use the Pam. Put the baking sheet in a 375 * F oven and bake about 15 minutes, check to see if browning on the bottoms, and turn them over. Check again in about 10 minutes, when crunchy all over (but not burned!!)

56. Home Made French Fries Recipe

Serving: 4 | Prep: | Cook: 20mins | Ready in:

Ingredients

- 4 Large russet potatoes
- salt
- Non-Stick cooking spray

Direction

- Preheat your oven to 425 degrees
- Wash the potatoes and cut into fry-size pieces (this depends on what you view as a fry size, feel free to use your judgement)
- In a large pot, put in your potato slices and cover with water
- Bring to a boil and cook until almost fork tender (time will vary depending on sizes and amount)
- Drain your potatoes and lay out evenly on a greased baking sheet
- Bake for 20 minutes or until the potatoes get a nice brown on top
- Flip over the potatoes and continue baking for an additional 5 minutes or until that side gets browned
- Sprinkle with salt immediately after removing from the oven

57. Homemade French Fries Recipe

Serving: 46 | Prep: | Cook: 45mins | Ready in:

Ingredients

- 6 good sized potatoes
- minced garlic
- dehydrated onion, minced
- seasoned salt
- olive oil

Direction

- Pre heat oven to 425.
- Slice the Potatoes. My Apple slicer is awesome to make the perfect steak fry. The piece that is supposed to be the apple core I just slice with a knife.
- In a bowl add Olive Oil to coat, desired onion, garlic, season salt and another seasoning. Toss together.
- Place on cookie sheet in a single layer and bake 15-20 min.
- Turnover and continue to bake another 15-20 min until desired doneness.
- Broil for a few minutes if you would crisper fries.
- I've also done these on the BBQ in an Aluminium Foil pack. I put enough holes in the pack to let out steam

58. Hooters Fries Recipe

Serving: 4 | Prep: | Cook: 20mins | Ready in:

Ingredients

- 4 large white russet potatoes
- coarse sea salt
- 4 Tbsp veg oil

Direction

- Preheat oven to 350F.

- Wash and peel potatoes.
- Cut into large, thick French fry wedges.
- Line a 9x13 baking pan with foil.
- Pour the oil in the pan.
- Put the potato wedges in the pan and toss them in the oil (use your hands).
- Shake the pan to distribute the potatoes evenly.
- Sprinkle with sea salt.
- Bake for 20 minutes, or until fries are the golden brown colour you prefer.

59. Italian Veggie Cheese Burger Wsweet Potato Fries Recipe

Serving: 2 | Prep: | Cook: 15mins | Ready in:

Ingredients

- 2 Morning Star Grillers or Grillers Prime
- Organic or regular ketchup
- 1 Green, Yellow, orange and red pepper
- 1/2 bag of Alexia sweet potato Julienne Fries or cut fresh
- 1 Large Organic or regular white onion
- Soybean or other cooking oil
- 1 oz. or 2 slices of your favorite cheese or cheddar cheese
- 1 Whole grain, Wheat or other healthy submarine sized long roll

Direction

- 1. Peel and cut a sweet potato into French fry shapes or use frozen bag of fries.
- 2. Heat up oil in shallow pan to cook fries if fresh or bake frozen fries for 15 min.
- 3. While cooking potatoes, slice onions and peppers into strips to be sautéed.
- 4. Heat a small amount of olive or any oil to sauté onion and pepper strips until clear.
- 5. Heat, microwave or bake 2 Morning star grillers/prime for 2 min. before fries are done.
- 6. Shred or place slice of cheese on top of burgers to melt cheese on top of burgers.
- 7. Cut burgers in half, cut the long roll open faced, squirt ketchup on both sides.
- 8. Place cut burgers along the right side of open bread, then sprinkle peppers on left side.
- 9. Last, place the fries in the middle, close the bread and put more ketchup on top of fries.
- 10. Cut in half and enjoy this Italian veggie cheese burger!
- 11. You can use Veggie hot dogs in place of the burgers for an Italian Veggie hot dog as well.

60. Masala Chips Recipe

Serving: 4 | Prep: | Cook: 30mins | Ready in:

Ingredients

- 4 washed potatoes medium sized)
- 2 tbsp olive oil
- 2 tsp mixed herbs
- pinch of chilli powder optional)
- salt and pepper (to taste)

Direction

- Cut potatoes into chip-like shapes
- Put into large bowl and mix in other ingredients
- Mix them with hand until they are properly coated
- Put them on a non-stick baking tray and pop into an oven at about gas mark 8 (230 C)
- Bake for 20 mins and check if they are soft.
- If not, leave in oven and check every 5 mins.
- Serve hot with Thai Chilli Sauce

61. No Fry Eggplant Parmesean Recipe

Serving: 68 | Prep: | Cook: 45mins | Ready in:

Ingredients

- 3 medium eggplants, washed and sliced thin
- olive oil
- 1 ball mozzerella cheese - sliced or grated
- 2-12oz. jars prepared Italian pasta sauce
- 1 - 1/2 cups Parmesean or romano cheese - grated
- 2 cups seasoned Italian breadcrumbs
- Pinches of salt.................

Direction

- Slice eggplant-salt
- Place on paper towels - dry for about 15 minutes then transfer to oil prepared cookie sheets (2 cookie sheets.
- Bake at 350 deg. for 35 minutes or until soft and brownish. Remove from oven
- Cover bottom of 13 x 9 dish/pan with tomato sauce................put slices of eggplant on top - then layer mozzarella cheese, breadcrumbs, parmesan or Romano cheese, more eggplant, etc. until all eggplant is used................
- Cover with aluminum foil...........Bake at 350 for 35 minutes or until bubbly.

62. No Guilt Oven Fries Recipe

Serving: 4 | Prep: | Cook: 25mins | Ready in:

Ingredients

- 3 large russet (baking) potatoes, about 8 ounces each, scrubbed clean (peeling is optional) and sliced lengthwise into about 12 evenly sized steak fries
- 4 Tbsp. canola or peanut oil
- 1 tsp. salt
- 1 tsp. pepper

Direction

- Preheat oven to 450 degrees.
- Place the sliced potatoes in a large bowl and cover with hot tap water; soak 10 minutes. Drain and pat dry with dishcloths or paper towels.
- Rinse and wipe out the large bowl; return potatoes to bowl and toss with the oil, salt, and pepper. Arrange potato slices in single layers on 2 heavy rimmed baking sheets.
- Bake for about 12 minutes; check that the bottoms of the potato slices are browning, and flip them with a spatula once the bottoms are nicely browned. Rotate the baking sheets so the potatoes will cook evenly. Bake for another 12 minutes or until the tops are browned and the potatoes are crispy on the outside, flaky on the inside.
- Transfer oven fries to a plate lined with paper towels to drain. Season with freshly chopped parsley and additional salt and pepper, if desired, and serve at once.

63. OVEN BAKED CARROT FRIES Recipe

Serving: 6 | Prep: | Cook: 20mins | Ready in:

Ingredients

- 1 1/2 lb carrots
- 1 tsp brown sugar
- 2 tbsp olive oil
- 1/2 tsp salt
- 2 tbsp finely chopped fresh dill
- Pinch of pepper

Direction

- Cut carrots in half crosswise, then cut lengthwise, then cut lengthwise again.
- In a mixing bowl, combine the carrot sticks, olive oil, dill, salt and pepper.
- Stir until all are evenly coated.
- Place carrots on a baking sheet, spreading sticks out as much as possible.
- Bake for 20 minutes or until carrots are tender.
- Serve hot.

64. Onion And Cheese Crusted French Fries Recipe

Serving: 8 | Prep: | Cook: 15mins | Ready in:

Ingredients

- 1 kg bag frozen french fries
- 2 or 3 egg whites
- 1 cup dried, fried onions (like the kind in a can - eg: French's brand)
- 1/3 cup parmesan cheese, grated
- pinch salt
- pinch pepper

Direction

- Bake the French fries until they are 3/4 of the way done. Remove from oven and allow to slightly cool while you prep the other steps.
- In a shallow dish, combine fried onions, parmesan cheese and a pinch each of salt and pepper. Mix until evenly distributed.
- In a separate shallow dish, lightly beat the eggs.
- Now, carefully place the French fries in the eggs and with a slotted spoon (or tongs) transfer over to the onion/cheese mix. Thoroughly coat the fries with the dry mix before transferring back to the baking sheet. Repeat steps as necessary. (You may need to do it in batches if all the fries won't fit in each dish at one time)
- Place back in the oven and allow to finish baking. By the time the fries are all the way done the cheese and onions should be nice and crispy on the outside.
- Eat and enjoy! (I like these w/ sour cream or real, Dutch Fritessaus... but ketchup is good too!)

65. Oven "fries" Recipe

Serving: 4 | Prep: | Cook: 65mins | Ready in:

Ingredients

- 1 and 1/4 pounds baking potatoes, peeled and cut into 1/2 inch strips
- 3/4 tsp. salt
- 1/2 tsp. sugar
- 4 tsp. oil (i use olive oil)
- 1 tsp. paprika

Direction

- Preheat oven to 450*F, spray a non-stick baking sheet with non-stick spray
- (Parchment paper works well)
- In a large bowl combine the potatoes, 1/4 tsp. of the salt
- Add the sugar with cold water to soak (water to cover the potatoes well)
- Soak 15 minutes then blot dry
- In another large bowl toss the potatoes with oil and paprika
- Place in a single layer on the baking sheet
- Bake, turning the potatoes over as they brown until cooked through and crispy, about 45 minutes
- Sprinkle with remaining 1/2 tsp. salt.

66. Oven Baked Carrot Fries Recipe

Serving: 6 | Prep: | Cook: 20mins | Ready in:

Ingredients

- 1-1/2 pounds carrots
- 2 tablespoons olive oil
- 2 teaspoons finely chopped fresh rosemary
- 1 teaspoon granulated sugar
- 1/2 teaspoon salt
- 1/8 teaspoon freshly ground black pepper

Direction

- Preheat oven to 425 then line a jellyroll pan with aluminum foil.
- Using sharp knife and cutting board clean and peel carrots then cut each carrot into 8 sticks.
- Combine carrot sticks, olive oil, rosemary, sugar, salt and pepper.
- Stir with rubber spatula until carrot sticks are evenly coated.
- Dump carrots onto foil lined pan spreading sticks out as much as possible.
- Bake 20 minutes then serve carrot fries hot or at room temperature.

67. Oven Baked Sweet Potato Fries Recipe

Serving: 4 | Prep: | Cook: 20mins | Ready in:

Ingredients

- 3 sweet potatoes, peeled and cut lengthwise 1/4-1/2 inch
- olive oil
- salt

Direction

- Preheat oven to 400
- Coat potatoes with olive oil
- Spread in a single layer onto a baking sheet
- Sprinkle with salt
- Bake for 20 minutes, flipping frequently to crisp

68. Oven Fried Cauliflower Recipe

Serving: 8 | Prep: | Cook: 100mins | Ready in:

Ingredients

- 1 cup mayonnaise
- 1 medium cauliflower broken into flowerets
- 1 cup Italian seasoned breadcrumbs

Direction

- Place mayonnaise in a large heavy duty plastic bag.
- Add cauliflower then seal and shake to coat.
- Place breadcrumbs in a large heavy duty plastic bag.
- Add half of cauliflower mixture then seal and shake to coal.
- Spread in a single layer onto a lightly greased baking sheet.
- Repeat with remaining cauliflower mixture and breadcrumbs.
- Bake at 350 for 1 hour.

69. Oven Fried Eggplant Recipe

Serving: 4 | Prep: | Cook: 35mins | Ready in:

Ingredients

- 1/2 cup fat-free mayonnaise
- 1 tablespoon minced onions
- 1 lb unpeeled eggplants, sliced (about 12 1/2 inch slices)
- 1/3 cup fine dry breadcrumbs
- 1/3 cup grated parmesan cheese
- 1/2 teaspoon dried Italian seasoning
- vegetable oil cooking spray

Direction

- Combine first 2 ingredients, stir well.
- Spread evenly over both sides of eggplant slices.
- Combine breadcrumbs, cheese, and Italian seasoning in a shallow bowl; dredge eggplant in breadcrumbs mixture.
- Place eggplant on a baking sheet coated with cooking spray.
- Bake@ 425 degrees for 12 minutes.
- Turn eggplant over; and bake an additional 12 minutes or until golden.

70. Oven Fried Garlic Fries Recipe

Serving: 6 | Prep: | Cook: 50mins | Ready in:

Ingredients

- 3 lbs. peeled baking potatoes, cut into 1/4-inch thick strips
- 4 tsp. vegetable oil
- 3/4 tsp. salt
- cooking spray
- 2 tbsp. butter
- 8 garlic cloves, minced
- 2 tbsp. finely chopped fresh parsley
- 2 tbsp. freshly grated parmesan cheese

Direction

- Preheat oven to 400 degrees.
- Combine potatoes, vegetable oil and salt in a large zip-top plastic bag, tossing to coat.
- Arrange potatoes in a single layer on a baking sheet coated with cooking spray.
- Bake at 400 for 50 minutes or until potatoes are tender and golden brown, turning after 20 minutes.
- Place butter and garlic in a large non-stick skillet; cook over low heat for 2 minutes, stirring constantly.
- Add potatoes, parsley, and cheese to pan; toss to coat.
- Serve immediately.

71. Oven Fried Green Tomatoes Recipe

Serving: 4 | Prep: | Cook: 30mins | Ready in:

Ingredients

- 4 medium to large green tomatoes
- 1 cup buttermilk
- flour to dredge (can add a little cornmeal)
- Spicy seasoning of your choice
- salt
- olive oil

Direction

- Slice Green Tomatoes into 1/4" to 1/2" slices (I like them at 1/2")
- Season flour with seasoning of your choice and salt (last night I used some leftover Dry Rub for Barbeque recipe that can be found on this site by Duggar)
- Dredge tomatoes in flour mixture and place on a non-stick baking pan sprayed with cooking spray.
- Drizzle with olive oil
- Bake for 30 minutes. I turn the broiler on for a few minutes to crisp up to tops.

72. Oven Fried Parmesan Chicken Strips Recipe

Serving: 5 | Prep: | Cook: 30mins | Ready in:

Ingredients

- 2 tablespoons butter
- 1/3 cup reduced-fat baking mix
- 1/3 cup grated parmesan cheese
- 1 1/2 teaspoons Old Bay Seasoning
- 1/8 teaspoon black pepper
- 2 pounds chicken breast strips

Direction

- 1. Melt butter in a 15- x 10-inch jelly-roll pan in a 425° oven.
- 2. Place baking mix and next 3 ingredients in a large zip-top plastic bag; shake well to combine. Add chicken, several pieces at a time, shaking well to coat. Arrange chicken in melted butter in hot baking dish.
- 3. Bake at 425° for 30 minutes or until chicken is done, turning once. Serve immediately.

- Note: To freeze, place uncooked, coated chicken strips on a baking sheet in the freezer. Once frozen, place strips in a zip-top plastic freezer bag, and freeze until ready to prepare. Bake frozen strips on a hot buttered jelly-roll pan (according to previous directions) at 425° for 35 minutes, turning after 25 minutes.

73. Oven Fried Potatoes Recipe

Serving: 12 | Prep: | Cook: 50mins | Ready in:

Ingredients

- 12 medium potatoes peeled and cubed
- 1/4 cup grated parmesan cheese
- 2 teaspoons salt
- 1 teaspoon garlic powder
- 1 teaspoon paprika
- 1/2 teaspoon pepper
- 1/3 cup vegetable oil

Direction

- Place potatoes in two large resealable plastic bags.
- Combine Parmesan cheese and seasonings then add to potatoes and shake to coat.
- Pour oil in two rectangular baking pans then add potato mixture.
- Bake uncovered at 375 for 50 minutes.

74. Oven Fried Sweet Potatoes Recipe

Serving: 8 | Prep: | Cook: 45mins | Ready in:

Ingredients

- 4 medium sweet potatoes peeled and cut into thin slices
- 1 tablespoon olive oil
- 1/4 teaspoon salt
- 1/4 teaspoon pepper
- vegetable cooking spray
- 1 tablespoon finely chopped fresh parsley
- 1 teaspoon grated orange rind
- 1 small garlic clove minced

Direction

- Combine the first 4 ingredients in a large bowl then toss gently to coat.
- Arrange sweet potato slices in a single layer on a large baking sheet coated with cooking spray.
- Bake at 400 for 30 minutes turning potato slices after 15 minutes.
- Combine parsley, orange rind and garlic in a small bowl and stir well.
- Sprinkle parsley mixture over sweet potato slices.

75. Oven Fried Tex Mex Onion Rings Recipe

Serving: 4 | Prep: | Cook: 15mins | Ready in:

Ingredients

- 1/2 cup plain dry bread crumbs
- 1/3 cup yellow cornmeal
- 1-1/2 teaspoons chili powder
- 1/4 teaspoon ground red pepper
- 1/8 teaspoon salt
- 1 tablespoon plus 1-1/2 teaspoons butter melted
- 1 teaspoon water
- 2 medium white onions sliced 3/8 inch thick
- 2 egg whites

Direction

- Preheat oven to 450.
- Spray large non-stick baking sheet with non-stick cooking spray then set aside.

- Combine breadcrumbs, cornmeal, chili powder, ground red pepper and salt in medium shallow dish then mix well.
- Stir in butter and water.
- Separate onion slices into rings.
- Place egg whites in large bowl and beat lightly.
- Add onions then toss lightly to coat evenly.
- Transfer to breadcrumb mixture then toss to coat evenly.
- Place in single layer on prepared baking sheet.
- Bake 15 minutes.

76. Oven Fried Zucchini Sticks Recipe

Serving: 4 | Prep: | Cook: 10mins | Ready in:

Ingredients

- canola oil cooking spray
- 1/2 cup whole-wheat flour
- 1/2 cup all-purpose flour
- 2 tablespoons cornmeal
- 1 teaspoon salt
- 1/2 teaspoon freshly ground pepper
- 1 1/2 pounds zucchini (about 3 medium), cut into 1/2-by-3-inch sticks
- 2 egg whites, lightly beaten

Direction

- Preheat oven to 475°F.
- Coat a large baking sheet with cooking spray.
- Combine flours, cornmeal, salt and pepper in a large sealable plastic bag.
- Dip zucchini in egg white, shake in the bag to coat, and arrange, not touching, on the baking sheet. Coat all exposed sides with cooking spray.
- Bake on the centre rack for 7 minutes. Turn the zucchini and coat any floury spots with cooking spray. Continue to bake until golden and just tender, about 5 minutes more. Serve hot.

77. Oven Fries Recipe

Serving: 4 | Prep: | Cook: 35mins | Ready in:

Ingredients

- 3 large all-purpose potatoes, such as Yukon Gold or Russet (1 1/2 pounds total), scrubbed and each cut lengthwise into 8 wedges
- 2 teaspoons extra-virgin olive oil
- 1/2 teaspoon salt
- 1/4 teaspoon paprika
- Freshly ground pepper to taste

Direction

- Set oven rack on the upper level and preheat oven to 450°F. Coat a baking sheet lightly with non-stick cooking spray.
- Combine oil, salt, paprika and pepper in a large bowl. Add potato wedges and toss to coat. Spread the potatoes on the prepared baking sheet and roast for 20 minutes. Loosen and turn the potatoes; roast until golden brown, 10 to 15 minutes longer.

78. Oven Home Fries With Peppers Onions Recipe

Serving: 6 | Prep: | Cook: 25mins | Ready in:

Ingredients

- 2-1/2 lbs. red skinned potatoes
- 3 Tbsp. extra virgin olive oil
- 1 green pepper, seeded & chopped
- 1 orange pepper, seeded & chopped
- 1 or 2 green onions, chopped (I use the whole thing)
- 1 Tbsp. grill seasoning (I use McCormicks Montreal steak seasoning)
- 2 tsp. sweet paprika

- ranch dressing for dipping, optional

Direction

- Pre-heat oven to 500 degrees.
- Coarsely chop potatoes & transfer to a non-stick baking sheet.
- Toss with oil, peppers, onion & seasonings.
- Bake in oven for 25 minutes, turning twice with a spatula
- Serve hot with ranch dressing.

79. Oven Roasted Chili Cumin Fries Recipe

Serving: 4 | Prep: | Cook: 30mins | Ready in:

Ingredients

- 4 med. russet potatoes, washed, scrubbed and dried
- 1 tb chile powder (I like Rancho Gordo's)
- 1-2 ts cumin, roasted and ground
- 1 tb kosher salt
- 1 tb olive oil
- Aioli for dipping

Direction

- Preheat oven to 425 F.
- Cut the potatoes into 1/2 inch sticks lengthwise, don't peel. In a bowl, mix with the other ingredients. Put the potatoes, in one layer, on a baking sheet, lined with parchment paper. Bake for 20 to 25 min., turning once, until cooked and nicely browned.

80. Oven Roasted Sweet Potato Fries Recipe

Serving: 4 | Prep: | Cook: 40mins | Ready in:

Ingredients

- 1 teaspoon seasoned salt
- 1/2 teaspoon paprika
- 1/4 teaspoon garlic powder With parsley (or add a 1/2 tsp of parsley)
- 1/4 teaspoon chili powder
- 1 1/2 pounds sweet potatoes, peeled and cut lengthwise into 1/2-inch-thick slices
- 3 tablespoons olive oil
- All seasonings are to your taste

Direction

- Preheat oven to 425 degrees F.
- In small bowl, combine Lawry's® Seasoned Salt, paprika, Lawry's® Garlic Powder with Parsley and chili powder; set aside.
- In large bowl, toss sweet potatoes with Olive Oil; sprinkle with seasoning mixture and toss to coat.
- On jelly roll pan sprayed with non-stick cooking spray, arrange potatoes in single layer.
- Roast, turning once, 40 minutes or until potatoes are tender and golden.
- Serve, if desired, with additional Seasoned Salt and sour cream

81. Oven Fried French Fries Recipe

Serving: 4 | Prep: | Cook: 40mins | Ready in:

Ingredients

- 3 large potatoes, cut lengthwise into 8 wedges
- 2 tsp olive oil
- 1/2 tsp salt
- 1/4 tsp paprika
- black pepper to taste

Direction

- Preheat oven to 450^F. In bowl, toss potatoes with oil, salt, paprika, & pepper. Place potatoes on baking sheet coated with cooking spray. Bake 40 minutes until golden brown, turning once.

82. Oven Fried Vegetables Recipe

Serving: 4 | Prep: | Cook: 40mins | Ready in:

Ingredients

- 1 cup broccoli flowerets
- 1 cup cauliflower flowerets
- 1 medium carrot, peeled and sliced (about 1 cup)
- 1 medium zucchini, sliced (about 1 cup)
- 1 medium yellow squash, sliced (about 1 cup)
- 3 tablespoons Italian-style dried bread crumbs

Direction

- Preheat oven to 350. F
- Spray a 15- x 10-inch jelly-roll pan with vegetable cooking spray.
- In a large non-stick skillet, bring 2 cups of unsalted water to a boil over high heat. Add broccoli, cauliflower and carrot to the skillet. Reduce heat to low and simmer vegetables until crisp-tender, about 5 to 6 minutes.
- Using a slotted spoon, transfer broccoli, cauliflower, and carrot to prepared pan. Add zucchini and squash to skillet and cook until crisp-tender, about 4 minutes.
- Drain zucchini and squash in a colander; place in prepared pan. Sprinkle with bread crumbs and toss gently to coat.
- Bake vegetables, turning once, until bread crumbs are golden, about 30 minutes. Serve immediately.

83. Oven Fried Zucchini Sticks Recipe

Serving: 4 | Prep: | Cook: 13mins | Ready in:

Ingredients

- olive oil cooking spray
- 1/2 Cup Whole-wheat flour
- 1/2 Cup all-purpose flour
- 2 Tbsp cornmeal
- 1 tsp salt
- 1/2 tsp pepper
- 3 medium zucchini, cut into 1/2 x 3 in. sticks
- 2 Large egg whites, lightly beaten

Direction

- Combine Flours, Cornmeal, and Salt & Pepper in a large sealable plastic bag.
- Dip zucchini in egg white, shake in the bag to coat.
- Arrange on baking sheet.
- Coat all exposed sides with cooking spray.
- Bake for 7 minutes.
- Turn zucchini and coat any floury spots with cooking spray.
- Continue to bake about 5 minutes more.
- Should be a golden brown.

84. Oven Fried Zucchini In A Crunchy Parmesan Crust Recipe

Serving: 4 | Prep: | Cook: 15mins | Ready in:

Ingredients

- 1 tablespoon extra-virgin 0live oil
- 1/4 cup fine dried bread crumbs
- 1/3 cup grated imported parmesan cheese
- 1/2 teaspoon dried rosemary, crumbled
- 2 to 3 dashed cayenne pepper
- 1/2 teaspoon salt
- 1/4 teaspoon freshly ground black pepper
- 1 large egg
- 4 small green or golden zucchini squash

Direction

- Preheat the oven to 400 degrees F. Lightly grease a heavy baking sheet with the oil and set aside.
- In a shallow dish, combine the bread crumbs, Parmesan cheese, rosemary, cayenne, salt and pepper, and mix well. In a second shallow dish, lightly beat the egg.
- Trim the ends of the squash. Cut each squash in half lengthwise. Lay the halves flat and cut in half lengthwise again. Then cut the strips in half crosswise. Dredge each piece first in the egg and then in the Parmesan mixture, coating evenly. Arrange well-spaced in a single layer on the prepared baking sheet.
- Bake in the oven for 5 to 7 minutes, then turn the squash over and bake 5 to 7 minutes longer, or until crisp and lightly browned. Serve hot or at room temperature.

85. Parmesan Oven Fries Recipe

Serving: 4 | Prep: | Cook: 50mins | Ready in:

Ingredients

- Combine:
- 1/4 cup Pamesan, grated
- 1/2 teaspon garlic powder
- 1/4 teaspoon paprika
- 1/8 teaspoon cayenne (optional)
- salt to taste
- Coat with and Roast:
- 3 russet potatoes, cut into 8 wedges each
- 3 tablespoons olive oil, divided
- 2 tablespoons chopped frsh parsley or dried parsely

Direction

- Preheat oven to 475 degrees with a baking sheet inside
- Combine Parmesan, garlic powder, paprika, cayenne, and salt in a small bowl.
- Coat potato wedges with 1 tablespoon oil in a large bowl, then add Parmesan mixture, tossing to coat.
- Remove baking sheet from the oven and coat with remaining oil.
- Place wedges on the pan and roast until golden, 15 minutes per side.
- Return fries to bowl and toss with parsley

86. Pizza Fries Recipe

Serving: 8 | Prep: | Cook: 5mins | Ready in:

Ingredients

- 1 bag (2 pounds) frozen french fry
- 1 cup Prego® Traditional Italian Sauce, any variety
- 1 1/2 cups shredded mozzarella cheese (about 6 ounces)
- Diced pepperoni

Direction

- Prepare the fries according to the package directions.
- Remove from the oven.
- Pour the sauce over the fries.
- Top with the cheese and pepperoni, if desired.
- Bake for 5 minutes or until the cheese is melted.

87. Ranch Tastic Butternut Fries With Bacon Recipe

Serving: 2 | Prep: | Cook: 20mins | Ready in:

Ingredients

- Ranch-tastic Butternut Fries with bacon
- PER SERVING (1/2 of recipe): 235 calories, 5.5g fat, 880mg sodium, 39g carbs, 5.5g fiber, 10g sugars, 8.5g protein -- POINTS® value 4*

- The salty taste of bacon, the natural sweetness of squash, the cool-yet-zesty taste of ranch -- yup, this recipe has it ALL!
- Recipe from hungrygirl.com - LOVE HER! She does makeover meals to make them healthier to eat!
- 1/3 cup fat-free sour cream
- 1/2 tbsp. dry ranch dressing/dip mix
- 1 butternut squash (about 2 pounds -- large enough to yield 20 oz. once peeled & sliced)
- 1/8 tsp. coarse salt
- 4 slices turkey bacon
- Optional topping: chopped scallions

Direction

- Directions:
- Preheat oven to 425 degrees.
- In a small bowl, combine sour cream with ranch mix and stir thoroughly. Refrigerate until ready to serve.
- Slice ends off squash, and then cut it in half width wise. Peel squash carefully with a vegetable peeler or knife. Cut the round bottom piece in half lengthwise and remove seeds.
- Using a crinkle cutter or knife, carefully cut squash into spears/French-fry shapes. (For exact nutritionals, weigh spears and use 20 oz.) Pat firmly with paper towels to absorb excess moisture. Sprinkle evenly with salt.
- Lay spears on a layer of paper towels, and let stand for at least 5 minutes, to allow salt to draw out excess moisture. Pat with paper towels.
- Spray a broiler pan, a baking rack placed over a baking sheet, or a baking sheet with non-stick spray, and lay spears flat on it. (Use two pieces of bake ware, if needed.)
- Bake in the oven for 20 minutes. Carefully flip fries, and bake for about 20 minutes longer, until tender on the inside and crispy on the outside.
- Meanwhile, bring a skillet sprayed with non-stick spray to medium-high heat on the stove. Cook bacon until crispy, and set aside to cool. Then cut each slice in half width wise, and cut each half into very thin strips lengthwise.
- Mix bacon strips with fries and drizzle or serve with ranch mixture. If you like, sprinkle with scallions, as well. Eat up!

88. Roasted Sweet Potato Fries Recipe

Serving: 4 | Prep: | Cook: 40mins | Ready in:

Ingredients

- 2 medium sweet potatoes
- 2 to 3 tablespoons olive oil
- coarse salt and pepper to taste
- -or-
- 1/8 brown sugar
- 1/4 teaspoon cinnamon
- dash of nut meg

Direction

- Preheat oven to 450 F.
- Do not peel the sweet potatoes, scrub and slice into 10 thick wedges each.
- Place the olive oil and potato wedges in a zip lock plastic bag.
- Shake to coat well.
- Arrange wedges on an oiled baking sheet making sure they do not touch.
- Bake 25 minutes, turn and bake another 15 minutes or until they are golden brown and crisp.
- Sprinkle with coarse salt and pepper to taste.
- -Or-
- Toss in another zip lock bag with the brown sugar and spices, my preference....
- If you use the brown sugar try taking an1/8 cup butter and adding again the sugar mixture, mixing it well and use it as a dipping sauce.

89. Rosemary Oven Fried Potatoes Recipe

Serving: 8 | Prep: | Cook: 30mins |Ready in:

Ingredients

- 8 russet potatoes
- 3 Tablespoons olive oil
- 2 Tablespoons fresh chopped rosemary
- salt and pepper to taste

Direction

- Slice potatoes into wedges and put into large bowl
- Drizzle olive oil over potatoes
- Sprinkle Rosemary over potatoes.
- Stir until oil and rosemary are evenly distributed
- Bake in 350 degree oven for 25 to 30 minutes.
- +++
- Adjust the olive oil and rosemary to your taste.

90. Rumbledethumps Scottish Fried Veggies Recipe

Serving: 6 | Prep: | Cook: 45mins |Ready in:

Ingredients

- Ingredients:
- 1lb 5oz/600g potatoes, peeled, boiled and mashed
- 14 oz/400g swede or turnip, peeled, boiled and mashed
- 3 oz/75g unsalted butter
- 9oz/250g savoy cabbage or kale, finely sliced
- salt and pepper
- 1 oz /25g cheddar cheese, grated

Direction

- Preheat the oven to 350F/180C/Gas 4
- Place the mashed potato and swede into a large saucepan.
- In a small frying pan melt 2 oz. / 50g of the butter, add the finely sliced cabbage or kale and cook gently for minutes until softened but not brown.
- Add the cabbage to the pan of potato and swede, add the remaining butter and mash together. Season with salt and pepper to taste.
- Place the mashed vegetables in an ovenproof baking dish, sprinkle the cheese on top, cover with a lid and bake in the oven for 30 - 45 mins until heated right through.
- Remove the lid and cook for a further 5 mins or until golden brown on the top.
- Serve piping hot as a side dish with a casserole, pie or any hearty foods.

91. Smash Fries Recipe

Serving: 3 | Prep: | Cook: 3mins |Ready in:

Ingredients

- ½ pound shoe string fries.
- 2 to 3 tablespoons olive oil
- 1 tablespoon fresh minced rosemary
- salt and pepper to taste

Direction

- 1. Cook shoestring fries as directed on package.
- 2. Meanwhile, in a small saucepan over low heat add olive oil and minced rosemary.
- 3. Once fries are done pour into a large bowl. Pour oil and rosemary mixture over fries, sprinkle with salt and pepper and toss to coat.

92. Spiced Country Fries Recipe

Serving: 4 | Prep: | Cook: 25mins | Ready in:

Ingredients

- 3 medium baking potatoes
- 1 egg white
- 1 tsp each paprika, black pepper and salt

Direction

- Preheat oven to 500F.
- Coat a baking sheet with non-stick spray.
- Cut potatoes into 36 wedges, place in bowl of cold water.
- Whisk egg white, paprika and salt in a large bowl until frothy.
- Dry potato wedges, add to egg white and toss to coat.
- Spread on baking sheet and bake on bottom rack 25 minutes, turning half way through.

93. Spicy Baked Sweet Potato Fries Recipe

Serving: 4 | Prep: | Cook: 60mins | Ready in:

Ingredients

- 6 sweet potatoes, cut into French fries
- 2 tbs. canola oil
- 3 tbs. taco seasoning mix
- 1/4 tps. cayenne pepper

Direction

- 1- Preheat oven to 425 F.
- 2- In a plastic bag, combine the potatoes, canola oil, taco seasoning, and cayenne pepper. Close and shake the bag until fries are evenly coated. Spread fries out in a single layer on two large baking sheets.
- 3- Bake for 30 minutes, or until crispy and brown on one side. Turn fries over using a spatula, and cook for another 30 minutes, or until they are all crispy on the outside and tender inside.

94. Spicy Buffalo Wing Style Fries Recipe

Serving: 6 | Prep: | Cook: 15mins | Ready in:

Ingredients

- 1 kg package frozen french fries (thick, extra crisp style works best)
- 1 1/2 tbsp butter
- 3 - 4 tbsp Frank's red hot sauce (or other similar hot pepper sauce)
- 1/2 cup ranch or bleu cheese dressing

Direction

- Bake the French fries according to directions.
- While the fries are baking, melt the butter in a pan and add in the hot sauce.
- When fries are finished baking, place them in a big bowl and drizzle with hot sauce and butter mixture. Toss to coat.
- Serve with ranch or bleu cheese dressing, on the side, for dipping. :) (You can also drizzle the ranch/bleu cheese just right on top too if you wish)

95. Spicy Steak Fries Recipe

Serving: 4 | Prep: | Cook: 35mins | Ready in:

Ingredients

- 2 large, unpeeled potatoes
- 2Tbs Mrs. Dash Extra Spicy seasoning Blend
- 2Tbs. olive oil
- 1 clove garlic, minced

Direction

- Wash and cut potatoes into wedges. Place potato wedges in paper towels and pat dry. In a large bowl, toss the potatoes with seasoning blend, olive oil and garlic.
- Coat baking sheet with cooking spray. Arrange potatoes in single layer on baking sheet.
- Bake at 425 for 20 mins. Turn potatoes and bake an additional 15 mins until browned and tender.

96. Sweet Garlic Butternut Fries Recipe

Serving: 2 | Prep: | Cook: 40mins | Ready in:

Ingredients

- Sweet-garlic Butternut Fries
- PER SERVING (1/2 of recipe): 189 calories, 1.5g fat, 453mg sodium, 45g carbs, 6g fiber, 13g sugars, 3.5g protein -- POINTS® value 3*
- Another Hungry Girl twist on fries!
- These fries are so good and sweet and garlicky, you'll FREAK when you taste 'em.
- 1 butternut squash (about 2 pounds -- large enough to yield 20 oz. once peeled & sliced)
- 1/4 tsp. coarse salt, divided
- 1/2 a head of garlic
- 1/2 tsp. olive oil
- 2 tbsp. sweet Asian chili sauce
- Optional: additional coarse salt

Direction

- Preheat oven to 425 degrees.
- Slice ends off squash, and then cut it in half width wise. Peel squash carefully with a vegetable peeler or knife. Cut the round bottom piece in half lengthwise and remove seeds.
- Using a crinkle cutter or knife, carefully cut squash into spears/French-fry shapes. (For exact nutritionals, weigh spears and use 20 oz.) Pat firmly with paper towels to absorb excess moisture. Sprinkle evenly with 1/8 tsp. salt.
- Lay spears on a layer of paper towels, and let stand for at least 5 minutes, to allow salt to draw out excess moisture. Pat with paper towels. If you like, sprinkle with more salt.
- Remove the outer layer of garlic, leaving the skins around the cloves intact. Slice 1/4 inch off the top of the garlic, exposing the tops of the cloves. Place garlic on a piece of foil, drizzle with oil, and use your fingers to make sure it's coated. Wrap foil tightly around the garlic, enclosing it completely.
- Spray a broiler pan, a baking rack placed over a baking sheet, or a baking sheet with non-stick spray, and lay spears flat on it. (Use two pieces of bake ware, if needed.) Place foil-wrapped garlic on it as well (or directly on oven rack).
- Bake in the oven for 20 minutes. Carefully flip fries, and then bake fries and garlic for 10 minutes longer.
- Carefully remove foil-wrapped garlic and set aside. Bake fries for 10 more minutes, or until tender on the inside and crispy on the outside.
- Once cool enough to handle, unwrap garlic, remove cloves (discard skin), and place in a small microwave-safe bowl. Add remaining 1/8 tsp. salt and mash with a fork until mostly smooth. Add chili sauce and mix well. Nuke for about 10 seconds, until softened.
- Plate fries and top or serve with garlic sauce. Consume immediately!
- MAKES 2 SERVINGS

97. Sweet Potato Fries Recipe

Serving: 4 | Prep: | Cook: 30mins | Ready in:

Ingredients

- 4 sweet potatoes
- extra virgin olive oil
- garlic salt or seasoned Salt
- cayenne pepper

- cooking spray

Direction

- Cut Sweet Potatoes into long French fry cuts
- Mix first 4 ingredients
- Everything is to your taste so sprinkle according to how you like
- Spray the cooking spray lightly on cookie sheet
- Cook in 350 Oven for 30 min or until golden brown
- Or put in foil and add a clove of Garlic and let cook on BBQ

98. Sweet Potato Fries With Banana Ketchup Recipe

Serving: 8 | Prep: | Cook: 20mins | Ready in:

Ingredients

- 4 sweet potatoes
- salt
- olive oil
- banana sauce
- 1 banana
- 1/2 cup of heinz tomato ketchup
- 1 tbs molasses
- 3 drops of Tabasco sauce, add to your liking
- or for a milder taste cayenne pepper

Direction

- Clean sweet potatoes
- Cut to your liking
- Season with salt and drizzle olive oil on top
- Bake @ 350 for 20 minutes
- If you want them golden broil for 2 minutes
- In a blender mix banana and all ingredients for the sauce till perfectly pureed.
- Tip.... for best presentation and a kick of extra flavour add some rosemary

99. Sweet Potato Fries With Spicy Mayo Recipe

Serving: 4 | Prep: | Cook: 30mins | Ready in:

Ingredients

- For the fries:
- 1 sweet potato, sliced into matchsticks
- olive oil
- Old Bay®
- For the Spicy mayo:
- mayonnaise or veganaise
- whole grain mustard
- Old Bay®

Direction

- Preheat oven to 425.
- Slice the sweet potato into batard/matchsticks NOT julienne slices.
- Toss in a bowl with a generous amount of olive oil and a good tablespoon of Old Bay®.
- Spray a cookie sheet with cooking spray (I like Grapeseed oil for high temperatures).
- Spread out the sweet potatoes in one even layer.
- Bake for 15 minutes, take out and flip them and bake for an additional 15 minutes.
- While they're baking, mix the ingredients for your spicy mayo, seasoning to taste, then devour.

100. Sweet Potatoe Fries Recipe

Serving: 4 | Prep: | Cook: 60mins | Ready in:

Ingredients

- 4 large sweet potatoes cut into wedges
- 2 tbsp veggie oil
- 2 tbsp ground cumin

- 1 tbsp chilli powder
- 1 tsp cayenne pepper

Direction

- Preheat oven to 400°F. Place a large baking sheet in the oven (yes put it in the oven without anything on it, we are making the sheet hot first). Remove from the oven after 15 minutes.
- While the sheet is heating up, place all ingredients in a large mixing bowl and toss to coat.
- Remove the sheet from the oven and carefully place all wedges on the pan, with one flat side down. You should hear a sizzle.
- Place in the oven for 1 hour. Turn the wedges over every 15-20 minutes.
- Serve as a side to fish or meat, or have as a snack on their own. Enjoy!

101. Toaster Oven Fried Potatoes Recipe

Serving: 4 | Prep: | Cook: 60mins | Ready in:

Ingredients

- Peeled potaoes thinly sliced
- oil
- salt
- ketchup

Direction

- Place potatoes in between slats
- Bake at 400F until desired doneness
- That it!

102. Wet Fries Recipe

Serving: 24 | Prep: | Cook: 25mins | Ready in:

Ingredients

- 1/2 Package (8 oz) frozen french fries
- 1 Can chili with or without beans(If you have made a good homemake chili this would be nice)
- 1 Cup Grated cheddar cheese (I like to melt down Velveeta,with Rotel tomatoes,for my cheese)
- Garnishes:
- Chopped fresh tomatoes
- Sliced jalapenos
- sour cream
- Slice black olives
- Chopped green chilies
- Slice green onion
- or any thing else that meets your fancy

Direction

- Heat French Fries in oven according to package directions
- Heat your chili
- Chop you Vegetables
- Arrange your garnishes
- Place fries on an oven proof plate
- Top with the chili, cheese
- Place in oven or microwave to melt cheese and heat through
- Top with your favourite Garnishes
- Lots and Lots of Napkins

103. Whacky Baked Carrot And Turnip Fries Recipe

Serving: 4 | Prep: | Cook: 20mins | Ready in:

Ingredients

- 4 or 5 large turnips
- 4 or 5 medium carrots
- 1 tbsp vegetable oil
- 1/3 cup grated parmesan cheese
- 1/2 cup garlic flavoured croutons ****
- salt and pepper, to taste

- ****note**** you may use plain croutons and add in a 1/2 tsp garlic powder

Direction

- Preheat oven to 425 F.
- Peel and cut turnips and carrots into skinny matchsticks. Place in a bowl and toss with vegetable oil until evenly coated. Set aside.
- In a large Ziploc bag, place the croutons and close the bag tight. With a rolling pin (or other heavy object) roll over the bag until the croutons are smashed into medium/fine crumbs.
- Open bag, add in parmesan and salt and pepper. Close bag and shake to combine.
- Drop the oil coated vegetable sticks into the bag with seasoned crumbs and shake until coated with crumb mixture. (You may have to do this in batches if all the sticks won't fit at once)
- Place coated sticks on a lightly oiled baking sheet and place in the oven. Bake for 15-25 minutes depending on vegetable thickness. Turn halfway through cooking to ensure even crispness. :)

104. Yuppie Fries Recipe

Serving: 4 | Prep: | Cook: 35mins | Ready in:

Ingredients

- 10-12 mini red potatoes
- 1 Tb. extra virgin olive oil
- 1/2 tsp. fresh ground black pepper
- 1 1/2 tsp. crushed dried rosemary
- 1 tsp. garlic powder
- 1 tsp. sea salt.

Direction

- Preheat oven to 425 degrees F.
- Cut potatoes into thin wedges, no more than 1/4 inch thick.
- Place potatoes and all other ingredients into a gallon storage bag.
- Shake until well coated.
- Spread potatoes onto a baking sheet lined with aluminum foil (shiny side down) in a single layer.
- Bake for 17 minutes.
- Remove from oven and turn potatoes.
- Bake for an additional 17 minutes or until desired crispness.
- Serve immediately.

105. Zucchini Oven Fries Recipe

Serving: 4 | Prep: | Cook: 15mins | Ready in:

Ingredients

- 2 medium zucchini
- 6 tablespoons low fat milk
- 2 egg whites
- 1 cup dry bread crumbs, can use seasoned
- 1 teaspoon kosher salt
- 1/2 teaspoon, or more, fresh ground pepper
- 4 tablespoons grated romano cheese
- cooking spray
- Dippers: ranch dressing, seasoned sour cream, warm marinara sauce.

Direction

- Preheat oven to 425°.
- Spray a rimmed baking sheet with cooking spray.
- Cut zucchini in half lengthwise and if the seeds are large, scoop out seeds and discard.
- Cut the zucchini into French fry type strips.
- In a bowl, whisk the egg whites and milk together.
- In a shallow dish, mix together bread crumbs, salt, pepper and cheese.
- Dip the zucchini strips into the egg white mixture until well coated.

- Dip the zucchini strips into the bread crumb mixture until well coated.
- Place the strips on the baking sheet leaving space between each stip.
- Bake about 6-7 minutes on each side.
- Handle gently with a spatula when turning so you don't lose any of the bread crumbs.
- Dippers: ranch dressing, seasoned sour cream, warm marinara sauce.

106. Hot Jacky Yam Fries Recipe

Serving: 2 | Prep: | Cook: 30mins | Ready in:

Ingredients

- large freezer size zip loc bag
- 1/2 yam per person
- crushed pepper
- garlic
- cayenne pepper
- allspice
- brown sugar
- jack daniels
- olive oil spray

Direction

- Slice yams into French fries slices....think steak fries. I like mine kind of thick you might like them skinny
- Put slices in gallon zip lock bag
- Add the rest of the ingredients to taste, I like a splash of jack Daniels and I prefer to spray the yams toss them in the bag and spray a little more so they are coated and everything sticks
- After you have rolled the slices around in the bag put them on a cookie sheet and bake for 30 mins at 350 degrees.
- I like to put them on aluminum foil before the cookie sheet...easy clean up.
- ENJOY!

107. Zucchini Fries Recipe

Serving: 6 | Prep: | Cook: 30mins | Ready in:

Ingredients

- 2 zucchini
- 1 egg white
- 1/4 cup milk
- 1/2 cup shredded Parmesan
- 1/2 cup seasoned breadcrumbs

Direction

- Preheat oven to 425
- Cut zucchini into 3 inch sticks.
- Whisk and egg white in a small bowl & add 1/4 cup milk
- Combine half cup shredded parmesan & half cup bread crumbs in a separate bowl. Dip zucchini in egg mix then bread crumb mix.
- Coat a baking sheet with cooking spray and place zucchini on sheet.
- Bake for 25 to 30 minutes, until golden and brown.

Chapter 3: Home Fries Recipes

***

108. Best Home Fried Potatoes Recipe

Serving: 4 | Prep: | Cook: 20mins | Ready in:

Ingredients

- 2 large baking potatoes

- 3 tablespoons unsalted butter
- 3 tablespoons vegetable oil
- 1 medium onion sliced thin and separated into rings
- 1 teaspoon salt
- 1 teaspoon freshly ground black pepper

Direction

- Peel potatoes then slice into thin slices.
- Heat butter and oil in heavy skillet then spread thin layer of potatoes into fat and cook for 5 minutes.
- Then layer onion rings and remaining potato slices in skillet and turn with broad spatula.
- Cook potatoes until golden brown then turn again.
- Cook and turn until potatoes are crisp and brown then season with salt and pepper.

109. Breakfast Home Fries Recipe

Serving: 2 | Prep: | Cook: 1hours | Ready in:

Ingredients

- 2 tbls. butter
- 1 tbls. olive oil
- red potatoes, diced and parboiled
- 1 small onion, chopped
- 2 cloves garlic, finely chopped
- salt and pepper to taste

Direction

- In skillet, add butter and oil: heat to medium
- Add remaining ingredients
- Fry, turning often until golden brown
- When plated, I love a dash of hot sauce (optional)

110. Chicago Style Home Fries Recipe

Serving: 6 | Prep: | Cook: 25mins | Ready in:

Ingredients

- 4 large Russet or yukon gold potatoes, cut into 2" (about 4.5 cm) chunks (leave the skin on) I Like Using Reds...
- 2 medium onions (or more–they do shrink down!), sliced thinly in half-moons
- 2 - 4 Tbsp. extra virgin olive oil
- 1 1/2 Tbsp. Chicago-Style steak seasoning (Any Brand) -
- McCormick Grill Mates is A Good One!!!

Direction

- Bring a large pot of water to the boil.
- Add potatoes and allow to boil for about 7 minutes, until just fork-tender. (Don't over boil, or these will turn to mush in the fry pan!) Alternately, if you're okay with a microwave, you can nuke these until just soft.
- Meanwhile, in a large skillet, heat the oil over medium heat and add the onion. Cover the pan and allow to cook for 5-10 minutes, stirring occasionally, until the onion is soft and just turning golden.
- Add the potato chunks to the pan, stir well to coat with the onion/oil mixture, and sprinkle with the steak spice. Continue to fry for about 5 minutes at a time before stirring, until the potato chunks are browned and have accumulated some nice crispy bits on them, another 10 minutes or so. Remove to a serving dish and dig in.

111. Deep Fried Home Made Potato Chips Recipe

Serving: 2 | Prep: | Cook: 15mins | Ready in:

Ingredients

- 2 to 3 medium potatoes unpeeled
- canola oil
- sea salt

Direction

- Very thinly slice the raw potatoes by hand or with a food processor
- Heat the canola in a deep kettle or fryer pot
- Add the chips a few at a time, and cook until golden brown.
- Sprinkle with sea salt and allow to dry.
- NOTE:
- You may need to turn these occasionally for even browning

112. Elaines Home Fries With A Plus Recipe

Serving: 4 | Prep: | Cook: 25mins | Ready in:

Ingredients

- 4 to 6 medium sized Idaho red potatoes
- 1 large red onion
- 1 tbsp butter
- 3 tbsp olive oil
- juice of 1/2 lemon
- salt & pepper to preference
- 1/2 tsp garlic powder (not garlic salt)
- OR, 1 garlic clove, minced
- dried parsley for sprinkling

Direction

- Prepare the pan with olive oil & butter, melted
- Cube the potatoes
- Chop onion coarsely
- Add to pan
- Add salt, pepper and garlic
- Fry until potatoes are lightly browned, then add the lemon juice and continue frying until golden
- Sprinkle with parsley and serve

113. Home Fried New Potatoes Recipe

Serving: 4 | Prep: | Cook: 15mins | Ready in:

Ingredients

- 10 baby new potatoes, quartered
- 2 tablespoons margarine
- salt and pepper, to taste
- 1 teaspoon dry parsley

Direction

- Melt margarine in sauté pan.
- Add potatoes and toss quickly to coat, salt and pepper and add parsley, toss to coat again.
- Fry on medium to medium-high heat until potatoes are browned, crisp and done all the way through.
- Serve hot

114. Home Fried Potatoes Recipe

Serving: 6 | Prep: | Cook: 15mins | Ready in:

Ingredients

- 3 medium baking potatoes
- 1 large white onion sliced thin
- 3-1/2 tablespoons bacon drippings
- 1/4 teaspoon seasoned salt
- 1/4 teaspoon garlic powder
- 1/4 teaspoon pepper

Direction

- Peel potatoes and place in a medium pan with enough cold water to cover them.
- Bring to a boil over medium heat then drain potatoes and refrigerate.
- While chilled cut into thin slices.

- In medium cast iron skillet sauté onions in bacon drippings then add potatoes.
- Add seasonings and periodically shake pan over medium heat until potatoes are golden all over.
- Serve hot.

115. Home Fries 1 Recipe

Serving: 6 | Prep: | Cook: 45mins | Ready in:

Ingredients

- 4 large unpeeled idaho potatoes (about 10 ounces each), well scrubbed
- 4 tablespoons unsalted butter (1/2 stick)
- 2 tablespoons olive oil
- 1 green bell pepper, seeds and membranes removed, finely chopped (about 3/4 cup)
- 2 shallots, peeled and minced
- 3 tablespoons minced Italian parsley

Direction

- Heat oven to 375°F.
- Halve potatoes lengthwise and place them, cut side up, directly on the oven rack. Roast until the entire cut surface of the potatoes has a golden-brown crust and the tip of a paring knife easily pierces the underside, about 45 minutes. Let potatoes cool until they are easy to handle, then cut them into large dice; you should have about 8 cups.
- Melt butter with oil in a heavy sauté pan over medium-high heat. When mixture foams, add bell pepper and shallots. Continue cooking until vegetables are softened and edges are beginning to colour, about 3 minutes.
- Add potatoes, tossing to coat, and cook until heated through, about 6 to 8 minutes. Turn them only once or twice so that they have a chance to get crisp. Liberally season potatoes with salt and pepper, and toss with parsley.

116. Home Fries Made Easy Recipe

Serving: 2 | Prep: | Cook: 10mins | Ready in:

Ingredients

- 2 medium potatoes cut into small squares
- All season salt
- dried parsley
- butter
- 1 small onion cut into rings
- garlic

Direction

- Sauté garlic then onions until caramelized while you microwave potatoes for 4-5 minutes to make them soft. Then sauté. Add All Season salt to taste. Sprinkle with dried parsley upon plating. Enjoy! :))

117. Indian Home Fries Recipe

Serving: 12 | Prep: | Cook: 50mins | Ready in:

Ingredients

- 6 medium boiling potatoes
- 4 tablespoons water
- 2 tablespoons grated fresh ginger
- 4 garlic cloves finely chopped
- 1 teaspoon salt
- 1/2 teaspoon turmeric
- 1 pinch ground red pepper
- 2 tablespoons vegetable oil
- 1 teaspoon fennel seeds

Direction

- In large pot cover potatoes with water and bring to a boil.

- Lower heat and simmer covered for 35 minutes.
- Drain and cool slightly then peel and cut into cubes.
- In a blender process water, ginger, garlic, salt, turmeric and red pepper until a paste is formed.
- In a large preferably non-stick skillet heat oil over medium high heat.
- When hot add the fennel and cook 30 seconds.
- Remove from heat and stir in spice paste then cook 2 minutes.
- Add potatoes and stir with a spatula to evenly coat with the spice paste.
- Fry 10 minutes turning occasionally until potatoes have a golden brown crust.

118. JKs Home Fries Recipe

Serving: 4 | Prep: | Cook: 60mins | Ready in:

Ingredients

- 1/2 lb purple peruvian potatoes, washed and cut in half - skin on
- 1/2 medium/large onion sliced thin
- salt and pepper to taste
- 1/4 tsp dried rosemary
- 1/8 - 1/4c vegetable oil

Direction

- Preheat oven to 450
- Take washed and halved potatoes and boil until fork tender
- Drain water and return potatoes to pan
- Toss potatoes and onions with vegetable oil
- Crush rosemary in finger tips and sprinkle on potatoes
- Season liberally with salt and pepper
- Add to roasting pan and put in oven
- Roast until golden brown and delicious.

119. Light Breakfast Potatoes Recipe

Serving: 4 | Prep: | Cook: 45mins | Ready in:

Ingredients

- 1 large sweet onion, diced
- 2 cloves garlic, minced
- 4 medium red potatoes, scrubbed and chopped
- 2/3 cup vegetable broth
- 1 tbsp Montreal steak spice seasoning (more, to taste)

Direction

- Heat a large non-stick skillet over medium high heat.
- Add the onion and a splash of water and cook 5 minutes, stirring occasionally and adding water as needed, until softened.
- Add garlic, potatoes and another splash of water and cook 5 minutes more.
- Add broth and steak spice, stirring well.
- Cover and simmer 15-20 minutes, until potatoes are just tender.
- Uncover and cook over high heat 5 minutes, until broth has evaporated.

120. Potato Frittata From Mrs. Dash Recipe

Serving: 4 | Prep: | Cook: 30mins | Ready in:

Ingredients

- Potato Frittata
- Ingredients:
- 3 Tbsp. Mrs. Dash® garlic & herb seasoning Blend
- 3 small russet potatoes, cooked, peeled and sliced in 1/4 slices
- 4 whole eggs or egg substitute
- cooking spray

Direction

- Directions:
- 1. Spray with cooking spray a 5 or 6 x 2 inch deep cake pan.
- 2. Layer pan with potato slices.
- 3. Stir eggs with Mrs. Dash® Garlic & Herb Seasoning Blend. Pour over potatoes and bake in a 375°F preheated oven until set, about 6-7 minutes.

121. Smokey Saucy Homefries Recipe

Serving: 2 | Prep: | Cook: 30mins | Ready in:

Ingredients

- 1 large potato, scrubbed not peeled. (The skin contains 70% of the nutrition!)
- 1\3 small onion, diced
- 2 garlic cloves, minced
- 1\3 cup of red bell pepper, diced
- Parsley, oregano, cumin, turmeric, smoked paprika, salt, white pepper, a half pinch of red pepper, a smidge of garlic powder to add 'oomph' and a heaping tablespoon of my beloved South African Smoke Seasoning blend from Trader Joe's.
- Oil for frying. I didn't have my usual grapeseed oil so I was forced to use canola. I hate canola oil.

Direction

- On a medium flame (and seriously, everything will burn if the flame is too high so keep it in check) add the onions and potatoes. Make sure to chop the potatoes thin and put them in first so they have time to cook. My ex used to par-boil her potatoes before frying them, but I don't have a dishwasher so I did it all in one pan.
- Add the garlic and peppers a few minutes in, after the onions and potatoes have begun sizzling.
- Add the spices to your specifications. You guys already know my taste buds are damaged so my level of seasoning is unbearable to most of you.
- Mix with a wooden spoon and let cook for about 15-20 minutes, or until the potatoes are tender. If it gets stuck to the bottom of the pan, don't be afraid to add some water and scrape all that great stuff up. It lends to the dish, trust me.
- Also, don't be afraid to taste it. How else will you know when it's done or what else it needs?
- When you're satisfied with it, mix well and shovel onto a plate. Serve with eggs and shovel liberally into noise hole.

122. Spicy Diner Style Home Fries Recipe

Serving: 4 | Prep: | Cook: 15mins | Ready in:

Ingredients

- 1 idaho potatoes- washed
- 1 medium white onion- thick diced
- 1 tbsp garlic powder
- 1/2 tbsp onion powder
- cayenne pepper- to taste
- salt-to taste
- coarse black pepper- few grinds
- PAM original flavor
- 1/2 tbsp olive oil (I use extra virgin)
- 2-3 tbsp cilantro- finely chopped (optional)

Direction

- 1. Ghetto style boiled potatoes. Wrap each potato in plastic wrap and microwave for about 4 minutes each until 4 tender. Set aside to cool. Dice into medium-sized cubes (same size as onions preferably).

2. Meanwhile in a large non-stick skillet spray with PAM and pour oil and set over medium flame. Add onions and sauté for 2 minutes. Add spices and sauté until fragrant and onions are soft- about 5-7 minutes. Add potatoes and combine with spices and onions. Sauté for about 8 minutes, with 5 minutes covered. This is when the potatoes will get crispy on one side- increase/decrease flame accordingly. I had it on medium-high flame. Uncover, taste for salt and spices. Place in serving dish and top with chopped cilantro (if desired). Serve with favourite breakfast meal!

123. Sweet Potato Home Fries Recipe

Serving: 4 | Prep: | Cook: 35mins | Ready in:

Ingredients

- 1 clove garlic
- about 3-4 green onions
- 4 medium sized sweet potatoes
- 2 tbsp peanut oil infused with red pepper flakes
- about 6 oz of shaved lean deli ham
- 1 sweet bell pepper
- garlic salt to taste
- pepper to taste
- paprika for taste and color
- handful of parsley or ive used cilantro as well
- 1/4 cup parmesan cheese

Direction

- Preheat oven to 350
- Mince garlic
- Chop green onion
- Chop bell pepper into bite size pieces
- Quarter sweet potatoes and then slice about 1/8 inch thick
- Mince parsley or cilantro
- Chop deli ham into small pieces
- Heat oil in a non-stick skillet over medium-high heat
- Add deli ham and allow to crisp up a bit
- Add garlic, bell pepper and sweet potatoes
- Season with a sprinkling of garlic salt, pepper and paprika (try to do a thin layer where each potato has a little season, not to heavy as you will season one more time after turning)
- Allow to cook with a lid on until bottom side is crisp, about 10 or 15 minutes
- Flip potatoes and break up a little, adding in green onions and one thinner layer of seasonings
- Cook for another 10-15 minutes until crisp on bottom
- Flip and break up potatoes, add parsley and mix through
- Sprinkle with parmesan cheese and put in oven about 10 minutes until cheese is melted and potatoes are crispy outside and tender inside
- Enjoy!

124. Truffled Home Fries Recipe

Serving: 2 | Prep: | Cook: 20mins | Ready in:

Ingredients

- 2 cups boiled yukon gold potatoes, roughly chopped
- 1 large onion, sliced into thin 1/2 rings
- 1 tbs. butter
- 1 tbs. olive oil
- 1 tsp.-1 tbs. truffle oil
- coarse salt and fresh ground black pepper

Direction

- Melt oil and butter together in a sauté pan over medium high heat. When the mixture starts to sizzle, add the onions. Sautee until edges are crispy and brown, about 10 minutes. Remove with a slotted spoon and set aside.

- Add the potatoes to the pan and fry until the outsides turn golden and crusty. Season with salt and pepper to taste.
- Mix onions into the potatoes and put the mixture into a serving dish. Drizzle with the truffle oil. Start with just a teaspoon and cautiously add more to taste. (I generally use truffle oil very sparingly as it can be overwhelming, but the potatoes and onions stand up to fit nicely and can carry a reasonably generous drizzle.)
- Sprinkle with coarse salt and freshly ground pepper and serve.

Chapter 4: Awesome French Fries Recipes

***

125. A And W Sauce For Coney Syle Fries Recipe

Serving: 6 | Prep: | Cook: 30mins | Ready in:

Ingredients

- 1/2 small onion, chopped.
- 1 pound lean hamburger meat.
- 1 can tomato soup undiluted
- 1/3 tomato soup can of water.
- 1 package of taco seasoning Mix.
- A few crushed chili flakes
- Prpeared French Fries

Direction

- Sauté onions in a little oil in a large sauce pan until opaque.
- Add hamburger meat and brown thoroughly.
- Add tomato soup and water.
- Mix in Taco Seasoning Mix and crushed chilies and stir well.
- Cover and simmer for about a half hour.
- Serve the meat sauce over freshly prepared French fries.

126. Air Fryer French Fries Recipe

Serving: 0 | Prep: | Cook: | Ready in:

Ingredients

- 1 pound russet potatoes, peeled
- 2 teaspoons vegetable oil
- 1 pinch cayenne pepper
- ½ teaspoon kosher salt

Direction

- Cut each potato lengthwise into 3/8-inch-thick slices. Slice sections into sticks also about 3/8 inch-wide.
- Cover potatoes with water and let soak for 5 minutes to release excess starches. Drain and cover with boiling water by a few inches (or place in a bowl of boiling water). Let sit for 10 minutes.
- Drain potatoes and transfer onto some paper towels. Blot off the excess water and let cool completely, at least 10 minutes. Transfer into a mixing bowl; drizzle with oil, season with cayenne, and toss to coat.
- Preheat the air fryer to 375 degrees F (190 degrees C). Stack potatoes in a double layer in the fryer basket. Cook for 15 minutes. Slide basket out and toss fries; continue frying until golden brown, about 10 minutes more. Toss fries with salt in a mixing bowl. Serve immediately.

127. Almanzo Wilders Fried Apples N Onions Recipe

Serving: 6 | Prep: | Cook: 15mins | Ready in:

Ingredients

- 1/2 lb bacon
- 6 yellow onions sliced
- 6 tart apples (i use granny smith or fugi) sliced
- 2 tbsp brown sugar

Direction

- In a large skillet fry the bacon until brown and crisp
- Remove bacon and put on a warming platter
- Drain all but 1 tbsp. of bacon grease
- Add the onion slices
- Cook over medium high heat for about 3 minutes
- Add the apple slices
- Stir in the brown sugar
- Cover the skillet and let cook until onions and apples are tender but not mushy
- Stir enough to prevent scorching
- Remove to large serving bowl and crumble bacon on top.
- Serve immediately.

128. Antique Recipe For Fried Potatoes Recipe

Serving: 6 | Prep: | Cook: 20mins | Ready in:

Ingredients

- boiled potatoes
- butter
- egg yoke
- bread crumbs
- lard

Direction

- Take cold, boiled potatoes, grate them, make them into flat cakes, and fry them in butter.
- You may vary these cakes by dipping them in the yolk of an egg and rolling them in bread crumbs, frying them in boiling lard.

129. Asian Crisp Fried Noodles And Chili Vegetables Recipe

Serving: 2 | Prep: | Cook: 10mins | Ready in:

Ingredients

- 1 3/4 ounces Chinese vermicelli
- oil
- 1/2 teaspoon oil
- 1 teaspoon grated fresh ginger
- 1/2 tablespoon chopped coriander
- 1/2 garlic clove
- 1/2 onion, cut in thin wedges
- 1/2 red chili pepper, finely chopped
- 1/2 green pepper, cut into fine strips
- 1/2 large carrot. cut into fine strips
- 7 ounces baby corn, fresh is best
- 7 ounces straw mushrooms
- 1/4 cup soy sauce
- 1/8 cup malt vinegar
- 1 teaspoon brown sugar
- 1/4 cup coriander leaves
- 1/2 teaspoon preserved chopped chili

Direction

- Deep fry the Chinese vermicelli in hot oil.
- Drain on absorbent paper.
- Place on a large serving plate and keep warm.
- Heat the teaspoon of oil in a large pan.
- Add the ginger, coriander and garlic and cook for 2 minutes.
- Add onion, red and green peppers and carrot.
- Stir fry for 3 minutes.
- Add the corn, mushrooms soy sauce, vinegar, brown sugar and chilli.

- Stir to combine and cook over a high heat for 3 minutes.
- Spoon the vegetables over the noodles, pour over any remaining sauce.
- Garnish with the coriander leaves and serve.
- Serves 2.

130. Asian Stir Fried Broccoli Recipe

Serving: 4 | Prep: | Cook: 10mins | Ready in:

Ingredients

- 1 tablespoon vegetable oil
- 2 cloves garlic minced
- 1 teaspoon grated fresh ginger
- 1 small white onion sliced
- 1 pound broccoli florets
- 1/2 red bell pepper sliced in thin strips
- 2 tablespoons water
- 1 tablespoon cooking sherry
- 1 tablespoon oyster sauce

Direction

- Heat oil in a heavy skillet.
- Add garlic and ginger then stir fry for 15 seconds.
- Add onions and stir fry until wilted.
- Add broccoli and red pepper and mix well.
- Add water and cover cooking over medium heat for 5 minutes.
- Mix sherry and oyster sauce or soy sauce in a small container.
- Drizzle over vegetables and toss well to mix.

131. Asparagus And Mushroom Stir Fry Recipe

Serving: 8 | Prep: | Cook: 10mins | Ready in:

Ingredients

- 2 lb thin asparagus
- 10 shiitake mushrooms, stemmed
- 2 tbsp olive oil
- 1 tsp chopped garlic
- 1/4 cup chicken stock
- 1 tbsp soy sauce
- 1 tbsp balsamic vinegar
- salt and freshly ground pepper
- 1/2 cup chopped chives

Direction

- Trim asparagus and break off hard end. Cut in 2-inch lengths.
- Slice shiitake mushrooms.
- Heat oil in skillet over medium-high heat.
- Add garlic and stir-fry for 30 seconds.
- Add asparagus and mushrooms and stir-fry for 1 minute or until mushrooms are slightly limp.
- Stir in stock, soy and vinegar.
- Bring to boil, cover pan and steam until asparagus is tender, about 2 to 3 minutes depending on thickness of asparagus.
- Uncover and season with salt and pepper.
- Stir in chives.

132. Authentic Chinese Fried Rice Recipe

Serving: 4 | Prep: | Cook: 10mins | Ready in:

Ingredients

- 12 oz. long-grain rice
- 3 pieces bacon
- 8 oz. Chinese barbecued pork tenderloin
- 1 cup cooked peas
- 3 eggs
- salt and pepper
- oil
- 2 tsp. grated green ginger
- 8 shallots or spring onions

- 1 lb. prawns
- 2 tbsp. oil, extra
- 2 tsp. soya sauce

Direction

- The day before:
- Make rice and spread evenly over two large cookie trays. Refrigerate overnight. Stir occasionally to allow rice to dry completely. If you want to serve rice the same day, spread out on shallow trays, put in moderate oven (325 F.) 15 to 20 minutes; stir rice every five minutes to bring the moist grains to the top.
- Finely dice bacon, fry until crisp, and drain; slice pork thinly. Beat eggs lightly with fork, season with salt and pepper. Heat a small quantity of oil in pan, pour in enough of egg mixture to make one pancake; turn; cook other side. Remove from pan, repeat with remaining egg mixture. Roll up pancakes, slice into thin strips. Finely chop shallots, shell and devein prawns, if large cut into smaller pieces. Heat extra oil in pan or wok. Sauté ginger one minute, stir in rice, stir five minutes. Add bacon, pork, shallots, peas, egg strips and prawns, mix lightly. When completely heated add soya sauce, mix well.

133. Baby Bok Choy Stir Fry Recipe

Serving: 4 | Prep: | Cook: 10mins | Ready in:

Ingredients

- baby bok choy Stir Fry
- 1 tbsp grapeseed oil
- 1 clove garlic, coarsely chopped
- 1 tsp coarsely chopped ginger
- 12 heads baby bok choy, washed, stem trimmed, cut in half
- 2 tbsp tamari or soy sauce
- 2 tsp black sesame seeds

Direction

- Heat grape seed oil in a wok or large sauté pan until almost smoking.
- Add the garlic and ginger.
- Stir-fry over high heat for 30 seconds.
- Add the baby bok choy and tamari.
- Cover for 1 to 2 minutes to steam bok choy.
- Remove from heat, toss with sesame seeds and serve.
- Add a dash of mirin.

134. Bacon Fried Green Beans Recipe

Serving: 24 | Prep: | Cook: 20mins | Ready in:

Ingredients

- 2-4 cans of any type green beans (DRAINED).. pick your favorite!
- I prefer french style but this pic below I used the french cut wides
- 1/2 lb of bacon chopped, or bacon drippings work the same.
- 1 iron skillet..works better then any other
- dash of salt not to much remember your bacon is salty
- pepper...all you like!!!

Direction

- Fry the chopped bacon, leave it in the pan or remove it and replace after beans are done...or if you're going without the bacon, heat the pan good and hot with the bacon drippings.
- When the skillet is sizzling. Toss those green beans in and let 'em fry. Either till they are browned nicely all over or just till they're wilted, either way.
- When I was a child my mama had this green bean dish at the table nearly every night. Sometimes it happened to be our main course. No complaints here I was a veggie lover n still am.

- Now a short funny story... since I've been down here in Mississippi, a lot of these folks don't realize the things you can do to make an extra dish they look at and say hmmmmm. The first week I was down here I cooked this along with pork chops and mashed potatoes. My man comes home from work, mind you never seeing a fried green bean in his life and stated "what in the world is THAT?" I said to him, "hush, taste it, and don't say another word till you've swallowed it". Well he liked them so well. I couldn't keep green beans on hand. He'd call ahead to see if I had green beans. Mind you...this man ate fried green beans for the next 2 weeks straight. I had a feeling the Piggly Wiggly store down here thought I was a bean fanatic buying them by the case. And today, that's his meal, fried green beans, pork chops and woops what else...oh my! I got to think of something before he's due in, he quit eating potatoes...oh well maybe an extra dab of beans will do him!
- Enjoy all. Some may think it's too bland, then spruce it up with some Chinese foods... you might be surprised as to how good this simple dish is. Ya I know greasy but hey how often do we really treat ourselves to something with great flavor and regret it later...hmmm?

135. Bacon Fried Rice Recipe

Serving: 4 | Prep: | Cook: 20mins | Ready in:

Ingredients

- ½ pound bacon, cut into 1/2-inch pieces
- 3 tablespoons vegetable oil
- 2 eggs, beaten
- 3 cups Cold cooked rice
- 1 ½ tablespoons soy sauce
- ½ cup Coarsely chopped green onions

Direction

- In a skillet, fry the bacon until crisp and drain on paper towels.
- In a wok or large skillet, heat 1 tablespoon of the oil. Add the eggs and cook, stirring, just until firm. Remove from the pan and reserve.
- Heat the remaining 2 tablespoons of oil in the pan and add the rice. Mix well.
- Add the soy sauce and mix well. Mix the eggs into the rice, breaking them into smaller pieces as you stir.
- Add the onions and bacon.
- Mix again to combine, and serve.
- Note: Cooked shrimp can be added with bacon, as well as water chestnuts.

136. Bacon And Cheddar Fries Recipe

Serving: 4 | Prep: | Cook: 5mins | Ready in:

Ingredients

- 1 pound regular cut fries with skin on
- 2 ounces shredded cheddar cheese
- 2 strips cooked diced bacon
- 3 ounces sour cream
- 3 tablespoons finely chopped green onions
- 2 tablespoons finely chopped jalapenos

Direction

- Deep fry regular cut fries at 350 for 4 minutes.
- Put fries on platter and top with cheese and bacon.
- Garnish with sour cream, green onions and jalapenos.
- Serve immediately.

137. Batter Fried Zucchini Flowers Recipe

Serving: 4 | Prep: | Cook: 10mins | Ready in:

Ingredients

- 18 zucchini blossoms
- A pint (500 ml) whole milk, or a mixture of beer and milk
- 3 heaping tablespoons flour
- An egg, lightly beaten
- salt
- olive oil or lard, for frying

Direction

- Trim the stems of the zucchini blossoms, remove the pistils, wash them gently and pat them dry just as gently.
- Prepare the batter by combining the milk, flour and egg.
- Heat the oil.
- Lightly salt the zucchini blossoms, dredge them in the batter, fry them until golden, drain them on absorbent paper, and serve them hot.

138. Bea Coles French Fried Onion Rings Recipe

Serving: 6 | Prep: | Cook: 5mins | Ready in:

Ingredients

- white onions
- milk for soaking
- 1 cup flour
- 1/2 teaspoon salt
- 2/3 cups water
- 2 tablespoons vegetable oil
- 1 egg white, beaten
- Crisco for frying
- *May sprinkle with cayenne pepper

Direction

- Slice and separate onions into rings
- Soak in milk for an hour
- Make a batter with the flour, salt, water, 2 tablespoons oil, beaten egg white
- Mix well
- Dip rings in batter and deep fry in Crisco until brown and crisp
- Drain on paper towel

139. Bears Fried Asparagus Recipe

Serving: 46 | Prep: | Cook: 15mins | Ready in:

Ingredients

- 1/2 cup cornstarch
- 3/4 cup flour
- 1 teaspoon salt
- 1/4 teaspoon black pepper
- 1/2 teaspoon white pepper
- 1/2 teaspoon celery salt
- 1/2 teaspoon baking soda
- 1 teaspoon baking powder
- 2 egg whites
- 2/3 cup cold flat beer
- 3 pounds (2 cups) raw, whole asparagus, cleaned and cut above white end

Direction

- Mix all ingredients except asparagus in a bowl with a wire whisk until well blended.
- Dip asparagus spears individually in the batter and deep fry them in at least 2 inches of peanut oil for 2 minutes or until golden brown.
- Dust generously with grated Parmesan cheese.

140. Beer Battered French Fries Recipe

Serving: 2 | Prep: | Cook: 8mins | Ready in:

Ingredients

- 2 large potatoes (russets are best for french fries)
- 2 whole eggs
- 2 1/2 cups flour
- 1 teaspoon baking powder
- 1/2 cup corn starch
- pinch salt and pepper
- 1 (12oz) bottle favorite beer
- milk enough to soak fries
- flour enough to dredge fries
- oil

Direction

- Combine dry ingredients in a mixing bowl. Add the beer and eggs mixing constantly. If the mixture seems too thick, adjust consistency by adding more beer or some water. Allow to rest at least one hour before using.
- Peel and cut the potatoes into fries. Soak in milk.
- Coat fries in the additional flour so the batter will adhere better to fries.
- Fill frying pan will oil (enough to complete cover fries). Heat oil to approximately 375 degrees Fahrenheit.
- Dip fries in batter and drop in oil. Cook until golden brown. Remove from oil and place on paper towels to dry.
- Variations: The same procedures will work well with shrimp, other vegetables, chicken strips or your own creations.

141. Best Fried Egg Sandwich Recipe

Serving: 1 | Prep: | Cook: 8mins | Ready in:

Ingredients

- 2 slices of beef bologna (or pork, if that's your thing)
- 1 large egg
- 2 slices of your favorite bread (I like that grainy whole wheat stuff)
- 1 (optional) slice of American cheese
- mustard
- black pepper

Direction

- Heat up the skillet, then toss the bologna in it and let it sizzle a moment - there's no oil necessary, since we're talking about bologna, here.
- When it's as hot as you want it on one side, flip it
- Stick the bread in the toaster - that is, if you like toasted bread.
- Take the bologna out and crack the egg into the skillet; add a little pepper to it, if you like
- Depending on your interest in the runny-ness factor, over-ease the egg (I tend to flatten my egg since I hate yellow egg goo)
- Pop out your toast, top one piece with the bologna, and cheese if you want it, and spread a little mustard and black pepper
- Top with the egg and the second piece of bread - the cheese will have melted in seconds and the whole thing should still be too hot to bite into right away.
- ENJOY!!

142. Blue Cheese Fried Potatoes Recipe

Serving: 4 | Prep: | Cook: 25mins | Ready in:

Ingredients

- 2 Tablespoons butter
- 2 russet potatoes, sliced into 1/4 inch slices
- 1 large onion, cut into 1/4-inch thick rings
- 1 (4ounce) package blue cheese crumbles
- 4 slices bacon, cooked and crumbled
- salt and ground black pepper to taste

Direction

- 1. Melt the butter in a large skillet over medium heat. Add the potatoes and onions. Cook until onions are golden brown and the potatoes are tender, 15 to 20 minutes. Stir in the blue cheese and bacon, continue to cook until the blue cheese begins to melt. Season with salt and pepper.

143. Bok Choy And Crimini Stir Fry Recipe

Serving: 1 | Prep: | Cook: 10mins | Ready in:

Ingredients

- 3 whole baby bok choy
- 1 cup crimini mushrooms, sliced
- 1/2 cup red onion, chopped
- 1 tbsp soy sauce
- 2 tsp sesame oil, divided
- 1 tsp honey
- 1 tsp red pepper flakes
- 1 tsp fresh ginger, minced

Direction

- Wash and quarter bok choy, reserving leafy tops.
- Heat wok and 1 tsp sesame oil over medium-high heat. Add onions, mushrooms, and lower halves of bok choy.
- Stir fry until veggies begin to turn a lovely golden color. Add leafy tops and stir until just wilted.
- Combine remaining ingredients and add to wok. Stir to coat and cook an extra 1-2 minutes.
- Enjoy!

144. Broccoli And Cauliflower Stir Fry Recipe

Serving: 2 | Prep: | Cook: 15mins | Ready in:

Ingredients

- Ingredients:
- 2 sun-dried tomatoes (not oil-packed)
- 4 tsp. Reduced-sodium soy sauce
- 1 Tbs. rice wine vinegar (or wine vinegar)
- 1 tsp. brown sugar
- 1 tsp. dark sesame oil
- 1/8 tsp. red pepper flakes
- 2 ¼ tsp. vegetable oil
- 2 cups cauliflower florets
- 2 cups broccoli florets
- 1 garlic clove, finely chopped
- 1/3 cup thinly sliced red or green bell pepper

Direction

- 1) Place tomatoes in a small bowl; cover with boiling water. Let stand 5 minutes. Drain; coarsely chop. Meanwhile, blend sauce, vinegar, sugar, sesame oil and red pepper flakes in a small bowl.
- 2) Heat vegetable oil in wok or large non-stick skillet over medium-high heat until hot. Add cauliflower, broccoli and garlic; stir-fry 4 minutes. Add tomatoes and bell pepper; stir-fry 1 minute or until vegetables are crisp-tender. Add soy sauce mixture; cook and stir until heated through. Serve immediately.
- Calories per serving: 214

145. Buttermilk Fried Corn Recipe

Serving: 6 | Prep: | Cook: 15mins | Ready in:

Ingredients

- 3 cups fresh corn kernels
- 2 1/4 cups buttermilk

- 1 cup all purpose flour
- 1 cup cornmeal
- 1 teaspoon salt
- 1 1/2 teaspoon pepper
- canola oil

Direction

- Stir together corn and buttermilk; let stand 30 minutes; drain.
- Combine flour and next 3 ingredients in a large heavy duty zip top plastic bag.
- Add corn to flour mixture, a small amount at a time, and shake bag to coat.
- Pour oil to a depth of 1 inch in a Dutch oven; heat to 375 degrees.
- Fry corn, in small batches, 2 minutes or until golden.
- Drain on paper towels.
- Serve immediately.
- Yield: 3 cups

146. Buttermilk Fried Green Beans Recipe

Serving: 6 | Prep: | Cook: 10mins | Ready in:

Ingredients

- 1 lb. green beans
- 1/2 cup buttermilk
- 2 cups flour
- 1/2 cup cornmeal
- 2 tsp. baking powder
- 2 tsp. salt plus more for sprinkling
- 1/4 tsp. cayenne (optional but delicious)
- oil for frying

Direction

- Preparation:
- Trim, rinse, and thoroughly dry the green beans.
- Put them in a medium bowl and toss with buttermilk to coat.
- Combine flour, cornmeal, baking powder, salt, and cayenne in a large bowl or re-sealable plastic bag.
- Drain green beans and toss them in the flour mixture to coat thoroughly.
- Bring about 1/2 inch oil in a wide, heavy pot to 350-375F degrees over high heat.
- Adjust heat to maintain that temperature range.
- Test temperature using a thermometer or by dipping the handle of a wooden spoon into the oil.
- If the oil bubbles around the handle, it is hot enough to fry the beans.
- Shake excess flour mixture off beans as you add enough of them to form a single layer in the oil.
- Fry until golden to medium brown and beans are tender, about 3 minutes.
- Transfer with tongs or a slotted spoon to a cooling rack set over paper towels.
- Sprinkle with salt and serve hot.
- Repeat with remaining beans.
- Makes about 6 servings Buttermilk Fried Green Beans.

147. CAMPFIRE FRENCH FRIES Recipe

Serving: 4 | Prep: | Cook: 45mins | Ready in:

Ingredients

- 4 potatoes, cut into strips
- 1 T. parmesan cheese
- 1 T. margarine
- 2 T. bacon bits

Direction

- Place each sliced potato on a square of heavy duty foil.
- Sprinkle with salt, pepper, cheese.
- Toss to coat.
- Dot with margarine, sprinkle with bacon bits.

- Seal foil, leaving a steam vent on top.
- Grill over hot coals 30-45 minutes, turning 2 or 3 times.

148. Cajun Fried Okra With Bacon Recipe

Serving: 4 | Prep: | Cook: 20mins | Ready in:

Ingredients

- 4-6 pieces of thick bacon, chopped small and fried in a large skillet
- 1 lb okra cut 1/2 inch thick (NOT breaded)
- 1 onion chopped
- 1 bell pepper chopped
- 1 or 2 cloves of garlic diced
- 1/2 cup chopped or dried parsley
- 1/2 tsp cumin
- A few dashes of soy sauce
- cajun seasoning to taste

Direction

- Fry bacon until crisp and drain.
- On medium high heat, cook vegetables in bacon grease until tender ~15 minutes.
- Add crumbled bacon to the veggies. And toss.
- Variation: When vegetables are tender, add one can of stewed tomatoes and reduce. Add Bacon when done.

149. Caribbean Stir Fried Shrimp Recipe

Serving: 6 | Prep: | Cook: 8mins | Ready in:

Ingredients

- 2 teaspoons vegetable oil, divided
- 1 medium onion, coarsely chopped
- 1 can (20 ounces) pineapple chunks in juice, drained, and patted dry
- 1 pound frozen, large shrimp, thawed, peeled and cleaned
- 1 clove garlic, minced
- Pinch crushed red pepper flakes (optional)
- 1 can (14.5 ounces) diced tomatoes, drained
- 1/4 cup canned, diced mild green chilies
- 1 teaspoon soy sauce
- 3 cups hot cooked rice (optional)

Direction

- Preparation Time: Approximately 5 minutes
- Cook Time: Approximately 8 minutes
- Preparation:
- Heat a large skillet or wok over medium-high heat. Add half the oil and heat until smoking, about 10 seconds. Add the onion and stir-fry until lightly browned, about 1 minute. Add the pineapple and stir fry gently until pineapple browns lightly, about 1 minute. Move pineapple to a bowl and set aside.
- Add remaining oil to the pan. Add shrimp and stir-fry until opaque, about 1 minute. Add garlic and red pepper, if desired, and stir-fry for 10 seconds.
- Add the tomatoes, chilies, and reserved pineapple and stir-fry until heated through, about
- 1 minute. Stir in soy sauce and serve over rice, if desired.
- Tip: We've kept the spiciness light (the canned chilies are mild) and the pinch of crushed pepper flakes is optional. If you want to add a little more heat, increase the pepper. Or for a completely family friendly version, eliminate the red pepper flakes, and your stir-fry will be as mild as a tropical breeze.
- Servings: 6
- Nutritional Information Per Serving: Calories 170; Total fat 3g; Saturated fat 0g; Cholesterol 115mg; Sodium 330mg; Carbohydrate 20g; Fibre 2g; Protein 16g; Vitamin A 6%DV*; Vitamin C 40%DV; Calcium 8%DV; Iron 15%DV
- *Daily Value

150. Cauliflower Potato Fry Recipe

Serving: 4 | Prep: | Cook: 30mins | Ready in:

Ingredients

- 1 small cauliflower, disassembled
- 2-3 medium potatoes (red skin, yukon gold, etc..), cut into cubes
- 3 red or mixed colour pepper, seeded, roughly chopped
- 1/2 Tbsp garam masala (optional)
- salt pepper to taste
- hot paprika to taste
- 4-6 Tbsp olive oil
- 2 medium onions
- 3 cloves garlic
- 2 slices ginger
- 1/2 cup water
- vinegar to taste

Direction

- In a large frying pan add all the ingredients up to and including the oil.
- Fry on medium.
- In a blender, purée all the rest of the ingredients except the vinegar, and add to the pan.
- Fry, turning occasionally, until the cauliflower and potato are cooked, all the liquid has evaporated, and the vegetables have browned. Season with the vinegar and serve.

151. Chicken Fried Rice Recipe

Serving: 1 | Prep: | Cook: 30mins | Ready in:

Ingredients

- 1/4 lb. chicken breasts, cut into 1/2-inch by 1/4-inch pieces
- 1 tbsp oil
- 1/2 Tbsp. fish sauce(nam pla)
- 1 clove garlic, smashed with the side of a cleaver or knife
- 2 1/2 Tbsp. vegetable oil
- 2 cups cooked jasmine rice, at room temperature or from the refrigerator
- 1 egg, lightly beaten with 1/2 tsp. water
- 1 tsp. thick soy sauce(Kikkoman or light soy sauce)
- 1/2 tsp. fish sauce
- 1/4 tsp. ground black or white pepper
- 1 cucumber, peeled and sliced 1/8 inch thick
- lime, fresh red chiles(optional) and scallion

Direction

- Heat 1 Tbsp. oil in a wok until hot, but not smoking, over medium high heat. Cook chicken until just cooked through, about 4 minutes. Add the 1/2 Tbsp. fish sauce, as you are cooking, to the meat. Remove from wok and set aside.
- Heat the additional 2 1/2 Tbsp. oil in wok. Add the smashed garlic, cook briefly (just 30 seconds). Add the rice, breaking it up with a wooden spoon or metal turner. Add the cooked chicken. Toss together in the wok. Add the soy sauce and 1/2 tsp. fish sauce. Add the beaten egg, and pepper. Continue to stir-fry until heated through and grains of rice are separated. Taste and adjust seasoning accordingly (add more fish sauce if it needs)
- Remove to serving dish and garnish with cucumber, scallion, lime wedge, and fresh red chile peppers.

152. Chicken And Sausage Sandwiches With Fried Bell Peppers Recipe

Serving: 4 | Prep: | Cook: 11mins | Ready in:

Ingredients

- 2 tablespoons olive oil, divided
- 2 medium red bell peppers, seeded and sliced into thin strips
- 1 cup onion sliced into half-moons
- salt and freshly ground black pepper to taste
- 1 pound cooked shredded chicken
- 1 cup diced chorizo, andouille, or other cooked spicy sausage
- 2 tablespoons balsamic vinegar
- 4 long rolls (submarine or hoagie rolls)

Direction

- Heat 1 tablespoon of the oil in a large skillet over medium-high heat. Add the bell peppers and onion and cook, stirring, until softened, about 5 minutes. Season with salt and pepper. Remove the vegetables from the skillet and set aside.
- Heat the remaining 1 tablespoon oil in the same skillet over medium-high heat. Add the chicken and cook until golden brown, 3 to 5 minutes. Add the sausage and vinegar and cook for 1 minute to heat through.
- Using tongs, arrange the chicken mixture on the open rolls, top with the fried peppers and serve.

153. Chili Fried Potatoes Recipe

Serving: 6 | Prep: | Cook: 25mins | Ready in:

Ingredients

- 5 medium potatoes, peeled and sliced thin
- Hot bacon drippings, oil, or Crisco for frying
- salt and pepper to taste
- 2 teaspoons chili powder, more or less to taste
- 1 small onion, chopped

Direction

- Prepare potatoes
- In skillet, heat drippings oil or Crisco
- Add potatoes, sprinkle with salt and pepper
- Cover and fry over medium heat, turning occasionally, until almost tender and lightly browned
- Remove lid, and sprinkle with chili powder
- Add the chopped onion
- Increase heat, and finish cooking, turning as needed, until potatoes are nice and brown
- Drain on paper towels

154. Chili Fried Onion Rings Recipe

Serving: 4 | Prep: | Cook: 2mins | Ready in:

Ingredients

- Onion rings are a classic accompaniment to burgers and steaks, but they can be tricky to cook right. The onions can turn out tough and stringy or the batter can be greasy and limp. We wanted crisp, toothsome onion rings coated in a crunchy, well-seasoned batter. Here's what we discovered:
- Test Kitchen Discoveries
- After trying a dozen different batters, we found we preferred a buttermilk and flour batter lightened with cornstarch. It fries up crisp, light, and delicate.
- For the cleanest flavor, fry the rings in either peanut or vegetable oil. And keep the heat high--fry at 400 degrees and don't let the temperature dip below 375 degrees. If the oil temperature dips too low, the onions' batter will absorb the oil and the rings will be greasy.
- Use sweet yellow onions for a bright but not too sharp flavor.
- Boost the heat of the chili powder with a hefty shot of cayenne pepper.
- A little sugar intensifies the flavor of both the onion and the spices. As an added bonus, it intensifies the browning of the batter.

Direction

- Hot and spicy as well as crispy, these onion rings are addictive. They partner perfectly with steaks. Use a deep-fry thermometer to monitor the temperature of the oil.
- 1 cup buttermilk
- 1 ¼ cups all-purpose flour
- ¾ cup cornstarch
- 3 tablespoons chili powder
- 1 teaspoon cayenne pepper
- 1 teaspoon sugar
- 1 ½ teaspoons table salt
- 1 teaspoon ground black pepper
- 6 cups peanut oil or vegetable oil
- 2 large yellow onions, sliced into 1/4-inch rounds and separated into rings
- 1. Adjust oven rack to middle position and heat oven to 250 degrees. Line rimmed baking sheet with paper towels and set aside.
- 2. Place buttermilk in medium bowl. Whisk flour, cornstarch, spices, sugar, salt, and pepper together in another bowl.
- 3. Heat oil in large Dutch oven over medium-high heat to 400 degrees. Meanwhile, dip one-third of onion rings in buttermilk and shake off excess liquid. Dredge rings in flour mixture, shake off excess, and place on large plate. When oil reaches proper temperature, scatter battered onions in single layer in oil and cook, stirring gently, until golden brown, 1 to 2 minutes (oil temperature should not dip below 375 degrees). Using tongs, transfer onions to prepared baking sheet. Place baking sheet in oven.
- 4. Repeat battering and frying process with remaining two batches of onions, making sure oil temperature returns to 400 degrees before adding each batch. Serve.

155. Chinese Style Fried Rice Recipe

Serving: 4 | Prep: | Cook: 40mins | Ready in:

Ingredients

- 2 cups uncooked basmati rice
- 2 cups water
- 1/2 cup ham steak (cut into cubes:pea size)
- 1/2 cup frozen peas & carrots
- 1 cup thinly sliced green onion
- 1/3 cup chopped shiitake mushroom
- 3 eggs, lightly beaten
- 3-4 tablespoons canola oil (or peanut oil)
- 1/4 teaspoon salt
- 1/4 tsp white pepper
- 1 Tbsp oyster sauce
- 1 tsp sugar

Direction

- Cook your rice (I use a rice cooker). You want it a bit on the crunchy side, so even though you might want to add more water, DON'T.
- Let your rice cool completely (I spread it out on a baking sheet and put it in the freezer if I'm in a hurry). You can even cook your rice the night before and let cool in the fridge.
- In wok or heavy large sauté pan over moderately high heat, heat oil until hot but not smoking. Add half of scallions (reserve remainder for garnish) about 1-2 minutes.
- Add eggs and rice and stir-fry until eggs are just set, about 1 minute. Add mushrooms, peas, ham, oyster sauce, sugar, salt, and pepper and stir-fry until heated through and fluffy, 4 to 5 minutes.
- Garnish with remaining scallions and serve.

156. Coconut Fried Rice Recipe

Serving: 4 | Prep: | Cook: 25mins | Ready in:

Ingredients

- 2 large eggs (use higher omega-3 fatty acid eggs if available)
- 1/4 cup egg substitute

- Canola cooking spray
- 1 tablespoon canola oil
- 1 sweet or yellow onion, finely chopped
- 2 to 3 teaspoons minced garlic (depending on your preference)
- 1/2 teaspoon salt (optional)
- 1/2 teaspoon black pepper
- 2 tablespoon catsup
- 1 cup finely diced tomato
- 1/4 cup low-fat milk (or substitute whole milk or fat-free half-and-half)
- A pinch or two of saffron (available in small jars in the spice section of your market)
- A pinch or two of curry powder
- 1/4 teaspoon coconut extract
- 4 cups cooked brown rice (use a rice cooker, or cook on the stove)
- 8 ounces or more frozen, cooked, shelled and de-veined shrimp, thawed; diced tofu; or cooked and shredded or diced chicken, beef, or pork (optional)
- 1/2 cup chopped green onions
- 1/4 cup chopped fresh cilantro leaves

Direction

- 1. Add eggs and egg substitute to medium bowl and beat with fork until well blended. Coat a large, non-stick wok or frying pan with canola cooking spray and start heating over medium-high heat. Pour in the egg mixture and either scramble or cook like an omelet (your choice). Set cooked eggs aside. If you made an omelet, cut into shreds before setting aside.
- 2. To the same wok or frying pan, add canola oil and heat over medium-high heat. Add onions and garlic and stir-fry until golden (a few minutes). Add salt (if desired), pepper, catsup, and diced tomato, and continue to stir-fry for a minute or two. Meanwhile, add the milk, saffron, curry and coconut extract to a 1-cup measure and stir to blend.
- 3. Add the brown rice, shrimp and coconut milk mixture to the wok with the onion mixture and continue to stir-fry for a couple more minutes. Stir in the cooked egg pieces or strips.
- 4. Arrange each serving of rice in a bowl and garnish with green onions and cilantro.

157. Copycat Kentucky Fried Chicken Potato Wedges Recipe

Serving: 4 | Prep: | Cook: 10mins | Ready in:

Ingredients

- 6 medium to large potatoes cut into wedges
- 2 tablespoons msg (Accent)
- 2 tablespoons onion powder
- 4 cups all-purpose flour
- 2 tablespoons salt
- 2 tablespoons cayenne pepper
- 2 teaspoons black pepper
- 2 tablespoons oregano flakes
- 8 chicken bouillon cubes, crushed
- 4 large eggs
- 1/2 cup milk

Direction

- Combine dry ingredients in mixing bowl.
- Mix milk and egg in separate bowl.
- Heat oil to 400 degrees.
- Dip potato wedges in milk/egg mixture and coat well, then place potato wedges in dry ingredient mix and coat well.
- Fry until golden brown.

158. Country Store Fried Apples Recipe

Serving: 8 | Prep: | Cook: 6mins | Ready in:

Ingredients

- 5 to 6 cups firm, tart apples, such as American Cameo or Granny Smith (about 2 1/2 pounds or 4 medium apples)
- 1/3 cup brown sugar
- 1 teaspoon ground cinnamon
- 1/4 teaspoon ground nutmeg
- 2 tablespoons cornstarch
- 1/2 cup apple cider

Direction

- Peel, core and slice apples into medium to thick slices.
- Place apples, brown sugar, cinnamon and nutmeg in small to medium slow-cooker.
- Dissolve cornstarch in apple cider and blend well.
- Pour over apples and stir to blend.
- Cover and cook on low 5 to 6 hours; stir halfway through cooking. Serves 8.
- ==
- Per serving: 102 calories
- (2 percent from fat), trace total fat (trace saturated fat), no cholesterol, 25 g. carbohydrates, trace protein, 6 mg. sodium, 3 g. dietary fibre.

159. Creamy Cheesey Confetti Fried Corn With Bacon Recipe

Serving: 6 | Prep: | Cook: 8mins | Ready in:

Ingredients

- 8 bacon slices, chopped
- 4 cups fresh sweet corn kernels (about 8 ears)
- 1 medium-size white onion, chopped
- 1/3 cup chopped red bell pepper
- 1/3 cup chopped green bell pepper
- 1 (8-ounce) package cream cheese, cubed
- 1/2 cup half-and-half
- 1 teaspoon salt
- 1 teaspoon pepper

Direction

- Cook chopped bacon in a large skillet until crisp; remove bacon, and drain on paper towels, reserving 2 tablespoons drippings in skillet.
- Set bacon aside.
- Sauté corn, onion, and bell peppers in hot drippings in skillet over medium-high heat 6 minutes or until tender.
- Add cream cheese and half-and-half, stirring until cream cheese melts.
- Stir in salt, and pepper.
- Top with bacon.

160. Creamy Fried Corn Recipe

Serving: 68 | Prep: | Cook: 22mins | Ready in:

Ingredients

- 8 slices bcon chopped
- 4 cups fresh sweet corn kernels{about 8 Ears}
- 1 medium size white onion chopped
- 1/3 cup chopped red bell pepper
- 1/3 cup chopped green pepper
- 1{8oz. pkg. cream cheese cubed
- 1/2 cup half and half
- 1 tsp. sugar
- 1 tsp. salt
- 1 tsp. pepper

Direction

- Cook chopped bacon in large skillet until crisp remove bacon and drain on paper towels reserving 2 Tbsp. drippings in skillet set bacon aside.
- SAUTE: Corn onion poppers in hot drippings over medium high heat 6 minutes till tender
- ADD: Cream cheese and half and half stirring until cream cheese melts. Stir in Sugar Salt, Pepper. Top with Bacon
- Prep-15 minutes-Cook 22 minutes

161. Crispy Cajun Fries Recipe

Serving: 6 | Prep: | Cook: 10mins | Ready in:

Ingredients

- 2 pounds russet potatoes, cut into fries
- 1 cup corn flour
- 2 tablespoons cornmeal
- 2 tablespoons cajun seasoning
- 1 quart oil for deep frying
- salt to taste

Direction

- Place cut potatoes into a large bowl of cold water. Soak for 10 minutes. In a large resealable plastic bag, combine the corn flour, corn meal, and Cajun seasoning. Shake the bag to blend. Drain the potatoes, but leave them wet. Place the fries in the plastic bag with the seasoning, and shake to coat.
- Heat the oil in a deep-fryer to 375 degrees F (190 degrees C).
- Cook fries in hot oil for 7 to 10 minutes, or until golden brown. Remove from the fryer to paper towels to drain. Season with a small amount of salt.
- NOTE: If you like it extra spicy soak the cut potatoes in hot sauce for a few seconds before shaking them in the dry batter.

162. Crispy Coated Cajun Fries Recipe

Serving: 6 | Prep: | Cook: 10mins | Ready in:

Ingredients

- 2 pounds russet potatoes, cut into fries
- 1 cup corn flour
- 2 tablespoons cornmeal
- 2 tablespoons cajun seasoning
- 1 quart oil for deep frying
- salt to taste

Direction

- Place cut potatoes into a large bowl of cold water.
- Soak for 10 minutes.
- In a large resealable plastic bag, combine the corn flour, corn meal, and Cajun seasoning.
- Shake the bag to blend.
- Drain the potatoes, but leave them wet.
- Place the fries in the plastic bag with the seasoning, and shake to coat.
- Heat the oil in a deep-fryer to 375 degrees F (190 degrees C).
- Cook fries in hot oil for 7 to 10 minutes, or until golden brown.
- Remove from the fryer to paper towels to drain.
- Season with a small amount of salt.

163. Crispy Fried Eggplant Recipe

Serving: 4 | Prep: | Cook: 20mins | Ready in:

Ingredients

- 1 medium eggplant, whole, sliced 1/8-inch thick
- 3 large eggs, beaten slightly
- 2 cups cornflake crumbs
- 1 cup grated romano/parmesan cheese
- 1/4 cup olive oil

Direction

- 1. Peel eggplant and slice 1/8 inch thick.
- 2. Whip eggs together and place in a shallow bowl for an egg wash.
- 3. Mix cornflake crumbs and Romano/parmesan cheese together in a

shallow container and dredge eggplant slices in the egg wash and then the dry mixture.
- 4. Put enough olive oil in a hot skillet to coat the bottom about 1/16 inch deep. Adjust to medium high heat.
- 5. Fry eggplant slices, turning frequently, until golden brown and crispy. Remove to paper towel to drain. Cover with second paper towel and add layers of eggplant as needed.
- 6. Place eggplant in a preheated 350 degree oven for a few minutes to crispen and degrease them. Remove and serve immediately.

164. Cumin Ketchup And Chili Salted French Fries Recipe

Serving: 2 | Prep: | Cook: 10mins | Ready in:

Ingredients

- 1/2 cup ketchup - Heinz, of course
- 1 t. cumin
- 1 t. balsamic vinegar or red wine vinegar
- 2 t. salt
- 2 t. chili powder - I like the Hot Mexican variety
- 3 large russet potatoes, peeled, wiped dry, cut into generous 1/4" thick sticks
- canola oil (for deep frying)

Direction

- Combine ketchup, cumin and vinegar in small bowl. Combine salt and chili powder in another small bowl.
- Arrange potatoes on absorbable kitchen towel. Roll up, enclosing potatoes, and let stand at least 30 minutes and up to 1 hour to dry.
- Pour oil into heavy, large saucepan to depth of 3". Heat oil to 320 degrees. Add 1/4 of potatoes and fry until just tender and barely colored, about 3 minutes. Transfer potatoes to wire rack set over paper towels to drain. Repeat with remaining potatoes. Cool fries completely.
- Reheat oil to 400 degrees. Fry potatoes in 3 batches until deep golden brown and beginning to blister, about 2 minutes. Transfer to a basket lined with several layers of paper towels. Sprinkle with chili salt and serve with cumin ketchup.
- Now wipe that silly French-fry induced grin off your face right along with the ketchup. They're worth the time and calories!

165. Dads Fried Cabbage Recipe

Serving: 8 | Prep: | Cook: 40mins | Ready in:

Ingredients

- 4 tbsps vegetable oil
- 1 large head cabbage, cored and chopped
- 1 large onion, diced
- 2 large carrots, pared and shredded
- 1/4 tsp garlic powder
- salt & pepper, to taste

Direction

- Add oil to large hot skillet over medium high heat.
- Immediately add all other ingredients. Continue frying mixture over medium high heat for a few minutes. When cabbage is slightly wilted, turn heat down to just under medium and cook for 20 minutes to a half hour, turning occasionally.
- Adjust seasoning, remove from heat and serve.

166. Dal Fry Recipe

Serving: 4 | Prep: | Cook: 30mins | Ready in:

Ingredients

- 1 cup of Toor Dal
- 1 onion cut into long stripes.
- 1 green chilly chopped.
- 1 tomato finely chopped.
- 1 tsp mixture of mustard seeds, whole coriander seeds, cumin seeds, fenugrek seeds.
- 1/2 tsp of tumeric
- 1 tsp chillie powder.
- 1 tsp of dry mango powder or dry anardana powder.
- 1/2 inch grated ginger.
- 2 tbsp of cooking oil.
- 2 tbsp of fresh chopped coriander.
- salt as per taste.

Direction

- Wash dal thoroughly and add 2 cups of water and cook the dal in a pressure cooker until done.
- Cool down cooker, remove dal & beat with spoon or a hand beater.
- Heat 2 tbsp. of oil in a pan. Add mixture of mustard, cumin, fenugreek & whole coriander seeds. When seeds starts popping add chopped onion, tomato, and grated ginger and cook it until soft.
- Add dry mango powder and tsp. of chilli powder and fry for a minute.
- Add dal mixture and bring to boil.
- Simmer for 5 to 10 minutes.
- Garnish it with chopped fresh coriander.

167. Dans Fried Green Tomatoes Recipe

Serving: 4 | Prep: | Cook: 10mins | Ready in:

Ingredients

- 1/2 Cup all-purpose flour
- 3 eggs, beaten
- 1/2 Cup yellow cornmeal
- 1 Lbs green tomatoes, sliced 1/2 thick
- 1/2 canola oil
- kosher salt

Direction

- Place the flour, eggs and cornmeal in three separate shallow bowls.
- Dip the tomatoes first in the flour, then the eggs (letting any excess run off) and finally the cornmeal, pressing gently to help it adhere.
- Heat the oil in a large skillet over medium high heat. Working in batches, cook the tomatoes until golden, 1 to 2 minutes per side.
- Transfer to a paper towel-lined plate. Season with salt before serving.
- Enjoy!

168. Deep Fried Asparagus Or Okra Recipe

Serving: 12 | Prep: | Cook: 10mins | Ready in:

Ingredients

- 1 pound fresh asparagus
- 1 cup flour
- 1 cup buttermilk
- 1 large egg
- 1 Tbs hot sauce (or as desired)
- 1 1/2 cup self rsing cornmeal mix
- 2 Tbs cajun seasoning
- vegetable oil to fry
- mustard Sauce
- 2/3 cup sour cream
- 3 Tbs creole mustard (or use coarse grain)
- 1 1/2 tsp dry ranch dressing mix
- 1 tsp fresh lemon juice
- 1/4 tsp onion pwder
- 1/4 tsp garlic powder
- 1/4 tsp salt or to taste
- pepper to taste

Direction

- Snap off tough ends of asparagus and rinse.
- Do not dry off.
- Place flour in dish and dredge asparagus in flour
- Whisk together buttermilk, egg and hot sauce.
- In another dish combine cornmeal and Cajun seasoning.
- Dip asparagus in buttermilk mixture and then into cornmeal mixture.
- Fry in 2 inches of hot oil at 360 F 4 to 5 minutes or golden.
- Drain on towelling paper.
- Serve with mustard sauce.
- Combine all mustard sauce ingredients.

169. Deep Fried Chicken Drumlets Recipe

Serving: 2 | Prep: | Cook: 10mins | Ready in:

Ingredients

- 6 chicken Drumlets or Wings (I bought wings and saved the mid joints for another dish)
- 1/2 tablespoon light soy sauce
- 1/2 ginger juice
- Plain flour with water for the batter
- breadcrumbs
- oil for frying

Direction

- Use a knife to cut around the rim of the drumlets.
- Use a knife to push the meat to the base.
- Season the drumlets with soy sauce and ginger juice for at least 1/2 hour.
- Coat the drumlets in batter then with the breadcrumbs.
- Deep fry the drumlets. Don't forget the bone too!
- Remove when turned golden brown and serve.

170. Deep Fried Corn On The Cob Recipe

Serving: 4 | Prep: | Cook: 3mins | Ready in:

Ingredients

- peanut oil (or personal favorite)
- 4 Fresh or fully thawed, ears of corn broken or cut in half.
- **** for Batter****
- 1/2 Cup buttermilk
- 2 eggs (well Beaten)
- 1/2 Cup corn Meal (may have to add more to make batter thick enough)
- ****for Coating****
- 1/2 Cup Self-Rising flour (may need more according to preference)
- 1/2 teaspoon garlic powder
- 1/2 teaspoon salt
- 1/8 teaspoon pepper (all of these can be added to according to taste preferences)

Direction

- In a Deep Fat Fryer or Deep Heavy Dutch Oven, Preheat oil to 375 degrees
- Make Batter with Cornmeal, Buttermilk, and Eggs (set aside)
- Combine Flour, Garlic powder, Salt, and Pepper (set aside)
- Dip Corn ears into Cornmeal batter to coat
- Roll in Flour mixture
- With Cooking Tongs, (holding at a safe distance) slowly place ears of Corn in hot Oil 1 at a time
- Fry for about 3 minutes or until golden brown.
- Drain on paper towels
- Serve with corn holders and season as desired.

171. Deep Fried Mac And Cheese Recipe

Serving: 4 | Prep: | Cook: 15mins | Ready in:

Ingredients

- peanut oil, for frying
- 1 recipe "The Lady's Cheesy Mac" prepared, chilled in the refrigerator overnight, and cut into 15 bite-sized squares, recipe follows
- flour, for dredging
- 1 egg, beaten
- Plain bread crumbs, for dredging

Direction

- Heat 2 inches of oil in a large, heavy Dutch oven to 350 degrees F.
- Dredge each Cheesy Mac square in flour, then egg, and then bread crumbs to coat. Fry for about 1 minute on each side until golden brown. Drain on paper towels before serving.
- "The Lady's Cheesy Mac":
- 4 cups cooked elbow macaroni, drained
- 2 cups grated Cheddar
- 3 eggs, beaten
- 1/2 cup sour cream
- 4 tablespoons butter, cut into pieces
- 1/2 teaspoon salt
- 1 cup milk
- Preheat oven to 350 degrees F.
- Once you have the macaroni cooked and drained, place in a large bowl and while still hot, add the Cheddar. In a separate bowl, combine the remaining ingredients and add to the macaroni mixture. Pour macaroni mixture into a casserole dish and bake for 30 to 45 minutes. Top with additional cheese, if desired.

172. Deep Fried Mars Bar Recipe

Serving: 2 | Prep: | Cook: 4mins | Ready in:

Ingredients

- 1/2 cup sifted flour
- 1/2 teaspoon salt
- 1/2 cup cold water
- Pinch baking powder
- 2 Mars Bars
- shortening or oil for frying

Direction

- Thoroughly mix flour, salt, and water.
- Let batter stand at room temperature for 20-30 minutes.
- Add the baking powder to the batter.
- Place shortening or oil in a deep fat fryer and begin heating over high heat (375F).
- Dip the Mars Bars into the batter, draining off the excess.
- Fry until crisp and golden.
- Drain on paper towel.
- * You can make these on a stick, too.
- +Good with vanilla ice cream.

173. Deep Fried Okra Recipe

Serving: 46 | Prep: | Cook: 15mins | Ready in:

Ingredients

- 1 - 2 pounds fresh okra
- 1 egg
- cornmeal
- vegetable oil for frying
- large skillet
- salt & pepper
- bowl with tight fitting lid
- paper towel lined plate

Direction

- Wash and cut tops and ends off of the okra. Cut into 1 - 2 inch pieces. Once the okra is cut up, place in the bowl with the tight fitting lid. Add egg to okra. Place lid over the bowl and shake the okra and egg so all pieces of okra are covered with the egg. Remove lid and add the corn meal. Just enough so the okra isn't gummy. Put lid back on and shake, shake shake until covered well with the cornmeal. Get skillet ready and have the oil hot. Add slowly to the hot oil. Turning often until browned. Once all pieces are browned remove and let drain on the paper towel lined plate. Sprinkle salt and lots of pepper over hot okra. Eat and enjoy!

174. Deep Fried Vegetables Recipe

Serving: 10 | Prep: | Cook: 15mins | Ready in:

Ingredients

- 1 head of broccoli, broken into florets
- 1 head of cauliflower, broken ino florets
- 2 eggs, beaten
- 1 cup grated parmesan cheese
- Enough vegetable oil for deep fryer

Direction

- Heat oil in deep fryer.
- Place broccoli and cauliflower florets into a bowl.
- Pour beaten egg over and toss making sure all florets is coated.
- Sprinkle grated parmesan cheese on top and make sure all florets is covered.
- Deep fry until light brown.
- Drain excess grease on a paper towel.
- Serve with ranch dressing (for dipping).

175. Deep Fried Oyster Po Boy Sandwiches With Spicy Remoulade Sauce Recipe

Serving: 4 | Prep: | Cook: 9mins | Ready in:

Ingredients

- 32 ounces shucked oysters
- 1 cup plus 1 tablespoon milk
- 1 tablespoon water
- 1/4 teaspoon cayenne pepper
- 2 eggs
- 1 cup all-purpose flour
- 1/2 cup cornmeal (recommended: Indian Head)
- 1/2 teaspoon freshly ground black pepper
- kosher salt
- vegetable oil, for frying
- 4 (6-inch) hoagie loaves
- Remoulade Sauce, recipe follows
- 4 leaves romaine lettuce
- 1 to 2 lemons
- Special equipment: brown paper bag
- Spicy Remoulade Sauce:
- 1 1/4 cups mayonnaise
- 1/4 cup stone-ground mustard
- 1 clove garlic clove, smashed
- 1 tablespoon pickle juice
- 1 tablespoon capers
- 1 teaspoon prepared horseradish
- 1/4 teaspoon cayenne pepper
- 1/4 teaspoon hot paprika
- 1/2 teaspoon hot sauce (recommended: Frank's Red Hot)
- Special equipment: a food processor

Direction

- Drain the oysters and place in a small bowl. Cover with 1 cup milk and let soak for 15 minutes. In a medium bowl, whisk together remaining milk, water, cayenne and eggs. Place the flour, cornmeal, black pepper, and salt into a brown paper bag, close and shake to mix.

- In a large heavy-bottomed pot, pour enough oil to fill the pan halfway. Heat until a deep-frying thermometer inserted in the oil reaches 360 degrees F.
- Drain the oysters from the milk. In batches dip oysters in the egg mixture then drop in the paper bag. Close and shake. Remove to a plate and repeat with the rest of the oysters. When oil is at 360 degrees F, fry oysters in batches. Do not overcrowd. Cook turning once until golden brown and cooked through, about 3 minutes. Remove to a paper towel. Repeat with remaining oysters.
- To serve, cut sandwich loaves in half horizontally. Slather a generous amount of Spicy Remoulade Sauce on the inside. Place a lettuce leaf inside and fill generously with oysters. Squeeze fresh lemon juice over oysters just before serving.
- Spicy Remoulade Sauce:
- Place all ingredients into a food processor and blend until smooth. Chill until ready to serve.
- Yield: 1 1/2 cups

176. Definitive Fries Recipe

Serving: 4 | Prep: | Cook: 10mins | Ready in:

Ingredients

- 4 large baking potatoes, russets are good
- oil for frying
- salt

Direction

- For the skinny fries, peel the potatoes (if desired) and cut each one lengthwise into slices 1/3 inch thick. Cut the slices lengthwise into sticks 1/3 inch thick. For the fat chips, prepare as above but slice the potatoes into 1/2 batons. Soak the potatoes in bowls of ice water for at least 30 minutes (as long as overnight) to release the excess starch.
- In a deep fat fryer or a heavy bottomed pot, preheat 3 inches of oil (or follow manufacturer's recommendations) to 300°F.
- Rinse potatoes in a few courses of clean water. Drain, then lay them out on a kitchen towel or paper towel and pat dry. Removing excess moisture at this stage will help reduce the oil from splattering when the potatoes hit the fat.
- Assemble your draining station. Take a baking rack and invert it so that the legs are pointing upwards. Place this on top of a few layers of newsprint.
- Fry the potatoes, in small batches until translucent and just starting to turn pale gold (approximately 6-8 minutes for the skinny fries, 8-10 for the thick ones). Do not overload the oil, or the temperature will drop too quickly and the potatoes will be uneven. Cooking times will depend on the size of batch and how well you can maintain the oil temperature. Using a spider, basket or tongs remove the first batch to the draining rack. Proceed with remaining potatoes until done. Allow to stand for at least 10 minutes, or up to 2 hours.
- When ready to serve, raise the heat of the oil to 375°F.
- Again working in batches, fry the potatoes until golden and crisp, about 2-3 minutes for the skinny and 3-4 for the thick. Remove to the draining rack (lined with fresh paper) for a moment to cool then transfer to a large bowl. Season liberally with salt and toss the fries to evenly coat. Serve immediately.

177. Delightful Tofu Fried Rice Recipe

Serving: 4 | Prep: | Cook: 20mins | Ready in:

Ingredients

- 2 cups uncooked instant rice
- 2 tablespoons vegetable oil, divided

- 1 (14-ounce) package reduced-fat firm tofu, drained and cut into (1/2-inch) cubes
- 2 large eggs, lightly beaten
- 1 cup (1/2-inch-thick) slices green onions
- 1 cup frozen peas and carrots, thawed
- 2 teaspoons bottled minced garlic
- 1 teaspoon bottled minced fresh ginger
- 2 tablespoons thai peanut sauce
- 3 tablespoons low-sodium soy sauce
- 1 tablespoon honey
- 1/2 teaspoon dark sesame oil
- Thinly sliced green onions (optional)

Direction

- Cook rice according to package directions, omitting salt.
- While rice cooks, heat 1 tablespoon vegetable oil in a large non-stick skillet over medium-high heat.
- Add tofu; cook 4 minutes or until lightly browned, stirring occasionally.
- Remove from pan.
- Add eggs to pan; cook 1 minute or until done, breaking egg into small pieces. Remove from pan.
- Add 1 tablespoon vegetable oil to pan. Add 1 cup onions, peas and carrots, garlic, and ginger; sauté 2 minutes.
- While vegetable mixture cooks, combine Thai peanut sauce, soy sauce, honey, and sesame oil.
- Add cooked rice to pan; cook 2 minutes, stirring constantly.
- Add tofu, egg, and soy sauce mixture; cook 30 seconds, stirring constantly.
- Garnish with sliced green onions, if desired.

178. Easy Stir Fried Spinach Ci Recipe

Serving: 6 | Prep: | Cook: 5mins | Ready in:

Ingredients

- 1lb fresh baby spinach
- 1 leek, diagonally sliced in 1inch pieces
- 2 cloves garlic
- 1 small can water chestnuts, sliced
- 3oz roasted red pepper, sliced
- 1T soy sauce
- squirt of fresh lime juice
- red pepper flakes and black pepper to taste
- about 2T peanut oil

Direction

- Heat oil, soy sauce, red pepper flakes and lime juice in wok or large stir fry pan.
- Add garlic and leek and cook until just tender, about 1-2 minutes
- Add spinach, water chestnuts and roasted red pepper, stir fry another couple of minutes until spinach is tender.
- Toss with another squirt of lime juice and black pepper before serving.

179. Elaines BBQ Stir Fry Recipe

Serving: 3 | Prep: | Cook: 20mins | Ready in:

Ingredients

- 1 ½ cups fresh baby carrots
- ¼ medium sized sweet spanish onion
- ½ green sweet bell pepper
- 1 small sweet red pepper
- 3 tbsp olive oil
- salt & pepper to taste

Direction

- Cut the veggies into thin slices (batonnet).
- Place in BBQ pan with the olive oil, salt & pepper.
- Cook over low flame until veggies are soft.

180. Elaines Chinese Fried Rice Recipe

Serving: 6 | Prep: | Cook: 30mins | Ready in:

Ingredients

- 2 cups brown rice
- 3 cups chicken stock
- 1 lemon
- 3 tbsp KIKKOMAN soy sauce (to me, this brand is the cadillac!)
- 4 tbsp canola oil
- 1 tbsp butter
- 2 medium sized carrots, finely cut
- 1 medium sized onion, finely chopped
- 1 large stalk celery, finely chopped
- 1/2 cup fresh or frozen peas
- 1/4 red pepper (sweet) finely chopped
- 2 cloves garlic, finely minced
- 4 tbsp fresh chives, finely chopped (or 3 tbsp dried)
- 1 tbsp Chinese five-spice mixture
- 1/2 tsp vanilla extract
- 1 tsp rice flour
- 1 egg
- salt and pepper to taste

Direction

- Prepare the rice by boiling in the chicken stock until el dente (still having some bite to it)
- Remove rice from pot RESERVING the liquid
- Transfer the rice to a deep frying pan or wok
- Before proceeding further, bring the stock to the boil, adding one whole lemon, cut in half to release its juices
- Continue boiling the stock on high heat, removing the lemon halves after 10 minutes.
- Boil the stock down to a reduction of 1/2 the original quantity.
- While the stock reduces:
- To the rice in the wok, add the oil, butter, Chinese five-spice, and soy sauce
- Mix well
- Heat should be medium to avoid scorching, and mixture should be stirred often
- Add the vanilla
- Crazy as this sounds, the vanilla serves to heighten the flavor of this dish
- Add the carrots, celery, onions, garlic, red pepper and peas, combining thoroughly and stirring frequently
- Now:
- Break one whole egg separately and whisk until well combined
- Add SLOWLY to the rice so it does not cook immediately in clumps like you see in egg foo young
- Add half the chives; reserve the other half for garnishing
- When the stock is reduced, add it to the mixture
- Add the rice flour, and stir well to help thicken the remaining reduction
- Add salt and pepper to taste, and serve.
- ENJOY!

181. Elaines Pepper Stir Fry Recipe

Serving: 4 | Prep: | Cook: 20mins | Ready in:

Ingredients

- 2 whole yellow sweet peppers
- 2 whole green sweet peppers
- 2 whole orange sweet peppers
- 4 large shallots
- 6 to 8 green onions
- mushrooms, no set amount

Direction

- Slice the peppers into long strips.
- Slice the shallots and onions thinly.
- Slice mushrooms to your preference.
- Place on a hot grill, on a baking sheet or tinfoil.
- Cook, turning frequently, until peppers are moderately soft, and the shallots are nicely caramelized.
- Add salt, pepper, whatever- to your taste.

182. Elaines Stir Fried Vegetable Medley With Port Wine Sauce Recipe

Serving: 2 | Prep: | Cook: 12mins | Ready in:

Ingredients

- 2 tbsp KIKKOMAN stir-fry sauce (most supermarkets carry it!)
- 1 green sweet bell pepper
- 1 orange sweet bell pepper
- 3 shallots
- 1 clove garlic, finely minced
- 1 ½ tbsp olive oil
- 4 oz fat-back bacon
- 1 cup Frozen 'Santa Fe Mix' vegetables. (These contain corn, green zucchini, red pepper, onions, yellow & green sweet peppers)
- ½ tsp salt
- pepper to taste (remember the Santa Fe mix has hot peppers in it!)
- 1 oz red port wine
- rice flour as needed for thickening the sauce

Direction

- Assemble all raw veggies and chop finely into thin batonnet strips; garlic, finely chop
- Slice the fatback bacon thinly
- In a saucepan, cook the bacon until crisp, and discard the fat.
- Chop up the bacon
- In a large pan, place the olive oil, salt, pepper, stir-fry sauce, and Port wine
- Add the raw vegetables and cook until crisp-tender, about 5 minutes
- Now add the frozen veggies, and continue cooking until thoroughly heated
- Add rice flour slowly, until the sauce thickens

183. FRENCH FRIED SKUNK Recipe

Serving: 46 | Prep: | Cook: 50mins | Ready in:

Ingredients

- 2 Skunks, skinned and cleaned
- 1 T salt
- water to cover
- 2 c Bear fat or lard
- 2 egg yolks, beaten
- 3 c milk or cream
- 1 1/2 c flour
- 1/2 ts salt
- 2 tb baking powder

Direction

- Clean and wash the skunks, making sure that the scent glands are removed. Cut up into small serving pieces. Put a soup kettle on the stove and add the meat. Cover with cold water and bring to a boil over high heat. Lower the heat and boil until the meat is tender, about 40 minutes. Remove all the scum that rises to the surface. Make a batter by mixing together the egg yolks, milk, flour, salt and baking powder. Mix real good [I didn't write this, folks] until the batter is about like cake batter. Heat the bear fat or lard in a deep fryer to about 360 degrees. Dip the pieces of skunk in the batter and then fry them in the deep fryer until golden brown. Drain well and serve.

184. FRIED CUCUMBERS Recipe

Serving: 4 | Prep: | Cook: 5mins | Ready in:

Ingredients

- 4 medium sized cucumbers
- 1 tsp. salt
- 1/4 tsp. pepper

- 3/4 C. dried bread crumbs
- 1 egg slightly beaten

Direction

- Peel cucumbers and cut into about 1/3 inch slices.
- Sprinkle with salt and pepper.
- Dip into crumbs, the egg then crumbs again.
- Fry in butter or hot oil until browned.
- Drain on absorbent paper towels.

185. FRIED FANTAIL SHRIMP IN BEER BATTER Recipe

Serving: 4 | Prep: | Cook: 8mins | Ready in:

Ingredients

- 1 c. sifted flour
- 1/2 tsp. sugar
- 1/2 tsp. salt
- 1 dash pepper
- 1 dash nutmeg
- 1 tsp. baking powder
- 1 beaten egg
- 1 c. beer
- 2 lbs. fresh shrimp
- cooking oil for frying

Direction

- Work the above ingredients, except for the shrimp, into a beer batter.
- Peel shell from shrimp, leaving the last section and tail intact.
- Cut almost through shrimp at the center back without cutting ends.
- Dry shrimp and dip into beer batter.
- Fry in deep, hot fat until golden brown, drain, serve at once.

186. FRIED GREEN TOMATOES Recipe

Serving: 4 | Prep: | Cook: 112mins | Ready in:

Ingredients

- 3 slices of bacon
- 4 medium green tomatoes
- 1 C. cornmeal
- salt and pepper to taste
- 1/2 C. milk

Direction

- Fry the bacon in heavy skillet.
- Transfer it to absorbent paper.
- Cut each tomato into 1/2" thick slices.
- Put sliced tomatoes on absorbent paper.
- Mix together the cornmeal, salt and pepper.
- Dip tomato slices into a small bowl of milk remove and coat with your cornmeal mixture.
- Fry tomatoes in the bacon fat over medium heat until the cornmeal browns, about 1 1/2 minutes on each side.

187. FRIED TOMATO SANDWICHES Recipe

Serving: 4 | Prep: | Cook: 4mins | Ready in:

Ingredients

- 2 Ripe tomatoes
- 1/2 cup mayonaise
- 1/2 cup grated cheddar cheese
- 2 tbsp fresh dill weed
- 2 tbsp chives;snipped
- lemon juice
- Salt & pepper
- 8 slices bread
- 2 eggs
- 1/4 cup milk
- 3 tbsp butter

Direction

- Peel the tomatoes, remove the seeds and cut into 1/4" slices. Combine mayo, cheese, dill & chives.
- Add lemon juice, salt & pepper to taste.
- Spread mayo mixture on the "inside" part of bread.
- Add tomatoes and top with another slice of mayoed bread.
- Press sandwich together slightly.
- In a shallow dish beat eggs and combine milk.
- Dip both sides of sandwich into mixture.
- Transfer to a buttered skillet. Fry 2-3 minutes on each side, or until golden brown.
- Serve

188. Fabulous Fried Cabbage Recipe

Serving: 6 | Prep: | Cook: 45mins | Ready in:

Ingredients

- 2 tsp butter
- 1 (15 oz.) can chicken broth
- 1 head cabbage, cored and coarsely chopped
- 1 pinch salt and pepper to taste

Direction

- Bring butter and chicken broth to a boil in large skillet. Reduce heat to low and add cabbage. Cover and cook over low heat to steam cabbage for about 45 mins. Stirring frequently, or till cabbage is tender and sweet. Season with salt and pepper and serve.

189. Faux Fried Chicken Nuggets Vegetarianvegan Recipe

Serving: 8 | Prep: | Cook: 10mins | Ready in:

Ingredients

- 1 teaspoon salt
- ½ teaspoon onion powder
- 1 teaspoon (fresh ground pepper)
- 1 teaspoon garlic powder
- 1/8 teaspoon cayenne
- 2 cups unbleached white flour
- 4 tablespoon nutritional yeast
- 3 tablespoons yellow mustard
- ½ cup water
- 2 tablespoons baking powder
- 1 pound faux chicken (I use Worthington Chicketts)
- vegetable oil for frying

Direction

- Mix together the salt, onion powder, pepper, garlic powder flour and nutritional yeast in a bowl.
- In a separate bowl dilute mustard with ½ cup water
- Add 1/3 cup of the flour mixture to the diluted mustard and whisk together.
- Add baking powder to the dry flour mixture and combine
- Dip chunks of the mock chicken into the mustard batter, then drop each chunk into the flour to coat with desired amount of flour mixture. Shake off excess flour.
- Preheat vegetable oil in a large heavy skillet or deep fryer to 350 degrees.
- Fry chunks in hot oil until crispy and golden brown turning as needed.
- Remove from oil drain on paper towels
- Serve with favourite dipping sauce or hot sauce

190. Franks Low Fat French Fries Recipe

Serving: 6 | Prep: | Cook: 40mins | Ready in:

Ingredients

- 4 large baking potatoes
- _____
- 1 Tbsp chili powder
- 1/2 tsp. garlic powder
- 1 tsp. garlic salt
- 1 egg white
- _____
- cooking spray

Direction

- Preheat oven- 450*
- Peel and slice potatoes into "meaty" wedges or slices.
- Mix powders and salt together in a large bowl or pan (to accommodate the potatoes)
- Wisk in egg whites.
- Coat potatoes in egg white mixture thoroughly
- Place on sprayed cookie sheet
- Bake 30-40 mins. or until tender (Check after 30 mins. for tenderness.)

191. French Fried Cauliflower Recipe

Serving: 46 | Prep: | Cook: 7mins | Ready in:

Ingredients

- 1 head cauliflower, cut into flowerets
- 3 eggs, beaten
- 1 sleeve round buttery crackers, crushed
- oil for deep frying

Direction

- Dip cauliflower into eggs; coat with cracker crumbs. Pour oil into a 1/2 inch depth heavy skillet; (I use a cast iron and it gives a great crunch) heat oil to 375F. Fry cauliflower 3 to 5 minutes or until golden brown; drain on paper towels.

192. French Fried Onion Rings Recipe

Serving: 4 | Prep: | Cook: 10mins | Ready in:

Ingredients

- 1 large sweet onion cut into 1/4" slices
- 1/2 cup milk
- 3/4 cup plain dried bread crumbs
- 1 teaspoon chili powder
- 1/2 teaspoon salt
- 1 tablespoon plus 1 teaspoon vegetable oil

Direction

- In rectangular glass baking dish combine onion and milk then let stand 30 minutes turning often.
- On wax paper combine bread crumbs, chili powder and salt.
- Preheat oven to 450 then spray non-stick jelly roll pan with cooking spray.
- Turn onion rings into bread crumb mixture to coat then place onion rings in pan.
- Drizzle evenly with oil then bake 5 minutes on each side.

193. French Fried Potatoes Recipe

Serving: 46 | Prep: | Cook: 25mins | Ready in:

Ingredients

- potatoes

- beef suet(has a higher melting point, you can get it hotter without smoking)
- Powdered mustard

Direction

- Take the potatoes, peel and cut lengthwise into sections about 1/2 inch thick.
- Dry, by rubbing in kitchen towel.
- Do not soak the potatoes in ice water or salted ice water.
- Doing this only makes the potatoes absorb more water and in turn makes them absorb grease too readily when cooked.
- Heat your beef grease to about 400 degrees.
- Beef grease makes the fries crisp and flaky.
- Do not use Lard or Shortening.
- Place the potatoes in the French fry basket, and put them down in the grease.
- Leave the potatoes until they are cooked and have a thin crisp skin formed on them (not all the way done) not a brown skin just a thin pale colored skin.
- This takes about 7 to 10 minutes.
- Remove them from the grease and let them drain, for about 2 to 4 minutes, until the grease is up to around 400 degrees again.
- Place the potatoes back in and leave them in until slightly brown.
- Shake a bit as the brown.
- This takes about 1-1/2 minutes.
- Take them out and let them drain on paper towel, place over a brown paper bag.
- Sprinkle lightly with powdered mustard.

194. French Fried Zuchini Recipe

Serving: 6 | Prep: | Cook: 35mins | Ready in:

Ingredients

- 3/4 c. all-purpose flour
- 1/4 tsp. garlic powder
- 1 tsp. salt
- 1/8 tsp. pepper
- 2 eggs, separated
- 2 Tbsp. salad oil
- 3/4 c. beer (fresh)
- 3 medium zucchini, sliced into french fry sliced strips
- oil for deep frying

Direction

- In medium bowl, combine flour, garlic powder, salt and pepper; mix well
- Combine beer, egg yolks and salad oil
- Add to dry mixture and stir just until lumpy.
- Cover with plastic wrap and set aside for 45 minutes
- After 45 minutes, whip egg whites; fold into the mixture.
- Dip zucchini into batter and deep fry at 375 degrees until golden brown

195. French Fry Eggplant Recipe

Serving: 6 | Prep: | Cook: 3mins | Ready in:

Ingredients

- eggplant
- salt
- water
- White self rising corn meal
- cayenne, paprika, optional
- Crisco for fryin'

Direction

- Peel and cut the eggplant into French fry strips
- Soak the eggplant in salted water for 1 hour or even a little more
- Drain WELL
- Toss in the corn meal that has been seasoned with a little cayenne and paprika
- Fry in Crisco on medium high heat until golden brown and crisp

- Drain on paper towels
- Serve immediately
- My mother sometimes cut a small eggplant in *rounds*, soaked it in salted water, and tossed it cornmeal before frying

196. French Fry Poboy Recipe

Serving: 1 | Prep: | Cook: 5mins | Ready in:

Ingredients

- 1 12 inch piece of French bread
- mayo lettuce and tomato or (dressed)... cheddar cheese slices are optional
- 1 large idahoan potato cut into steak fries
- lots of roast beef gravy

Direction

- Cut potato into steak fries and fry in deep fryer for five min
- Take piece of French bread and cut it almost all the way (side to side) leaving one side intact and open like a book
- Next spread mayo on bread put lettuce and tomato and cheese (optional)
- Remove fries from oil when done and place them on the po'boy
- Finally generously spoon or pour on hot roast beef gravy should be heated while fries are cooking
- Close it up cut in half and eat it or eat it when you're stoned
- It's messy but it's awesome!

197. French Fried Potato Skewers Recipe

Serving: 2 | Prep: | Cook: 5mins | Ready in:

Ingredients

- 2 medium sized raw potatoes cut into chunks
- canola oil
- salt and pepper to taste
- beef gravy from roast, or canned gravy

Direction

- Skewer the potato pieces onto a wooden skewer
- Do not allow the pieces to touch each other to ensure even browning
- Heat the canola oil on medium heat
- Deep fry until warm, golden brown
- Serve in a dish with hot gravy!
- Simple yet it adds a delightful bit of flair to the main course!
- NOTE:
- This recipe very easily doubles, triples, etc.

198. Fresh Corn And Veggie Summer Stir Fry Recipe

Serving: 8 | Prep: | Cook: 5mins | Ready in:

Ingredients

- 4 ears of corn, uncooked, kernels cut from cob
- 1 red bell pepper, diced
- 1 large onion, diced
- 2 hot peppers, Hungarian yellow, banana, jalepeno - hot kind, finely minced
- 1 yellow squash, quartered lengthwise and sliced across into quarters
- 1 zucchini, quartered lengthwise and sliced across into quarters
- 1 tablespoon olive oil
- 2 tablespoons butter
- seasoned salt, Jane's Crazy Salt - to taste
- 1 teaspoon chicken soup base

Direction

- Melt butter and oil together in large skillet. Add all veggies at the same time. Stir and cook for about 15-25 minutes depending upon

volume. When squash is cooked add Crazy salt, pepper and chicken soup base. Stir well and serve.
- NOTE: I've added eggplant to this as well. You can add a can of black beans and diced fresh tomatoes and a little balsamic vinegar to cold leftovers and toss it with cooked bow ties for a nice salad, too.
- Also, I know the chicken soup base might sound weird...use it! It just add a nice mellow, smoothness and depth of flavor to the dish.

199. Fried Apple Jacks Recipe

Serving: 18 | Prep: | Cook: 10mins | Ready in:

Ingredients

- 1/2 of a 21 ounce can apple pie filling
- 18-20 wonton wrappers
- vegetable or canola oil
- About 1/2 cup powdered sugar

Direction

- Cut apples in pie filling into small pieces. Separate wonton wrappers. Place 1 tablespoon filling in centre of each wonton wrapper. Moisten inside edge of wonton with a little water and fold in half diagonally. Press with tines of folk to seal.
- Pour 2 inches of oil in an electric skillet. Set heat control to 350 degrees F.
- When oil is at 350 degrees F, cook Apple Jacks until they are golden brown on each side, turning over with tongs.
- Drain on paper towels. Cool slightly. Place powdered sugar in sifter and sprinkle sugar over Apple Jacks. Serve.
- Yield: 18-20 servings

200. Fried Apples And Onions Recipe

Serving: 4 | Prep: | Cook: 10mins | Ready in:

Ingredients

- 1/2 pound bacon sliced
- 2 pounds onions
- 2 pounds apples tart chopped
- 2 tablespoons sugar brown

Direction

- Fry bacon slices in skillet until brown and crisp then set aside on a warm serving platter.
- While meat is frying peel onions leaving stems to hold for slicing.
- Slice onions as thin as possible and discard stems.
- Core apples and cut crosswise in circles about 1/4" thick.
- Drain all but 1 tablespoon fat from skillet then add onion slices.
- Cook over medium high heat about 3 minutes.
- Cover with apple slices in an even layer then sprinkle brown sugar over all.
- Cover skillet and cook until tender about 5 minutes.
- Stir to prevent scorching.
- Remove to warm plate with bacon slices.

201. Fried Apples Recipe

Serving: 6 | Prep: | Cook: 20mins | Ready in:

Ingredients

- 6 large apples sliced
- 1/4 cup butter
- 1/4 cup water
- 1/3 cup light brown sugar
- 2 tablespoons lemon juice
- 1 teaspoon cinnamon

Direction

- Core peel and slice apples into thick slices.
- Place in medium skillet with butter and water.
- Cook over medium heat stirring to prevent sticking.
- Continue cooking until barely tender.
- Mix brown sugar and cinnamon together.
- Sprinkle apples with brown sugar and lemon juice.
- Toss and cover skillet then let stand for 10 minutes.

202. Fried Apples With Bacon Recipe

Serving: 8 | Prep: | Cook: 20mins | Ready in:

Ingredients

- 4 large granny smith apples cored and cut into thick slices
- 1/3 cup granulated sugar
- 2 tablespoons fresh lemon juice
- 3/4 teaspoon ground nutmeg
- 1/4 teaspoon ground cinnamon
- 1/8 teaspoon ground cloves
- 1/2 pound bacon chopped

Direction

- Place apples in bowl then add sugar, juice, nutmeg, cinnamon and cloves then toss to coat.
- Sauté bacon in skillet over medium heat until crisp then drain bacon on paper towels.
- Add apples to bacon drippings in skillet and sauté until apples are tender about 10 minutes.
- Transfer apples and juices in skillet to bowl then sprinkle with bacon.

203. Fried Apples Classic And Deluxe Recipe

Serving: 0 | Prep: | Cook: 20mins | Ready in:

Ingredients

- 6 medium-sized tart apples
- 2 tablespoons butter
- 1/4 to 1/2 cup brown sugar

Direction

- Cut the apples into quarters and remove the cores.
- Cut each quarter lengthwise into three or four slices. (Cut out any blemishes or brown spots, but leave the peel on.)
- Melt the butter over low heat in a skillet with a cover.
- Add the apples, and stir lightly with a spatula to coat them with butter.
- Cover and cook for about 5 minutes to soften.
- Sprinkle the sugar over the apples. (Use the larger quantity if the apples are especially tart.)
- Turn them again with the spatula to spread the sugar around.
- Cook over medium-low heat for another 10 to 15 minutes, until the apples are soft and the sugar has begun to thicken into a light syrup.
- Serve warm.

204. Fried Artichokes Recipe

Serving: 4 | Prep: | Cook: 20mins | Ready in:

Ingredients

- 4 medium sized artichokes (look for vegetables with soft, long, flexible stems)
- 1 lemon
- Plenty of olive oil
- sea salt to taste

Direction

- Fill a large bowl with water and the juice of one lemon.
- Working one artichoke at a time, trim the stem to 1 1/2 – 2 inches.
- Using a vegetable peeler, remove the outer dark green layer of the stem, revealing the softer, lighter green centre.
- Cut off the artichoke's thorny top (horizontally) using a serrated knife and then carefully slice the artichoke in half, (vertically).
- Remove the artichoke's tough outer leaves until only the soft inner leaves remain.
- Using a small spoon, remove the hairy "choke" at the centre of each artichoke half. (It may seem like you are wasting a lot of the plant --which is kind of true.)
- Fry step 1: Select a pot that is large enough to comfortably hold all of the artichoke halves.
- Place them in the pot, fill with oil until chokes are half covered.
- Then add water to cover.
- Bring pot to a simmer and cook, uncovered, about 15 minutes until they are cooked but not too soft.
- Remove with tongs, drain and place on a platter.
- Fry step 2: Heat about one inch of oil in a cast iron pan (or other heavy pan).
- Using a pair of tongs, and lots of care, place the choke halves side down in the oil.
- Be really careful--hot oil splatters and hurts.
- Fry for about 12 minutes, flipping the chokes halfway through, until brown and crispy on both sides.
- Turn off the heat and remove the fried chokes with tongs.
- Place onto paper towels to drain.
- Sprinkle with salt and serve warm.

205. Fried Asparagus Recipe

Serving: 5 | Prep: | Cook: 3mins | Ready in:

Ingredients

- 1 pound of asparagus, trimmed
- 1 medium egg
- 4 ounces of freshly-grated romano cheese
- 1 cup of fine dry breadcrumbs
- 1 tablespoon of milk
- olive oil, for frying
- salt and pepper

Direction

- In boiling, salted water, cook the asparagus spears until just tender.
- Drain on paper towels.
- In a bowl, beat the egg with milk.
- Dip the asparagus in the egg/milk mix, then into the breadcrumbs.
- Heat enough olive oil to cover the asparagus in a deep fryer or a large skillet.
- Fry the asparagus until lightly browned.
- Drain on paper towels.
- Season with your desired amount of salt and pepper.
- Sprinkle with grated Romano cheese.

206. Fried Baby Artichokes Recipe

Serving: 4 | Prep: | Cook: 10mins | Ready in:

Ingredients

- 12 baby artichokes (they should be no larger than 3" wide. any bigger than that I wouldn't consider them babies - I'd probably call them adult runts with pokey chokey chokes)
- 1 lemon, halved & squeezed into a large glass bowl with water.
- 3 cloves garlic, minced
- olive oil to fry
- kosher salt & pepper
- a nice squeezin' of a lemon half to finish off the dish

Direction

- 1. Clean and prepare your baby 'chokes: Have your bowl with lemon/water ready. Snap off the outer layers of the leaves until you get to smooth, light pale green leaves. With sharp paring knife again, peel the dark green layer off the stem. Also cut off the top 1" of the artichoke. Now, with top of the artichoke facing down against the cutting board, cut the artichoke into thin 1/4" slices. Place slices in lemon water. Repeat with remaining artichokes.
- 2. In a large skillet, put enough olive oil to at least cover the bottom of the pan. Let the olive oil heat up over medium-high heat. When hot, add the garlic and fry until fragrant, about 15 seconds. Add only enough artichoke slices to make 1 layer in the pan (you may have to do this in a couple of batches). You don't want to overcrowd the pan, otherwise the artichokes will steam, not fry. Fry the artichokes until the edges are a little charred and crispy, about 5 minutes. Repeat with remaining. Top with a sprinkling of kosher salt, pepper and a squeeze of lemon.

207. Fried Bananas Kluay Tod Thailand Recipe

Serving: 4 | Prep: | Cook: 30mins | Ready in:

Ingredients

- 1 pound of bananas, about 6 to 8. Traditionally small asian bananas are used. But you can use any banana you choose.
- 3/4 cup rice flour.
- 1/4 cup tapioca flour.
- 1/2 cup tsp baking soda.
- 2 tbsp sugar.
- 1 tsp salt
- 1/2 cup shredded coconut.
- 1 cup water
- 4 cups oil for deep frying

Direction

- Peel and slice each banana lengthwise into four slices.
- In a mixing bowl combine rice flour, tapioca flour, sugar, salt, coconut and baking soda.
- Add water a little at a time.
- Mix well to form a thick batter.
- Heat the oil in a deep fryer or wok to 375°F.
- Dip each piece of banana into the batter to completely coat,
- Deep fry until golden brown.
- Remove from oil and drain on paper towels.
- Serve as a snack or with Thai ice cream.

208. Fried Bell Pepper Rings With Horseradish Dip Recipe

Serving: 6 | Prep: | Cook: 10mins | Ready in:

Ingredients

- PEPPERS:
- 3 large bell peppers - Green, Red, or Yellow (I use one of each)
- 2 large eggs, lightly beaten
- 2 cups milk
- 2/3 cup Italian-seasoned bread crumbs
- 1/2 cup grated parmesan cheese
- 1 cup all-purpose flour
- vegetable oil
- DIP:
- 1 (8 oz.) pkg. cream cheese
- 2 tbsp. milk
- 3 tbsp. cream style horseradish
- 1/4 tsp. worcestershire sauce
- 1/8 tsp. salt
- Combine the cream cheese and milk, beating until smooth. Add the horseradish, worcestershire sauce and salt; mix well. Serve with cauliflowerets, carrot sticks and celery strips.

Direction

- PEPPERS:
- Slice peppers into 1/4-inch rings; remove and discard seeds and membranes.
- Set aside.
- Combine eggs and milk, stirring well.
- Combine bread crumbs and cheese, stirring well.
- Dip pepper rings in egg mixture, and dredge in flour.
- Dip again in egg mixture, and dredge in bread crumb mixture, coating well.
- Pour oil to depth of 2 inches into a Dutch oven; heat to 375 degrees. Fry green bell pepper rings 1 to 2 minutes or until golden, turning once.
- Drain on paper towels.
- Serve immediately.
- DIP:
- Combine the cream cheese and milk, beating until smooth.
- Add the horseradish, Worcestershire sauce and salt; mix well.

209. Fried Bologna Sandwich Recipe

Serving: 4 | Prep: | Cook: 5mins | Ready in:

Ingredients

- 4 Sandwich rolls
- 8 Thick slices of deli bologna (Sliced thick)
- 2 tbs butter
- 4 Slices of cheese (your favorite)
- Fresh lettuce
- mustard
- Mayonaise
- BBQ Sauce
- Sliced bananna peppers (hint, great addition)
- pickles

Direction

- Put butter in a frying pan and heat to medium.
- Add the bologna and fry a few minutes till turning light brown.
- Remove the meat from the pan.
- Toast the bread in the pan, add the cheese on top of the bread the last few seconds and let melt slightly. Remove.
- Add the bologna to the sandwich and garnish with the rest of the ingredients.
- Serve with chips and pickles.
- P.S- If using the BBQ sauce, reduce the amount of butter to 1 TBS and fry the bologna in 2 TBS of BBQ sauce!
- Easy and so good. Enjoy!

210. Fried Cabbage Recipe

Serving: 6 | Prep: | Cook: 25mins | Ready in:

Ingredients

- 3 slices bacon, chopped
- 1/4 cup onion, chopped
- 6 cups cabbage, cut into thin wedges
- 2 tablespoons water
- 1 pinch white sugar
- salt and pepper to taste
- 1 tablespoon cider vinegar

Direction

- Place bacon in a large, deep skillet.
- Cook over medium high heat until evenly browned and crisp.
- Remove bacon and set aside.
- Cook onion in the hot bacon grease until tender.
- Add cabbage.
- Stir in water, sugar, salt and pepper.
- Cook until cabbage wilts, about 15 minutes.
- Stir in bacon.
- Splash with vinegar before serving OR serve with vinegar on the side.

211. Fried Cabbage With Bacon Onion And Garlic Recipe

Serving: 6 | Prep: | Cook: 45mins | Ready in:

Ingredients

- 6 slices of bacon chopped and fried
- 1 Head of cabbage, cored and sliced
- 2 cloves of garlic minced
- 1 Large onion diced
- 1 1/2 tsp salt
- 1 tsp pepper
- 1/2 tsp onion powder
- 1/4 tsp garlic powder
- 1/8 tsp paprika

Direction

- In a large stock pan, fry bacon till crispy. Add onion and garlic in with bacon and grease and stir till caramelized, add cabbage immediately. Stir continuously for about 10 minutes. Add salt, pepper, onion powder, garlic powder and paprika. Cover, lower heat and continue cooking for 20 minutes stirring occasionally.

212. Fried Catfish Sandwiches With Spicy Mayonnaise Recipe

Serving: 4 | Prep: | Cook: 10mins | Ready in:

Ingredients

- • 1/2 cup mayonnaise
- • 3/4 teaspoon fresh-ground black pepper
- • 1/8 teaspoon cayenne
- • 4 large crusty rolls, split
- • 3/4 cup cornmeal
- • 1 1/4 teaspoons salt
- • 1/2 teaspoon dried thyme
- • 2 pounds catfish fillets
- • 2 eggs, beaten to mix
- • 1/4 cup cooking oil
- • 3 cups tender greens, such as spinach or leaf lettuce (about 2 ounces)

Direction

- • In a small bowl, combine the mayonnaise, 1/2 teaspoon of the black pepper, and the cayenne. Spread the mayonnaise mixture on the rolls.
- • In a shallow bowl, combine the cornmeal with the salt, thyme, and the remaining 1/4 teaspoon black pepper. Dip the fillets into the beaten eggs and then into the seasoned cornmeal. Shake off the excess cornmeal.
- • In a large non-stick frying pan, heat the oil over moderate heat. Add the cornmeal-coated fish and fry, turning once, until golden on the outside and just done in the center, about 4 minutes per side for 3/4-inch-thick fillets. Drain the fish on paper towels. Sandwich the catfish and greens in the rolls.
- • Fish Alternatives: Substitute moderately firm, lean fillets for the catfish. Scrod, rockfish, ocean perch, haddock or tilefish are good options.
- • Wine Recommendation: Choose a gamay from California or a Beaujolais from France, which is also made from the gamay grape. Chill the wine slightly for maximum enjoyment.

213. Fried Cauliflower Recipe

Serving: 46 | Prep: | Cook: 20mins | Ready in:

Ingredients

- 1 medium cauliflower
- 2 eggs
- 2 T flour
- 1 tsp salt
- 1/4 tsp pepper
- 1 1/2 cups oil for frying

Direction

- Cut cauliflower in flowerettes and parboil.
- Drain and set aside.
- Slightly beat eggs, with flour, salt & pepper.
- Heat oil in skillet.
- Dip each flowerettes into the egg mix.
- Fry in the oil until golden brown.
- Drain on a paper towel.
- Serve still warm.

214. Fried Chocolate Tofu Recipe

Serving: 4 | Prep: | Cook: 30mins | Ready in:

Ingredients

- 1 block of firm tofu - pressed and dried for 1 - 12 hours
- 5 tsp espresso powder
- 1 cup semisweet chocolate chips
- 2 tsp ginger
- 2 tsp cayenne powder
- 2 tsp cinnamon
- 1/2 cup oil
- 2 cups water
- 2 eggs
- flour

Direction

- Heat water and espresso until simmering
- Add ginger, cayenne powder, cinnamon, stir
- Add chocolate chips progressively, stirring
- Making sure chocolate doesn't burn, cut tofu down to bite size, thinner could allow you more concentrated taste
- When chocolate is at a medium watery boil, add tofu, stirring until chocolate is thick and you can just smell it starting to burn
- Drain tofu from chocolate
- Whisk 2 eggs and toss tofu in, covering
- Toss tofu in flour and slide into wok you have already heated with oil and 2 more tsp. of cayenne
- While frying keep chocolate liquid simmering uncovered until reduced, drizzle on tofu when done
- Serve hot

215. Fried Corn From Texas Recipe

Serving: 6 | Prep: | Cook: 25mins | Ready in:

Ingredients

- 6 ears corn
- 1/4 cup bacon drippings
- 2 tablespoons flour
- 1 tablespoon sugar
- 1 cup water
- 1/4 cup milk
- 1 teaspoon salt
- 1 teaspoon freshly ground black pepper

Direction

- Shuck corn then wash and remove silk then cut corn cobs in half then cut kernels off.
- Scrape juice out of corn from cob.
- Heat drippings in large skillet then add corn, flour, sugar, water, milk, salt and pepper.
- Bring to boil stirring constantly then cover and reduce heat then simmer 25 minutes.

216. Fried Corn Off The Cob Recipe

Serving: 4 | Prep: | Cook: 30mins | Ready in:

Ingredients

- 4 ears leftover corn on the cob (or fresh corn)
- 3 tbsp flour
- 2 tbsp bacon drippings
- salt & pepper to taste

Direction

- Cut the corn off the cob preserving as much of the oil as possible.
- Break up the slices in a large skillet. Add enough water to cover.
- Bring to a boil over high heat and then reduce heat to a constant simmer.
- Cook until corn is tender and water has reduced.
- Add flour and bacon drippings to thicken and flavour the mixture.
- Continue cooking until corn starts to stick the skillet and brown.
- Add salt and pepper to taste, cook until it reaches desired colour.

217. Fried Corn On The Cob Recipe

Serving: 2 | Prep: | Cook: 5mins | Ready in:

Ingredients

- 1 cup milk
- 1 egg, beaten
- 1 1/2 cups flour
- 1 teaspoon seasoning salt
- 1/2 teaspoon pepper
- 6 ears corn, husks and silk removed boiled your corn before frying
- oil (for frying)

Direction

- Combine milk and egg in shallow dish and mix well.
- Combine flour, seasoned salt and pepper in shallow dish and mix well.
- Dip each ear of corn into milk and egg mixture, then roll in seasoned flour. Knock off excess flour.
- In a large skillet, heat oil to 350 degrees.
- Add corn and fry for 5 minutes or until golden brown (approximately 2-1/2 minutes on each side).
- Drain on paper towels.

218. Fried Corn Recipe

Serving: 4 | Prep: | Cook: 30mins | Ready in:

Ingredients

- 9 Ears fresh corn
- 1/2 C. bacon drippings
- 1 C. Half & Half (you could use whole milk)
- salt & pepper to taste
- A Sharp Knife
- A Cast Iron Skillet (well seasoned)

Direction

- Into a bowl:
- Run your knife down the cobs to slice off the corn (you just want the top of the corn)
- Then use the back of your knife and scrape the cob until all of the corn juice/corn mush is removed
- Into a hot cast iron skillet add the bacon drippings.
- Once the drippings are sizzling, add your corn stirring constantly so it doesn't stick or burn (you want it to get a little brown and crispy though)
- Cook until thick (about 6-7 minutes) DON'T STOP STIRRING!
- Pour in the half &half, and salt and pepper.
- Cover and cook slow for another 10-15 minutes (you could also finish it in the oven)
- Let it cool a bit then serve! It's best to serve it straight out of the skillet so it will stay warm.

219. Fried Corn Tennessee Style Recipe

Serving: 4 | Prep: | Cook: 20mins | Ready in:

Ingredients

- 6 ears fresh corn (Though not as flavorful as fresh corn, frozen corn kernels also can be used.)
- 4 slices bacon
- 1/2 cup milk
- 1 tsp. salt
- 1/4 tsp. freshly ground black pepper
- Pinch sugar

Direction

- With sharp knife, cut corn kernels from cob. Also scrape pulp out with back of knife. Set aside.
- Cut bacon in half and fry in heavy iron skillet until crisp. Drain on paper towelling.
- Discard all but 4 Tbsp. bacon fat. Add corn. Cook, without stirring, until bottom is browned (lift corn from the side with a spatula to check).
- When well browned, add milk and seasonings, stirring until well combined. Cover and cook over low heat 10 min. longer. Arrange bacon over the top and serve.

220. Fried Dill Pickles Recipe

Serving: 20 | Prep: | Cook: 3mins | Ready in:

Ingredients

- 2 pints sliced dill pickles, undrained
- 1 large egg, lightly beaten
- 1 tablespoon, all purpose flour
- 1/2 teaspoon hot sauce
- 1 1/2 cups all purpose flour
- 2 1/1 teaspoons ground red pepper
- 1 teaspoon garlic powder
- 1/4 teaspoon salt
- vegetable oil

Direction

- Drain pickles, reserving 2/3 cup pickle juice. Press pickles between paper towels to remove excess moisture. Combine 2/3 cup pickle juice, egg, 1 tablespoon flour, and hot sauce; stir well and set aside.
- Combine 1 1/2 cups flour and next 3 ingredients; stir well. Dip pickles in egg mixture; dredge in flour mixture.
- Pour oil to depth of 1 1/2 inches if using a skillet. Fry coated pickles, in batches, in hot oil (375 degrees) for 2 to 3 minutes or until golden, turning once. Drain on paper towels. Serve Immediately.
- Yield: about 10 1/2 dozen

221. Fried Dogs And Sausages In BBQ Sauce Recipe

Serving: 8 | Prep: | Cook: 120mins | Ready in:

Ingredients

- 1 pkg. of hot dogs
- 1 pkg. of mild sausage
- 1 pkg. of hot sausage
- 1 pkg. of smoked sausage
- 1 - 28 oz bottle of ketchup
- 1 can of coca-cola classic
- 1 cup chopped onion
- 1 cup chopped green pepper
- 1 T horseradish
- 1 tsp. vinegar
- pinch of brown sugar

Direction

- Chop ALL hot dogs and sausages into bite-sized pieces

- Fry in a skillet until brown. Place in crock pot and add remaining ingredients. Cook for 2 hours on low.

222. Fried Fish In A Pocket Recipe

Serving: 4 | Prep: | Cook: 20mins | Ready in:

Ingredients

- 1 1/2 to 2 pounds hlibut or other fillets
- 1/2 cup all-purpose flour
- 1/4 teaspoon salt
- 1/4 teaspoon cumin, optional
- 1/2 cup beer or milk
- 1 egg, beaten
- oil for frying
- 4 pita (pocket) bread, White or whole wheat
- 1 cucumber, thinly sliced
- 1 ren onion, chopped
- 1 tomato, seeded and chopped
- 1/4 to 1/2 cup plain yogurt or sour cream or a combination
- 1 cup crumbled feta cheese
- 1/4 teaspoon ground black pepper, optional

Direction

- Cut fish into 2-inch pieces.
- In a bowl, mix flour, seasoning and beer or milk and egg.
- Pour oil to 1/4-inch depth in skillet and heat.
- Dip fish in batter. Fry until lightly browned. Drain and keep warm.
- Slice the bread in half, making 2 pockets per person. Fill each one with equal amounts of fish and vegetables.
- Top with yogurt or sour cream and feta cheese. Sprinkle with pepper if desired.

223. Fried Fish Sandwich Recipe

Serving: 4 | Prep: | Cook: 4mins | Ready in:

Ingredients

- 2 pounds grouper, mahi mahi, cod, or halibut fillets
- 2 teaspoons Greek seasoning, divided
- 1 1/2 teaspoons salt, divided
- 1 teaspoon freshly ground pepper, divided
- 2 1/4 cups all-purpose flour
- 1/4 cup yellow cornmeal
- 2 teaspoons baking powder
- 2 cups cold beer
- 1 large egg, lightly beaten
- vegetable oil
- 4 sesame seed hamburger buns
- tartar sauce or mayonnaise
- 4 green leaf lettuce leaves
- 4 tomato slices

Direction

- Preparation
- 1. Cut fish into 3-inch strips. Sprinkle evenly with 1 tsp. Greek seasoning, 1 tsp. salt, and 1/2 tsp. pepper.
- 2. Combine flour, cornmeal, baking powder, remaining 1 tsp. Greek seasoning, 1/2 tsp. salt, and 1/2 tsp. pepper; stir well. Add 2 cups cold beer and egg, stirring until thoroughly blended and smooth.
- 3. Pour oil to a depth of 2 to 3 inches into a Dutch oven; heat to 375°.
- 4. Dip fish strips into batter, coating both sides well; shake off excess. Fry fish, in batches, 2 minutes on each side or until golden (do not crowd pan). Drain on paper towels.
- 5. Spread top half of each bun evenly with tartar sauce. Place 1 lettuce leaf and 1 tomato slice on bottom half of each bun; top each with 2 fried fish strips and top halves of buns.

224. Fried Fish Tacos Recipe

Serving: 6 | Prep: | Cook: 60mins | Ready in:

Ingredients

- 1 quart vegetable oil
- 12 to 16 corn tortillas
- 1 cup all-purpose flour
- 2 teaspoons salt
- 1 cup beer (not dark)
- 1 pound cod fillet, cut into 3- by 1-inch strips
- Accompaniments: shredded lettuce, sour cream, avocado slices, chopped or sliced radish, red or green salsa, and lime wedges

Direction

- Preheat oven to 350°F.
- Heat 1 inch oil in a 10-inch heavy pot (2 to 3 inches deep) over moderate heat until a deep-fat thermometer registers 360°F.
- Meanwhile, separate tortillas and make 2 stacks of 6 to 8. Wrap each stack in foil and heat in oven 12 to 15 minutes.
- While tortillas warm, stir together flour and salt in a large bowl, then stir in beer (batter will be thick). Gently stir fish into batter to coat. Lift each piece of fish out of batter, wiping any excess off on side of bowl, and fry fish in batches, turning once or twice, until golden, 4 to 5 minutes. Drain on paper towels.
- Increase oil temperature to 375°F and refry fish in batches, turning once or twice, until golden brown and crisp, about 1 minute. Drain on paper towels.
- Assemble tacos with warm tortillas, fish, and accompaniments.

225. Fried Green Beans Recipe

Serving: 6 | Prep: | Cook: 15mins | Ready in:

Ingredients

- 1 pound fresh green beans snapped and cleaned
- 1/4 pound salt pork
- 1 medium white onion chopped
- 2 teaspoons minced garlic
- 1-teaspoon salt
- 2 teaspoons freshly ground black pepper
- 1/4-cup water

Direction

- Fry salt pork in skillet.
- Remove salt pork after there is at least 2 tablespoons grease in skillet.
- Fry onions in grease until translucent then add green beans and garlic.
- Cook and stir frequently on medium high heat for about 5 minutes.
- Turn to simmer and cook 15 minutes longer.
- Stir occasionally and add water if needed.

226. Fried Green Beans Dry Recipe

Serving: 2 | Prep: | Cook: 5mins | Ready in:

Ingredients

- ¼ lb or fist full Fresh of green beans (snapped)
- 1 Tbsp favorite seasoning (I use Italian)
- 1 tsp seasoned pepper
- 2 tsp corn starch
- cooking spray
- 3 Tbsp water

Direction

- Spray with oil and heat a large skillet on medium high
- Rinse the green beans and shake off excess water (you don't want them dry)
- Put your seasonings and corn starch in a large plastic bag
- Add the beans and shake to coat

- Put them in your skillet and cook; add water and cover for 2 minutes
- Uncover and cook until done 4 minutes or so
- They should be hot and crisp

227. Fried Green Tomato Slices Recipe

Serving: 12 | Prep: | Cook: 10mins | Ready in:

Ingredients

- 4 green tomatoes thickly sliced
- 1/2 cup cornmeal
- 1/4 teaspoon salt
- 1 teaspoon freshly ground black pepper
- 1/3 cup bacon drippings

Direction

- Dip tomato slices in cornmeal mixed with salt and pepper.
- Heat bacon drippings in a heavy skillet and sauté slices quickly until browned on both sides.

228. Fried Green Tomatoes N More Recipe

Serving: 68 | Prep: | Cook: 10mins | Ready in:

Ingredients

- olive oil
- margarine/butter
- 4 dashes hot sauce
- 1/2 c. flour
- 1/2 c. cornmeal
- 1/4 t. cayenne pepper
- seasoned salt
- 4 - 6 med/large green tomaotes, sliced medium
- 1 yellow squash, sliced medium
- 1 zuchinni, sliced medium
- 1 med. white onion, rough chopped
- 1 tub fresh mushrooms, sliced thick
- 1 red pepper, rough chopped
- 2 T. chopped garlic
- 2 roma tomatoes, chopped (less water)
- 1 cup shredded parmesan
- fresh ground black pepper

Direction

- Combine flour, cornmeal, cayenne pepper and seasoned salt
- Add about 3 T. extra virgin olive oil to large skillet and add a part of margarine
- When heated, add onion and red pepper
- While onion and pepper are sautéing, dredge zucchini, squash, green tomatoes and mushrooms in flour mixture
- Add to pan
- Add Garlic
- Add hot sauce
- Fry until desired brown-ness, turning infrequently
- Drain on paper-towel lined plate
- Add chopped roma tomatoes and fresh grated parmesan cheese

229. Fried Green Tomatoes With Crabmeat Remoulade Recipe

Serving: 8 | Prep: | Cook: 20mins | Ready in:

Ingredients

- Remoulade:
- 1 1/2 cups mayonnaise
- 2 teaspoons creole mustard
- 2 tablespoons fresh lemon juice
- 1/4 cup chopped onions
- 2 tablespoons chopped fresh flat-leaf parsley

- 2 tablespoons finely chopped green onions (green part only)
- salt, freshly ground black pepper, and hot sauce, to taste
- 1 pound lump crabmeat, picked over for shells and cartilage
- Fried Green Tomatoes:
- 2 pounds green tomatoes, trimmed and cut crosswise into 1/2-inch-thick slices
- salt and freshly ground black pepper, to taste
- 3/4 cup vegetable oil for deep-frying
- 1 1/4 cup all-purpose flour
- 3/4 cup yellow cornmeal
- 3/4 cup buttermilk
- 2 eggs, lightly beaten
- 4 cups baby salad greens

Direction

- Directions for Remoulade:
- Combine the mayonnaise, mustard, lemon juice, onions, parsley, and green onions in a bowl and stir to blend. Season with salt, pepper, and hot sauce. Add the crabmeat and gently toss to coat evenly. Cover and refrigerate.
- Directions for Green Tomatoes:
- Season the tomato slices with salt and pepper. Heat the oil in a large skillet over medium heat. Put the flour in a shallow bowl and the cornmeal in another shallow bowl. Combine the buttermilk and eggs in another bowl. Dredge the tomatoes first in the flour, coating evenly on both sides, and shaking off any excess flour.
- Then dip them in the egg and buttermilk mixture, coating evenly. Then dredge them in the cornmeal, coating evenly and shaking off any excess cornmeal. Add the tomatoes, 3 or 4 at a time, to the hot oil and fry until golden brown, about 2 minutes on each side.
- Drain on paper towels and repeat with the remaining tomatoes. To assemble, arrange equal amounts of the greens in the centre of 6 salad plates. Top with fried green tomatoes slices and the crabmeat mixture. Serve immediately.

230. Fried Haloumi Lemon Dressing Recipe

Serving: 4 | Prep: | Cook: 10mins | Ready in:

Ingredients

- 1/2 lb halloumi, thickly sliced
- 1/4 cup seasoned flour
- oil for shallow frying
- 1 cup baby spinach leaves
- 1 avocado, seeded, peeled and sliced
- 1/4 cup basil
- juice of 1 lemon
- 1/4 cup olive oil
- black pepper, freshly ground
- wedges of lime

Direction

- Dust cheese slices in flour, shaking off excess. Heat oil in a frying pan until a bread cube sizzles as soon as it is added.
- Fry cheese in batches until golden both sides. Drain on crumpled kitchen paper.
- Serve, while still hot, on a bed of combined spinach leaves, avocado and basil. Drizzle liberally with combined olive oil, juice and pepper. Serve immediately with lime wedges.
- Note: Haloumi cheese slices can also be oiled and grilled or barbecued. They are great on toast.

231. Fried Hot Dog Sandwich Recipe

Serving: 1 | Prep: | Cook: 4mins | Ready in:

Ingredients

- All beef hot dogs

- Crushed wheat bread (preferred)
- Mayo - Best Foods
- yellow mustard

Direction

- Cut dogs down the center like the pic so they lay flat in the pan.
- Cook on medium and let the cut side get a little black like the pics.
- Turn and let the other side get a little black.
- Toast the bread when you flip the dogs.
- First spread edge to edge mayo - no dry spots
- The best taste is from using yellow mustard see pic.
- Mix the mustard into the mayo and spread it around so the mixed mayo and mustard is edge to edge.
- A great crunchy taste!

232. Fried Okra Recipe

Serving: 8 | Prep: | Cook: 30mins | Ready in:

Ingredients

- 2 lbs okra, 1/2" slice
- buttermilk
- 1 cup flour
- salt and pepper, to taste
- 1/4 tsp cayenne pepper flakes (optional)
- cooking oil or bacon drippings

Direction

- Marinate okra in buttermilk for about an hour; drain well.
- Over medium high heat, add enough oil or drippings to coat the bottom of a very large skillet or cast iron pan.
- Combine flour, salt, pepper and cayenne. Dredge okra in flour mixture. Add to hot oil and fry, turning occasionally, until nicely browned, about 30 minutes.
- Serve.

233. Fried Peanut Butter And Banana Sandwich Recipe

Serving: 1 | Prep: | Cook: 4mins | Ready in:

Ingredients

- 1 small ripe banana
- 2 slices bread
- 3 Tbs.peanut butter
- 2 Tbs.butter

Direction

- In a small bowl, mash the banana with the back of a spoon. Toast the bread lightly. Spread the peanut butter on one slice of toast and the mashed banana on the other. Fry the sandwich in melted butter until each side is golden brown.
- Cut diagonally and serve hot.

234. Fried Peanut Butter And Banana Sandwiches Recipe

Serving: 4 | Prep: | Cook: 10mins | Ready in:

Ingredients

- 1/2 cup butter, softened
- 3/4 cup crunchy peanut butter
- 3 T honey
- 1 1/2 t ground cinnamon
- 2 to 3 ripe bananas
- 8 slices white bread
- ===================================
- Topping:
- 1/4 cup sugar
- 1 tablespoon ground cinnamon

Direction

- In a frying pan, melt 3 tablespoons of the butter. Make sure butter does not burn.
- In a small bowl mix together the peanut butter, honey, and cinnamon.
- Slice the bananas into 1/4-inch thick slices.
- Spread the peanut butter mixture on 4 slices of bread and cover with banana slices.
- Top with the remaining 4 slices of bread. Spread the remaining butter on both sides of the sandwiches.
- Grill the sandwiches in the frying pan until each side is golden brown.
- For topping, combine the sugar and cinnamon in shallow plate. Coat the grilled sandwiches with the mixture. Cut diagonally and serve hot.

235. Fried Pickles Recipe

Serving: 4 | Prep: | Cook: 10mins | Ready in:

Ingredients

- 1 cup all-purpose flour
- • 1/4 cup cornstarch
- • 1 teaspoon baking powder
- • 1/4 teaspoon salt
- • 1 cup ice water
- • 1 egg yolk
- • 2 tablespoons dill pickle juice
- • 4 cups drained dill pickle slices or equivalent amount of medium to large pickles, sliced 1/4-inch thick
- • vegetable oil for frying

Direction

- 1. In a large bowl, combine the flour, cornstarch, baking powder, and salt.
- Make a well in the centre.
- All at once, add the water, egg yolk, and pickle juice.
- Stir the mixture with a wire whisk to make a smooth batter.
- Cover the bowl and refrigerate for 30 minutes
- 2. In a deep fryer or large saucepan, heat at least 2 inches of oil to 375° F.
- In batches, dip pickle slices in the batter, lightly and evenly coating them.
- Without crowding, place coated slices in the hot oil.
- Fry until golden and crisp, 1 1/2 to 2 minutes.
- Drain on paper towels and serve immediately.

236. Fried Plantains Recipe

Serving: 5 | Prep: | Cook: 5mins | Ready in:

Ingredients

- 1 riped plantain (in banana family but larger)
- salt to taste
- 1/4 vegetable oil

Direction

- Peel Plantain
- Cut up into 10 slices about 1/8 thick
- Sprinkle with salt and set aside
- In small frying pan heat oil
- When oil is hot, add plantain slices
- Turn when lightly browned
- Remove when both sides are lightly browned
- Serve with rice dishes 2 per person

237. Fried Potato Patties With Dry Shrimp Recipe

Serving: 2 | Prep: | Cook: 5mins | Ready in:

Ingredients

- 4 med potatoes
- 1/3 cup dry shrimp
- 2 egg yolks
- 1/4 cup onion, chopped
- 1/8 cup bell pepper, chopped

- 1 cup vegetable oil
- 1 jalapeno pepper (chopped)
- or hotter 2
- 1/4 cup plain bread crumbs
- 1/8 cup celery, chopped
- 1/8 cup parsley, chopped

Direction

- Boil 1 cup water, add dry shrimps. Let remain in water for 5 minutes. Drain water, chop dry shrimp fine.
- Boil potatoes. In large mixing bowl, mash the boiled potatoes and season as desired. Add egg yolks, bread crumbs and chopped dry shrimp. Mix well. Add onion, bell pepper, celery, parsley and jalapeno pepper. Mix well.
- Makes 6 potato patties.
- In frying pan, add vegetable oil. Heat on medium flame until oil is hot. Place potato patties in pan, let fry for about 3-1/2 minutes or until potato patties are lightly brown. Remove from flame. Let drain on paper towel. Serve hot.

238. Fried Potato Salad Recipe

Serving: 10 | Prep: | Cook: 10mins | Ready in:

Ingredients

- 5 lbs potatoes, peeled, cut into 1/2-inch dice
- 1 1/2 C cornichon, sliced
- 5 C sweet onion, small dice
- 5 C celery, small dice
- 1 1/4 C flat leaf parsley, chopped
- 2 1/2 C mayonnaise, plain
- 1 1/4 C buttermilk
- 1 1/4 tsp white pepper, ground
- 1 tsp kosher salt, to taste
- 5 C mashed potatoes, prepared, seasoned, warm
- As Needed seasoned flour for breading
- As Needed Mixture of 2C egg whites and 2C buttermilk, whisked well for breading
- As Needed Instant-Mash potato flakes for breading

Direction

- Cover diced Potatoes with cold water and add 1 tablespoon kosher salt. Bring to a boil and cook until just tender. Drain and shock to cool. Combine cooled potatoes with remaining ingredients through mashed potatoes in a large bowl and mix gently but completely.
- Taste for seasoning. Refrigerate 1 hour until well chilled. Have pans of flour ready, seasoned with salt and pepper, egg white/buttermilk mixture and Instant Mash Potato Flakes for breading.
- Using a #12 (2-2/3 oz.) disher, scoop portions of potato salad into the seasoned flour, coat well and shake off excess flour. Dip floured potato salad into buttermilk mixture and finally roll in potato flakes. Place on sheet pans to hold for service.
- At service, deep fry 350°F for 15-20 seconds until crispy on the outside and still cold inside.

239. Fried Potatoes With Hoisin Sauce Recipe

Serving: 3 | Prep: | Cook: 30mins | Ready in:

Ingredients

- 4 medium-sized potatoes.
- salt
- pepper
- sugar
- 1/2 cup of flour
- 1 Tbsp of hoisin sauce
- cooking oil for deep frying

Direction

- Wash the potatoes well. Do not peel them.
- Slice the potatoes into thin rings.
- Season with salt, pepper and sugar.

- Toss in flour.
- Heat the cooking oil in a pan. Fry the potatoes in batches until golden and crispy. Drain on paper towels.
- Pour the Hoisin sauce into a large bowl.
- Add the fried potatoes and toss gently to coat each piece well.

240. Fried Potatoes With Onions Recipe

Serving: 4 | Prep: | Cook: 44mins | Ready in:

Ingredients

- 2 pounds potatoes, cubed
- 4 1/2 ounces of butter
- 1 red onion, cut into 8 wedges
- 2 garlic cloves, crushed
- 1 tsp lemon juice
- 2 T thyme
- salt and pepper

Direction

- Cook the cubed potatoes in a pan of boiling water for 10 minutes.
- Drain the potatoes thoroughly.
- Melt the butter in a large frying pan over low heat.
- Add the onion wedges, garlic and lemon juice.
- Cook for 2-3 minutes, stirring.
- Add the potatoes to the pan and mix well to coat with the butter mixture.
- Reduce the heat and cover the frying pan.
- Cook for 25-30 minutes or until the potatoes are golden and tender.
- Sprinkled the thyme over the top of the potatoes and season with salt and pepper.
- Serve immediately.

241. Fried Potatoes With Tartar Sauce Recipe

Serving: 4 | Prep: | Cook: 5mins | Ready in:

Ingredients

- 4 medium-sized potatoes.(Don`t peel them)
- 1/2 cup flour
- salt
- pepper
- sugar
- cooking oil for frying
- tartar sauce

Direction

- Wash the potatoes properly. Do not peel them.
- Slice the potatoes thinly. But not too thin, otherwise you`ll be cooking potato chips.
- Place the sliced potatoes in a bowl.
- Season with salt, pepper and sugar to taste.
- Pour in the flour. Hand-mix them until every slices are coated with flour.
- In a non-stick pan. Fry them until golden brown.
- Place the fried potatoes in paper towel.
- Serve with tartar sauce.

242. Fried Shrimp PoBoy Recipe

Serving: 1 | Prep: | Cook: 5mins | Ready in:

Ingredients

- Handful of raw shrimp, shelled and deveined
- 1 c. buttermilk
- 1 c. corn meal
- 1 T. creole seasoning
- French bread
- lettuce
- tomato
- Pickle
- creole mustard

Direction

- Peel and devein your raw shrimp
- Soak the shrimp in buttermilk
- Mix the cornmeal together with the creole seasoning
- Coat the shrimp in the cornmeal seasoning mix
- Deep fry the shrimp in 350 degrees until cooked through
- Open your French bread
- On top side coat with creole mustard
- On bottom put lettuce, tomato, and pickle
- In between these add your shrimp and enjoy.

243. Fried Spinach Patties Recipe

Serving: 4 | Prep: | Cook: 25mins | Ready in:

Ingredients

- 1 box frozen spinach
- 1/4 cup uncooked rice
- 1/2 cup romano cheese
- 3/4 cup seasoned bread crumbs
- 3 large eggs
- salt & pepper to taste

Direction

- 1- Boil frozen spinach and drain well. Hand squeeze off excess water from spinach.
- 2- Cook rice until done and rinse rice well. Drain and hand squeeze off excess water.
- 3- Mix together spinach, rice, eggs, salt and pepper. Add Romano cheese and bread crumbs. Mix well
- 4- Make small thin patties out of batter and fry in a little oil until both sides are brown.

244. Fried Squid Po Boy With Avocado And Black Chile Oil Recipe

Serving: 4 | Prep: | Cook: 3mins | Ready in:

Ingredients

- 1 lb small squid (bodies and tentacles), cleaned
- 3 lemons
- kosher salt
- vegetable oil for frying
- all-purpose flour
- 1 ripe avocado, halved, and pitted, peeled, and sliced
- 4 soft hero rolls, split
- 4 tsp Black Chile oil (recipe below)
- Black Chile Oil: Yield 1 14/ cups
- 8 dried chipotle chiles
- 2 dried ancho chiles
- 3/4 cup grapeseed oil
- 2 tbs white wine vinegar
- 2 tbs sugar
- 1 tbs minced garlic
- 1 tbs kosher salt
- juice from 1/2 lime

Direction

- Rinse the squid and cut the bodies into 1/4-inch rounds. In a bowl, toss the squid in the juice from 1 lemon and season with salt. Fill an 8-to-10-inch skillet with enough vegetable oil to come about 2-inches up its side. Make sure the pot is deep enough to leave at least 4-inches above the oil. Heat the oil to 350-360 degrees. The oil is ready when you can see it moving around in the skillet; test with a small piece of squid, making sure that the oil sizzles when the squid is added.
- In a bowl, toss the squid in a generous amount of flour and shake off any excess. Working in batches, fry the squid until golden and crisp, about 2 to 3 minutes. Using a slotted spoon, transfer the squid to paper towels to drain. Sprinkle with salt.

- Layer the avocado on the bottom half of each hero roll and coat the top halves with the chili oil. Stuff the oils with the squid and squeeze a generous amount of juice from the remaining lemons on top. Close the sandwiches and serve.
- Black Chile Oil:
- Place an oven or cooling rack on top of a gas burner. Place the chilies on the rack and char over an open flame. Using tongs, turn the chilies as they char. The chilies will puff up and turn completely black. Remove from the heat and cool.
- Discard the stems from all the chilies as well as the seeds from the anchos. Add the chilies and all the remaining ingredients to a food processor or blender and mix until fully incorporated. Use immediately or transfer to a container and refrigerate for 2 to 4 weeks.

245. Fried Sweet And Sour Potatoes Recipe

Serving: 6 | Prep: | Cook: 50mins | Ready in:

Ingredients

- 4 strips bacon
- bacon drippings or small amount of oil
- 1/4 cup onion, finely chopped
- 1 Tbsp. sugar
- 1/2 cup water
- 4 medium potatoes, peeled, washed and diced
- 1/4 tsp. salt
- 1/4 cup wine vinegar

Direction

- Fry bacon until crisp. Set aside. Add potatoes to drippings or oil. Cook about 20 minutes.
- Add onions, sugar, salt and water and simmer for 15 minutes.
- Remove from heat and pour vinegar over potatoes.
- Cover and let stand for 15 minutes.
- Crumble bacon and add to potato mixture.
- Reheat until hot to serve or this may be served as a cold dish.
- This is best when made several hours ahead of time so flavours can mingle.

246. Fried Tofu With Peanut Recipe

Serving: 4 | Prep: | Cook: 3mins | Ready in:

Ingredients

- 1 bag tofu - cubed deep fried
- FOR SAUCE:
- 1 tablespoon vinegar
- 2 tablespoons sugar
- 1 pinch salt
- 2 tablespoons peanuts, roasted and crushed
- 1 teaspoon ground fresh chili paste
- 5-7 sprigs cilantro, chopped

Direction

- Cut the tofu cubes into half and place them in a toaster oven or oven at 350 degrees on a cookie sheet. You just want to toast them. If you like them crispy, use lower heat and leave them in the oven longer. Flip every few minutes to toast all sides.
- FOR SAUCE: In a microwavable bowl, combine sugar, ground fresh chili paste, salt and vinegar.
- Heat up for a minute or until sugar is dissolved. Mix in the chopped cilantro. Top with peanuts.
- Sauce can mix into tofu...or on the side

247. Fried Tofu With A Special Dipping Sauce Recipe

Serving: 8 | Prep: | Cook: 10mins | Ready in:

Ingredients

- 1 Cup cornmeal
- 1 teaspoon red pepper flakes, or more if desired
- fresh black pepper
- sea salt
- 1 package extra firm tofu, drained and pressed and cut into 1/2" cubes
- canola oil
- 2 Tablespoons organic apricot fruit spread
- 1 teaspoon fresh ginger, minced
- 1/4 Cup tamari or shoyu
- 1/4 Cup water

Direction

- In a medium fry pan add enough oil for tofu to fry in. (The oil should come to the middle of the tofu but does not need to cover it as you can turn the tofu)
- Bring oil to medium high heat. You want the oil to fry the tofu but you DO NOT want the oil to bubble or boil. Be careful to watch this does not happen.
- In medium bowl add cornmeal, red pepper flakes and a sprinkle of salt and pepper.
- Add tofu and coat well.
- When oil is hot add tofu cubes about 8 pieces at a time. They should cook in about 30 seconds.
- Remove to a paper towel lined plate to drain off excess oil.
- Season with sea salt. Repeat with remaining tofu.
- For the dipping sauce:
- In a medium bowl add apricot spread, ginger, water and tamari.
- Mix well.
- If sauce is not thick enough add more apricot fruit spread, one teaspoon at a time until you have reached your desired consistency.
- Serve with toothpicks.

248. Fried Whole Okra Recipe

Serving: 6 | Prep: | Cook: 8mins | Ready in:

Ingredients

- 1 lb. young okra
- 1/2 cup corn meal
- dash of cayenne pepper
- 1/2 tsp salt
- 1/8 tsp pepper

Direction

- Cut off stem and tip of okra pods; wash thoroughly. Cook in boiling salted water for 8 minutes. Drain and dry completely. Roll in seasoned corn meal. Fry in deep fat at 350* or sauté in butter until brown. Serve immediately.

249. Fried Yellow Squash Recipe

Serving: 6 | Prep: | Cook: 4mins | Ready in:

Ingredients

- Nice fresh yellow squash (maybe 6 or 8 medium squash)
- 1 cup self-rising flour
- 1 cup pancake mix
- 1 teaspoon paprika
- buttermilk
- salt and pepper
- Crisco for fryin'

Direction

- Wash squash, peel if needed, slice in rounds, not too thick
- Salt and pepper squash
- Pour buttermilk in bowl
- Whisk dry ingredients in another bowl
- Dip each round of squash in buttermilk, THEN

- Coat in breading mix
- Drop gently in hot oil and brown until golden
- Remove from pan, drain on paper towel
- Oh, so good!

250. Fried Yucca And Mojo Recipe

Serving: 4 | Prep: | Cook: 45mins | Ready in:

Ingredients

- 1 cup Goya olive oil
- 1/2 cup Goya cider vinegar
- 1/2 cup coriander chopped
- 1 bay leaf
- salt and pepper to taste
- Goya Yucca; 1 – 24 oz package
- Goya vegetable oil – to fry

Direction

- 1. Fry yucca according to the instructions in the package.
- 2. Mix all the other ingredients - blend into a dressing.

251. Fried Cucumbers Recipe

Serving: 4 | Prep: | Cook: 7mins | Ready in:

Ingredients

- cucumber sliced in 1/8 inch thick slices (you decide how many you want for how many people. 1 small cuke will easily do 4 people)
- butter
- salt and pepper
- flour

Direction

- Slice cucumber to 1/8 inch thick rounds, or, if you feel fancy on the bias (angle)
- Roll in flour
- Heat butter in a skillet till bubbly
- Lay cukes in butter and fry till light brown
- Add salt and pepper to taste
- ***for a variation fry in bacon fat (you've been saving from some of my other recipes) or extra virgin olive oil
- *** Also goes great with sour cream or sour cream and dill also on top when served with fish

252. Fried Peanut Butter And Bannan Sandwich Recipe

Serving: 4 | Prep: | Cook: 10mins | Ready in:

Ingredients

- 1/2 cup butter, softened
- 3/4 cup crunchy peanut butter
- 3 tablespoons honey
- 1 1/2 teaspoons ground cinnamon
- 2 to 3 ripe bananas
- 8 slices white bread
- Topping:
- 1/4 cup sugar
- 1 tablespoon ground cinnamon

Direction

- In a frying pan, melt 3 tablespoons of the butter.
- Make sure butter does not burn. In a small bowl mix together the peanut butter, honey, and cinnamon. Slice the bananas into 1/4-inch thick slices.
- Spread the peanut butter mixture on 4 slices of bread and cover with banana slices.
- Top with the remaining 4 slices of bread.
- Spread the remaining butter on both sides of the sandwiches. Grill the sandwiches in the frying pan until each side is golden brown.

- For topping, combine the sugar and cinnamon in shallow plate. Coat the grilled sandwiches with the mixture.
- Cut diagonally and serve hot.

253. Fry Free Samosas Recipe

Serving: 4 | Prep: | Cook: 30mins | Ready in:

Ingredients

- 14 ounces low-fat extra-firm tofu, frozen for 24 hours and thawed
- 1 medium onion, minced
- 1/2 cup peas
- 2 roma tomatoes, diced
- 1 tablespoon fresh grated ginger
- 1 jalapeno pepper, stemmed, seeded and finely diced
- 1/2 - 3/4 cup water
- 1 lb yukon gold potatoes, cooked, peeled and diced
- 1/2 teaspoon salt
- 2 teaspoons curry powder
- 1/4 tsp cinnamon
- 3/4 teaspoon ground cumin
- 1/4 teaspoon cayenne
- 1 tablespoon lemon juice

Direction

- Drain and press tofu to remove excess water, and cut into 1/4-inch cubes.
- Heat a little water in a deep non-stick skillet and add the onion.
- Cook on medium-high for 5-6 minutes, until the onion begins to brown.
- Add peas, tomatoes, ginger, jalapeno pepper, and another splash of water.
- Cook, stirring, until peas thaw (about 2 minutes).
- Add potatoes and tofu to skillet along with 1/2 cup more water, salt, curry powder, cinnamon, cumin, cayenne, and lemon juice.

- Cover and simmer for about 10 minutes, adding more water if necessary.
- Raise heat and cook until almost all the liquid is gone.

254. Fry Bread Tacos Recipe

Serving: 4 | Prep: | Cook: 60mins | Ready in:

Ingredients

- 1 pound ground beef
- 1 (1.25 ounce) package taco seasoning mix
- 1 (15.5 ounce) can pinto beans, with liquid
- 1 cup shredded cheddar cheese
- 2 cups shredded iceberg lettuce
- 1/2 cup picante sauce
- FRY BREAD:
- 2 cups all-purpose flour
- 1 tablespoon baking powder
- 1 teaspoon salt
- 1 cup milk
- 4 cups oil for frying, or as needed

Direction

- Combine beans and 2 tablespoons of picante sauce in a small saucepan over low heat. Cook until heated through. In a large skillet, over medium-high heat, cook the ground beef with taco seasoning mix according to seasoning mix package directions. Cover, and keep warm while you prepare the fry bread.
- In a medium bowl, stir together the flour, baking powder, and salt. Stir in milk, and mix until the dough comes together. Add more flour if necessary to be able to handle the dough. On a floured surface, knead the dough until smooth, at least 5 minutes. Let the dough rest for 5 minutes.
- Heat oil in a large, deep heavy skillet to 365 degrees F (180 degrees C). Oil should be about 1 1/2 inches deep. Break off 3/4 cup sized pieces of dough, and shape into round discs 1/4 inch in thickness, making a thinner

depressed area in the center. Fry breads in the hot oil until golden on both sides, turning only once. Drain on paper towels.
- Top fry bread with beans, ground beef, lettuce and cheese. Spoon picante sauce over. You can also top with other of your favorite taco toppings, such as onion, sour cream or guacamole.

255. Fryed Cabbage Recipe

Serving: 68 | Prep: | Cook: 12mins |Ready in:

Ingredients

- 1 head mountain cabbage
- 6 slices Fat back
- 1/4 tsp salt
- 1/4 tsp black pepper
- crushed red pepper
- sugar
- water

Direction

- Slice cabbage in long thin strips (remove Cobb).Fry fatback mid-high heat in large skillet until golden brown. Remove fatback. Add cabbage let it pile up. Salt & pepper to taste. Use same amount sugar as the salt. Sprinkle 1/4to1/2 tsp. of crushed red pepper on top. Use red pepper +/- for the heat factor you like. Add about 1 tbsp. water cover simmer until cooked down or slightly colored. Stir frequently but keep covered. Serve

256. Garlic Fried Asparagus Recipe

Serving: 2 | Prep: | Cook: 12mins | Ready in:

Ingredients

- asparagus
- butter or olive oil
- garlic powder -- or you can omit garlic.

Direction

- Wash and trim asparagus to fit large enough frying pan.
- Add your favourite [butter is mine] butter or olive oil to pan. Add it to your taste, but don't be too stingy with it.
- Fry with slow to medium heat, gently sprinkling just a hint of the garlic powder over all. Thicker asparagus pieces cook best in centre of the pan.
- You will have to experiment a little according to how you like your asparagus done. If you like it more al-dente, cook it less. But about when half way cooked turn each piece over, cooking till done. Mine is very slightly browned on each side when done. Once you have done this you'll know exactly for next time. The asparagus gets darker green, stays firm and to me has a far better flavour cooked this way.
- Of course you have to add butter when serving! You've seen the Butterworth family in the TV ad I hope, with a stick of butter sticking vertically out of each baked potato.

257. Garlic Fried Potatoes Recipe

Serving: 4 | Prep: | Cook: 10mins |Ready in:

Ingredients

- 2 ounces butter, softened
- 1 1/2 tablespoons garlic, minced
- canola oil
- 2 large idaho potatoes (12 to 14 ounces each), peeled and cut into 1-inch pieces
- kosher salt
- black pepper

Direction

- Combine butter and garlic in a small bowl and set aside.
- Using a large, heavy bottomed pot, fill halfway with oil and heat to 325°F. Blanch diced potatoes in oil until tender, but not browned, about 4 minutes.
- Drain on paper towels and transfer to a small sheet pan. Freeze or chill potatoes until ready to serve.
- When ready to serve, reheat oil to 325°F and fry frozen or chilled potatoes until golden browned, about 3 minutes. Drain potatoes on paper towels, and transfer to a mixing bowl. Add 1 or 2 tablespoons of the softened garlic-butter, tossing to coat. Season with salt and pepper.
- Serve immediately.

258. Garlic And Pepper Stir Fry Recipe

Serving: 4 | Prep: | Cook: 15mins | Ready in:

Ingredients

- 2 tablespoons soy sauce
- 1 teaspoon toasted sesame oil
- 1/4 teaspoon cracked black pepper
- 1 tablespoon cooking oil or peanut oil
- 3 cloves garlic, minced
- 2 cups red, yellow, and/or green sweet peppers, cut into bite-size strips; carrot slices; and/or fresh pea pods (stems and ends removed)
- 1 medium onion, sliced and separated into rings
- 2 cups sliced fresh mushrooms
- sesame seeds, toasted

Direction

- In a small bowl, stir together soy sauce, sesame oil, and black pepper; set aside. In a 12-inch skillet or wok heat cooking oil over high heat for 1 minute. Add garlic; cook and stir for 1 minute. Add sweet pepper and onion; cook and stir for 3 minutes. Add mushrooms; cook and stir for 2 to 3 minutes more until vegetables are crisp-tender.
- Add soy sauce mixture to skillet or wok. Cook and stir to coat vegetables. Transfer mixture to a serving dish. Sprinkle with sesame seeds.

259. Garlicky Stir Fried Shanghai Bok Choy Recipe

Serving: 6 | Prep: | Cook: 10mins | Ready in:

Ingredients

- 2 lb baby bok choy
- 2 fl oz. vegetable oil
- 8 garlic cloves, sliced thinly
- salt, as needed
- sugar, as needed

Direction

- Cut the bok choy lengthwise in half. Score the cores to promote even cooking.
- Blanch the bok choy in boiling salted water, shock in an ice bath, and drain well.
- Heat the oil in a wok, add the garlic, and stir-fry until aromatic and light brown.
- Add the bok choy and stir-fry to complete the cooking process. Add a small amount of water to the wok to keep the garlic from burning, if necessary. Season with salt and sugar.
- Serve immediately.
- That's it!

260. Ginger Fried Rice Recipe

Serving: 4 | Prep: | Cook: 10mins | Ready in:

Ingredients

- 1/2 cup peanut oil
- 2 tablespoons minced garlic
- 2 tablespoons minced ginger
- salt
- 2 cups thinly sliced leeks, white and light green parts only, rinsed and dried
- 4 cups day-old cooked rice; Vongerichten recommends jasmine but this is the perfect way to use up any leftover rice you have, especially from Chinese delivery
- 4 large eggs
- 2 teaspoons sesame oil (for some heat but the same awesome
- flavor, use hot sesame oil)
- 4 teaspoons soy sauce

Direction

- In a large skillet, heat 1/4 cup oil over medium heat.
- Add garlic and ginger and cook, stirring occasionally, until crisp and brown.
- With a slotted spoon, transfer to paper towels and salt lightly.
- Reduce heat under skillet to medium-low and add 2 tablespoons oil and leeks.
- Cook about 10 minutes, stirring occasionally, until very tender but not browned.
- Season lightly with salt.
- Raise heat to medium and add rice.
- Cook, stirring well, until heated through. Season to taste with salt.
- In a non-stick skillet (it just makes it easier) fry eggs in remaining oil, sunny-side-up, until edges are set but yolk is still runny.
- Divide rice among four dishes.
- Top each with an egg and drizzle with 1/2 teaspoon sesame oil and 1 teaspoon soy sauce.
- Sprinkle crisped garlic and ginger over everything and serve.

261. Glazed Teriyaki Chicken Stir Fry Sub Recipe

Serving: 4 | Prep: | Cook: 10mins | Ready in:

Ingredients

- ¼ C. French's® honey dijon mustard
- 2 T. teriyaki sauce
- 1 T. light brown sugar
- 1 T. grated, peeled ginger root
- 1 T. red wine vinegar
- 1 T. vegetable oil
- 1 lb boneless skinless chicken, cut into thin strips
- 1 C. red and yellow bell peppers, coarsely chopped
- ½ C. red onion, coarsely chopped
- ½ C. plum tomatoes, coarsely chopped
- 4 Italian heros, split (about 8 inches each)
- 2 C. shredded napa cabbage or romaine lettuce

Direction

- Combine mustard, teriyaki sauce, sugar substitute, ginger and vinegar in small bowl; set aside.
- Heat oil in large skillet or wok over high heat. Stir-fry chicken 5 min until no longer pink. Add vegetables and stir-fry 2 min until just tender. Pour sauce mixture over stir-fry and cook 1 min.
- Arrange cabbage on rolls and top with equal portions of stir-fry. Close rolls. Serve warm.
- Tips: Serve this stir-fry just over shredded Napa cabbage for a dinner entree. If desired, substitute 1 pound sliced boneless pork or steak for the chicken.

262. Gluten Free Fried Eggplant Recipe

Serving: 4 | Prep: | Cook: 15mins | Ready in:

Ingredients

- 1 med. eggplant (about 2lbs)
- 1/2 cup cornmeal
- 1/2 cup extra fine cornmeal
- 1/2 cup garfava flour*-or chickpea flour
- 1/4 cup potato starch
- 1/4 cup rice flour
- 1/4 cup parmasean cheese
- 1/2 tsp.garlic powder
- 1/2 tsp.salt
- 1/2 tsp.pepper
- 1/4 tsp. or more to taste cayenne
- 2 eggs
- 1/2 cup buttermilk
- 3/4 cup vegetable shortening

Direction

- Peel eggplant, slice lengthwise into about 1/4 to 1/2 inch thickness, then cut in half crosswise. In a large shallow bowl place eggplant slices in heavily salted water, 3-4 inches of water above eggplant. Set aside for 30 minutes. This will keep eggplant from turning brown and absorbing all the oil. (About 4-6 tablespoons salt for water)
- In a shallow dish mix dry ingredients. In a medium bowl beat eggs and add buttermilk. Set aside.
- In a large skillet melt shortening over medium-high heat. Reduce heat to medium when melted.
- Rinse and drain eggplant well, pat dry with paper towels. Dip slices in egg mixture, then coat them in the shallow dish with flour mix. You can dip and coat all at once and place on a large plate.
- Turn oven on warm setting.
- Fry a few slices at a time until golden brown, turning once. Place cooked pieces on a baking sheet and keep in warm oven as you continue to fry remaining eggplant slices.
- Serve with favourite sauce, use for eggplant parm or enjoy just as they are.
- *fava bean/chickpea flour mix

263. Grandmas Fried Potatoes Recipe

Serving: 6 | Prep: | Cook: 17mins | Ready in:

Ingredients

- 5 or 6 idaho potatoes
- oil
- 1 Tbs. butter (optional)
- 1 tsp. parsley flakes (optional)

Direction

- Peel and wash potatoes.
- Cut into little cubes.
- Put enough oil in the bottom of skillet to cover bottom of skillet well.
- Heat oil over medium heat until hot.
- Carefully put in the potatoes, cover with a lid and stir occasionally.
- Fry for about 10 minutes covered then remove lid and fry until browned a little.
- If you want butter and parsley add this last 5 minutes of cooking.
- Place on paper towels to drain oil.

264. Greek Fries Recipe

Serving: 6 | Prep: | Cook: 20mins | Ready in:

Ingredients

- 3 medium russet potatoes, sliced into fries
- 4oz feta cheese, crumbledd
- 1/4 cup kalamata olives, sliced
- 2-3T balsamic vinegar
- 1t lemon grass, chopped*
- 1/2t dried oregano
- 1t parsley flakes
- 1t paprika
- 1/2t sea or kosher salt
- 1 clove garlic, crushed or minced

- 1/4 cup dressing quality olive oil
- peanut oil for frying, if desired
- *if lemongrass is unavailable, you can use green onion tops and a touch of lemon juice to replace part of the vinegar

Direction

- Fry potatoes in 375degree oil for 5-7 minutes, until golden brown. (Or, bake in 450 oven for about 35-40 minutes, until cooked though)
- Meanwhile, in large bowl, combine vinegar and spices and slowly whisk in oil to combine.
- Drain fried potatoes on brown paper or paper towels then add to bowl
- Toss to combine.
- Arrange on serving plates or on platter, and top with feta cheese and sliced olives.
- ~you can place fries in 250 oven for a few minutes to rewarm, if needed, before adding the cheese and olives---these don't need to be served steaming hot, but you will probably need a fork! :)

265. Green Banana Fries Recipe

Serving: 6 | Prep: | Cook: 30mins | Ready in:

Ingredients

- • 5 small unripe (green) bananas
- • 1 quart oil for frying, or as needed
- • salt to taste

Direction

- Peel the bananas using a knife, as they are not ripe and will not peel like a yellow banana. Slice into long thin wedges or strings to make fries.
- Heat the oil in a heavy deep skillet over medium-high heat. If you have a deep-fryer, heat the oil to 375 degrees F (190 degrees C). Place the banana fries into the hot oil, and fry until golden brown, 5 to 7 minutes. Remove from the oil, and drain on paper towels. Pat off the excess oil, and season with salt. Serve immediately.

266. Green Beans With Almonds And Fried Onions Recipe

Serving: 6 | Prep: | Cook: 10mins | Ready in:

Ingredients

- 1 pound fresh green beans
- kosher salt
- 1 to 2 tablespoons unsalted butter
- 1/4 cup slivered almonds (2-ounce package)
- 1/2 lemon, juiced
- ground black pepper
- 1 can fried onions

Direction

- Bring 1 inch of water to a boil in a high-sided sauté pan.
- Cut beans lengthwise while you wait for the water to boil.
- Add salt and green beans to boiling water and cook until just tender.
- Drain beans and rinse under cold water to stop the cooking.
- Return the skillet to medium heat and add butter.
- When butter is melted, add the almonds and cook until golden brown.
- Return the green beans to the pan, along with the juice of 1/2 a lemon
- Add salt and pepper, to taste.
- When warmed through, top with fried onions

267. Grilled Fiesta Fries Recipe

Serving: 2 | Prep: | Cook: 15mins | Ready in:

Ingredients

- 1 bag Extra Crispy Crinkle-cut frozen fries (such as Ore-Ida)
- 1-1/2 ounces real bacon bits
- 1 cup of cheddar cheese, shredded
- 1/4 cup sour cream
- 1/4 cup guacamole (make your own favorite recipe)
- 2 tablespoons tomatoes, diced
- 2 tablespoons black olives, sliced
- taco seasoning

Direction

- Preheat grill to medium heat (450°-500°)
- Line a foil pan with some aluminum foil and spray with non-stick cooking spray.
- Place frozen fries in a single layer.
- Place the pan on the grill.
- Cook for 10 minutes.
- Turn fries, spray on a bit more cooking spray and sprinkle with taco seasoning.
- Cook for 5-10 more minutes.
- Remove pan from grill.
- Top with bacon and cheese.
- Return to grill and cook 2 minutes more or until cheese melts.
- Remove from grill and top with sour cream, guacamole, tomatoes and black olives.

268. Grilled Steak Fries Recipe

Serving: 8 | Prep: | Cook: 15mins | Ready in:

Ingredients

- FRIES:
- 4 large russet potatoes, each cut into 8 wedges
- 3 Tbsp. EVOO
- Kosher salt and black pepper to taste
- 1 cup shredded cheddar cheese
- SAUCE:
- 1 cup mayonnaise
- 2 Tbsp. Dijon mustard
- 2 strips bacon, diced and fried until crisp
- 2 Tbsp. chopped scallion

Direction

- Preheat grill to medium
- Toss potato wedges with oil, salt, and pepper.
- Grill potatoes, uncovered, until tender when pierced, 10-15 minutes.
- Turn potatoes halfway through to create grill marks on both sides.
- Transfer potato wedges to a foil pan or baking dish; Sprinkle with Cheddar.
- Turn off grill; place pan on grill to allow residual heat to melt Cheddar.
- Combine mayonnaise and Dijon for the sauce in a small bowl.
- Garnish with bacon and scallions.

269. Harvest Cider Poutine Recipe

Serving: 8 | Prep: | Cook: 30mins | Ready in:

Ingredients

- • 8 Medium Sized Yukon Gold Potatoes
- • 2L canola oil
- • 12 oz. cheese Curds (3 oz. per person)
- • 12 oz. Pulled Pork (3 oz. per person)
- • 3 cups of Your Favourite Gravy
- • Approx. 3 cans Molson Canadian cider
- • 1 Bag Coleslaw Mix (purple cabbage, green cabbage, carrots)
- • 3 Granny Smith apples
- • 1/8 cup apple cider vinegar
- • 1/2 cup Olive Oil
- • 1 tsp Dry Mustard
- • 1/2 tsp celery Seed

- • 1 tbsp Sugar
- • 1/2 tsp Salt

Direction

- 1. Prepare the fries by cutting 8 med-sized Yukon Gold potatoes into 3/8" strips. Soak in water for 15 minutes and then blanch in canola oil for 5 min at 300 F. Drain and let cool. Raise temperature to 350F and cook for approx. 5-7 minutes (until crispy on the outside and sweet & moist inside). Note: Colour of fries may vary but golden brown is the ideal!
- 2. Next prepare the gravy. Infuse your favourite gravy with Molson Canadian Cider. Mix a ratio of 10:1 --> Gravy: Molson Canadian Cider (adjust according to taste). Combine in a saucepan and simmer for 10 minutes.
- 3. While simmering the gravy, prepare the coleslaw. Combine 1/8 cup of Molson Canadian Cider, apple cider vinegar, olive oil, dry mustard and salt in a bowl and add in one bag of coleslaw mix. Stir in 1 Granny Smith apple finely sliced into 1' bite-size pieces.
- 4. Once you have prepared all toppings place 1 cup of cooked fries in a shallow bowl (one bowl per person), add tempered curds and pour on gravy. Top with pulled pork and ¼ cup of coleslaw.
- 5. Pair with a glass of Molson Canadian Cider and ENJOY!
- For this recipe and more visit molsoncanadian.ca/cider

270. Herbfarm Roasted Asparagus Salad With Fried Sage Recipe

Serving: 6 | Prep: | Cook: 15mins | Ready in:

Ingredients

- 2 lbs asparagus
- 1 tablespoon fresh sage, finely chopped
- 1 1/2 tablespoons olive oil
- salt
- 1 cup olive oil, for frying
- 30 medium sage leaves, patted dry
- a wedge of parmigiano-Reggiano cheese
- --> Dressing
- 1 large lemon, thinly sliced, zested
- 3 tablespoons lemon juice
- 1 tablespoon fresh sage, chopped
- 1/4 teaspoon salt
- freshly ground coarse black pepper
- 1/4 cup extra virgin olive oil

Direction

- Preheat oven to 450 degrees F.
- Trim the bottoms of the asparagus spears at the point where they turn pale and tough. If the spears are medium to thick, peel the lower 2/3 of the trimmed spears with a sharp vegetable peeler. Thin spears do not need to be peeled. Place them in a bowl and toss with the chopped sage, olive oil and a light sprinkle of salt. Spread the asparagus in a single layer on a baking sheet and roast until the spears are slightly limp when you hold them from the bottom, 4-8 minutes depending on their thickness. They will continue to cook once you remove them from the oven. Let cool.
- Fried Sage: Heat the oil in a 1 1/2 to 2-quart saucepan. Drop in half of the sage leaves and turn them in the oil with a wire skimmer or slotted spoon. They'll sizzle loudly at first, but if they're dry, they won't splatter. Fry for only 10 to 15 seconds, then remove them to paper towels to drain. Do not let the leaves brown. Fry the remaining sage leaves and sprinkle them all lightly with salt. They should crisp when they cool. The sage can be fried up to 1 day ahead of time; it will stay crisp if stored in an airtight container at room temperature.
- Cheese: Hold a wedge of Parmigiano in your hand and use a sharp vegetable peeler with light pressure to shave thin curls of the cheese into a bowl. You'll want to shave off 2 ounces, about 1 cup.

- Dressing: Combine all the dressing ingredients except the olive oil in a small mixing bowl, then whisk in the oil.
- Assembling the salad: When ready to serve, toss the asparagus with the dressing in a large bowl. Arrange the asparagus in a fan shape on a serving platter or individual plates. Sprinkle with the Parmigiano shavings and then with the fried sage leaves. If you have a sage plant that's flowering, sprinkle the salad with some of its blossoms.
- Variation, Warm Roasted Asparagus with Sage Butter: Roast the asparagus spears as directed. While they are roasting, melt 4 tablespoons unsalted butter in a small (8-inch) skillet over medium-low heat. Add the 30 sage leaves and cook, stirring often, until the butter begins to brown slightly and the sage gives off a nutty, toasty aroma, 3 to 4 minutes. Stir in the finely sliced zest of 1 lemon, 3 tablespoons lemon juice, and 1/4 teaspoon salt. Transfer the asparagus to a warm platter and spoon the sage leaves and lemon butter on top. Sprinkle with the Parmigiano shavings and sage blossoms if available.
- Note: You can roast the asparagus ahead of time, but don't dress the spears until ready to serve, since the lemon juice drains their colour.

271. Iron Skillet Fried Squash Recipe

Serving: 4 | Prep: | Cook: 25mins | Ready in:

Ingredients

- 5 medium summer squash, peeled and sliced 1/4 inch thick
- 1/2 large onion, sliced 1/8-inch thick
- 1 tablespoon bacon drippings
- salt and pepper, to taste

Direction

- Peel and slice squash 1/4 inch thick.
- Slice onions about 1/8 inch thick.
- Place both in iron skillet or sauté skillet, cover with water and cook covered on medium high heat about 15 minutes, until tender.
- Drain in colander . Return to skillet on low heat to drive off excess moisture. Add salt and pepper to taste.
- Add 1 tbsp. of bacon drippings, mix in, turn heat to medium high, pat down into skillet and let fry until slightly crispy.
- Serve right out of the skillet.

272. KFC Original Fried Chicken Recipe

Serving: 8 | Prep: | Cook: 30mins | Ready in:

Ingredients

- 8 Desired Pieces of chicken
- 1 1/2 Cups flour
- 1 Packet Dry Italien DRESSING seasong
- 1 envelope Lipton tomato soup
- 2 eggs Well Beaten
- 2/3 Cup milk
- vegetable oil to cover bottom of skillet 1/2 inch deep

Direction

- Combine Eggs and Milk- Set aside
- Combine Flour w/ Italian Dressing & Soup Mix
- Dip Chicken into Egg mixture & then into Flour mixture repeat
- Fry Pieces over Medium Heat for 25-30 minutes Turning Often
- Remove, Drain, Serve

273. Kai Lan Stir Fry Recipe

Serving: 4 | Prep: | Cook: 5mins | Ready in:

Ingredients

- Kailan (chinese broccoli) - 1 bunch , wahed and cut the stalks into thirds .
- olive oil
- Sauce (heat it for 1 min) :
- 2 tbsp oyster sauce
- 2 tsp olive oil
- 1 tbsp garlic , chopped
- 2 slices ginger , julienned
- 2 tsp sugar
- 2 tbsp stalk (optional)

Direction

- Cut the stems into thin slices, tops into florets.
- Boil water and add salt, oil and the vege.
- Cook until tender and crisp like for 3 mins.
- Drain and place on a serving plate.
- Drizzle the sauce on top.

274. Lanas Country Cream Gravy For Fried Chicken More Recipe

Serving: 4 | Prep: | Cook: 10mins | Ready in:

Ingredients

- Cream gravy
- 2 tablespoons butter
- 4 tablespoons flour
- salt and pepper, to taste
- 1 cup milk
- 1 cup water
- Crispy pieces left in pan after cooking fried chicken,
- pork chop, or steak. (add last)

Direction

- (Please note, I have posted my fried chicken recipe! :)
- To make cream gravy:
- (Save all crispy pieces after you cook chicken, fried steak, or pork chops!)
- Pour off all but about 2 tablespoons of the fat from the skillet.
- Add 2 tablespoons butter and 4 tablespoons flour; blend and cook until golden brown, scraping browned bits from bottom of skillet.
- (I use these last)
- Gradually stir in 1 cup milk and 1 cup hot water. Stir until smooth and thickened; add salt and black pepper.
- Serve with hot biscuits, potatoes, or rice.

275. Leahs French Fried Onion Circles Recipe

Serving: 4 | Prep: | Cook: 6mins | Ready in:

Ingredients

- One large yellow or vidalia onion for each 2 people
- 2 large eggs
- 1/8 cup corn starch
- 1/2 cup all purpose flour
- 4 good shakes of red chili peppers
- 2-3 tablespoons jerk seasonings
- 1 teaspoon freshly cracked tri-colored pepper
- 1/4 to 1/2 cup water/milk

Direction

- Despite the amount of spices, these are not hot, yet they have some zest.
- Slice onions 1/4 inch thick, do not make into rings, but try to keep slices 'whole'
- Place into batter and carefully flip them over to coat.
- Place bowl with batter and onions into refrigerator until ready to fry.
- These cook up quickly, and I did them last after frying up my shrimp I had made for dinner.
- Take onion slices out of batter, let excess batter drip off, and carefully place into hot oil.

- Flip over when one side has been browned and let cook on other side.
- Let cooked onion slices drain of fresh paper towels, and sprinkle with a little kosher salt once right out of the hot oil.
- Serve as a side dish and garnish with fresh chopped parsley or chives for added colour if you so wish.

---

276. Lemony Chickpea Stir Fry Recipe

Serving: 4 | Prep: | Cook: 20mins | Ready in:

Ingredients

- 2 tablespoon ghee or extra-virgin olive oil
- fine grain sea salt
- 1 small onion or a couple shallots, sliced
- 1 cup cooked chickpeas (canned is fine, if you don't want to cook up a pot of dried chickpeas)
- 8 ounces extra-firm tofu
- 1 cup of chopped kale
- 2 small zucchini, chopped
- zest and juice of 1/2 a lemon

Direction

- Heat 1 tablespoon of the ghee/olive oil. In a large skillet over medium-high heat and stir in a big pinch of salt, the onion, and chickpeas.
- Sauté until the chickpeas are deeply golden and crusty.
- Stir in the tofu and cook just until the tofu is heated through, just a minute or so.
- Stir in the kale and cook for one minute more.
- Remove everything from the skillet onto a large plate and set aside.
- In the same skillet heat the remaining tablespoon of ghee/olive oil, add the zucchini and sauté until it starts to take on a bit of color, two or three minutes.
- Add the chickpea mixture back to the skillet, and remove from heat.
- Stir in the lemon juice and zest, taste, and season with a bit more salt if needed.
- Turn out onto a platter and serve family style.
- Servings 4
- 1 cups per serving
- Calories 232.25
- Fat 11.625
- Carbs 31.25
- Protein 19.85
- Fiber 4.725

---

277. Lone Star Bacon And Cheddar Fries Recipe

Serving: 4 | Prep: | Cook: 3mins | Ready in:

Ingredients

- Lone Star bacon and Cheddar Fries
- Serves 4.
- 1 pound (3/8-inch) regular cut fries with skin on
- 2 ounce shredded cheddar cheese
- 2 strips cooked diced bacon
- 3 ounces sour cream
- Finely chopped green onions, for garnish
- jalapeno peppers, for garnish

Direction

- Deep-fry regular cut fries (350-360 degrees F) for 3 to 3 1/2 minutes or until golden brown and crisp.
- In fry serving basket, arrange hot fries. Top with cheese and bacon. Garnish with sour cream and green onions. If desired, garnish with jalapenos. Serve immediately.

---

278. MIMMIES FRIED APPLE PIES Recipe

Serving: 16 | Prep: | Cook: 30mins | Ready in:

Ingredients

- PASTRY: 2 cup sifted flour
- ¼ tsp salt (see note at butter)
- ½ cup butter (if using salted butter, reduce salt above)
- 6 Tbsp ice water
- powdered sugar
- FILLING: 4 large granny smith apples
- ½ stick butter (lightly salted is OK)
- ½ cup loosely packed light brown sugar
- 2 tsp ground cinnamon
- dash allspice

Direction

- PASTRY: Sift flour with salt into mixing bowl. Cut in butter. Add enough ice water to make a stiff dough.
- Work with half of the dough at a time. Roll out to approx. ¼ inch thickness or less.
- Cut squares of pastry approx. 4 inches on each side. Set aside while preparing filling.
- FILLING: Peel and core apples and cut into small pieces about ½ inch thick
- Melt butter in a heavy skillet on medium high heat. Add brown sugar, cinnamon, and allspice. Stir to dissolve sugar.
- Add apples to the mixture, stir to coat well and reduce heat to simmer. Simmer until apples are fork tender but remain in wedges.
- PIES: Assemble all pies as below before frying. In a skillet, place 1½ cups oil and bring to temperature on medium high heat.
- Place about a tablespoon or two of apples on one side of each square of pastry.
- Fold each pie into a triangle. Lightly dampen the edges with ice water and use a fork to press and seal the edges together.
- Prick each side of each pie with a fork 2-3 times.
- Fry the pies in the hot oil until brown on each side.
- Drain well on a paper towel and sprinkle tops with powdered sugar while pies are still hot.

279. Maple Fried Apples Recipe

Serving: 23 | Prep: | Cook: 15mins | Ready in:

Ingredients

- 6-8 apples*
- 1/4 cup butter
- 1/2 cup brown sugar
- 1 tbsp maple syrup
- * I use honey Crisp or Cripps Pink because I like sweet-tart hard apples. Pick what you prefer, but crispy apples will retain their crunch in this recipe.

Direction

- Get a large and deep pan to do the work. Apples take up a lot of room!
- Melt the butter and brown sugar together into a syrupy mix on medium-low heat.
- Add apples at you cut them, I usually double quarter them.
- Pour in the maple syrup, to which I usually mix in what I think it needed. I say a tablespoon but add what you want, really.
- Sauté for 15 to 20 minutes, or until apples are tender. Crisper apples will be tender on the outside but will still have a crunch inside.

280. Maw Maws Fried Green Tomatoes Recipe

Serving: 6 | Prep: | Cook: 10mins | Ready in:

Ingredients

- green tomatoes
- cornmeal, coarse grind if you can find
- salt
- pepper
- buttermilk or egg (Optional, might not need}

- bacon drippings or peanut oil

Direction

- Heat oil is large cast iron skillet, enough bacon grease or oil to cover bottom, but not so much that when you put the tomato in that it floats.
- Slice tomatoes about 1/4" thick. You don't want them too thin or they fall apart during frying.
- Season both sides with salt and pepper.
- Dredge in cornmeal and fry to brown on both sides.
- My Maw Maw would sometimes dip in buttermilk or egg depending on what was in the house first and then dredge and fry because she said sometimes the cornmeal won't adhere right to the tomato and you won't have enough breading.

281. Mexican Fried Rice Recipe

Serving: 4 | Prep: | Cook: 20mins | Ready in:

Ingredients

- 1 cup uncooked jasmine rice
- 1 1/2 cups water
- 1 egg
- 1 tablespoon garlic-flavor olive oil or olive oil
- 1 pound fresh chicken tenders
- 1/2 cup chopped onion
- 2 cloves garlic, minced
- 1 (15 ounce) can black beans, drained
- 1 (11 ounce) can whole kernel corn, with Red and green peppers
- 1 (7 ounce) jar sliced roasted red bell peppers, drained
- 1 (8 ounce) jar taco sauce
- 1/4 cup chopped green onions
- 1/4 cup chopped fresh cilantro

Direction

- Cook rice in water as directed on package.
- Meanwhile, spray 12-inch skillet with non-stick cooking spray. Heat over medium heat until hot. Beat egg in small bowl. Add egg to skillet; cook 1 minute or until firm but still moist, stirring frequently. Remove from pan; cover to keep warm.
- Heat oil in same skillet over medium heat until hot. Add chicken, onion and garlic; cook and stir 4 to 6 minutes or until chicken is no longer pink in centre. Add beans, corn and roasted peppers; mix well. Cook 1 minute or until thoroughly heated, stirring constantly and breaking up chicken and roasted peppers as mixture cooks.
- Add cooked egg and rice; cook and stir 1 minute. Stir in taco sauce; cook 2 minutes or until thoroughly heated, stirring occasionally. Stir in green onions. Spoon mixture onto serving platter. Garnish with cilantro.

282. Mexican Stir Fry Recipe

Serving: 24 | Prep: | Cook: 10mins | Ready in:

Ingredients

- cooking oil spray
- 1/2 med onion, diced
- 3 lg cloves garlic, minced
- 1 t to 1 T chili powder (to taste)
- 1/2 t cumin powder
- 1/2 t kosher salt
- 1 lg cactus (nopale) pad, spines removed & julienned
- 2 chayote squash, pit removed and julienned
- 6 tomatillos, husks removed & chunked
- 1 handful of fresh cilantro, chopped
- juice of 1/2 lime
- sour cream, plain yogurt, or buttermilk if necessary to cut the "heat" if you added too much chili powder.

Direction

- Heat a large nonstick skillet to med-high.
- Sauté the onions, garlic, & spices in cooking spray for 2-3 minutes.
- Adjust heat to high and add cactus & chayote, stirring constantly, for 4 more minutes.
- Add the tomatillos & cilantro and cook for another 2-3 minutes.
- Add lime juice, taste & adjust seasonings, & serve.
- CEA-HOW Note: If it's too hot, you can always subtract some of your protein serving and use a bit of plain yogurt or buttermilk on this dish to cool down the heat-factor.

283. Moms Winter FryUp Recipe

Serving: 2 | Prep: | Cook: 10mins | Ready in:

Ingredients

- 4 Veggie sausages
- 1 Medium Waxy potato
- 1/2 Small parsnip, peeled
- 1 red onion
- 1 Shiny red apple
- 1 pear (I'm no expert, use whichever you like best)
- olive or vegetable oil
- salt, pepper and rosemary

Direction

- Chop fruit and veggies into large chunks, about an inch square. Keep them apart as we'll be cooking them in stages.
- First heat some oil in a large (REALLY large) frying pan, and add the potato and parsnip.
- Stir around for a couple of minutes, and add the sausages to the pan. Once the sausage and veggies are looking golden, add the onion.
- And once that's looking cooked, add the fruit. It's best not to cook it too long in case it burns.
- If the sausages look ready you can remove them from the pan.
- Season with salt, pepper and rosemary and give it all a big stir.
- Divide the sausages and fruit/veggie mixture between two plates. Serve with crusty wholemeal bread.

284. Mountain Country Fried Green Onions Recipe

Serving: 4 | Prep: | Cook: 20mins | Ready in:

Ingredients

- Mountain Country Fried green onions
- =======================================
- I wasn't sure if yal would like this or not, but we
- are gonna post it anyway!! :)
- If you do not eat bacon you may substitute butter
- or margarine.
- =======================================
- 3 or 4 slices of bacon
- 2 cups of green onions including tops, chopped into small pieces (about 1/2")
- 1/2 teaspoon of salt
- 1/8 teaspoon of black pepper
- 1 teaspoon of sugar

Direction

- Fry the bacon in a heavy skillet until crisp, drain on paper towels and crumble into small pieces.
- Remove all but about 1 tablespoon of the bacon grease from the pan and add the chopped green onions, salt, black pepper, sugar, and the crumbled bacon.
- Stir in 1/2 cup of hot water and simmer for 20 to 25 minutes.
- Serve hot.

285. Multi Flavored Thai Fried Rice Recipe

Serving: 4 | Prep: | Cook: 10mins | Ready in:

Ingredients

- 3 cups jasmine rice
- 7 oz. pork loin (sliced thin & lengths approx. 2 inches long)
- 6 large shrimp (uncooked)
- 3 large eggs
- 2 slices boiled ham (diced)
- 1/3 cup sweet red pepper (diced)
- 1/4 cup sweet green pepper (diced)
- 1/2 cup mixed vegetables
- 1/3 cup black raisins
- 1 cup pineapple chunks
- 2 tbsp. soy sauce
- 3 tbsp. brown sugar
- 1 tbsp. garlic (chopped)
- 1 tbsp. paprika
- 3 tbsp. olive oil

Direction

- Using a rice cooker, or other method, cook the rice prior to starting this recipe.
- Wash the pork and slice it thin into 2 inch long strips.
- Heat the olive oil in a pan, add the garlic and fry until golden brown.
- Then, add the pork and stir for several minutes until well done.
- Add the shrimp to the pan and continue to stir until the shrimp turns pink, then add the ham and stir the pork, shrimp and ham together for a few minutes.
- Add the mixed vegetables, pineapple, raisins, sweet red pepper, green pepper, paprika and rice to the pan, then stir and mix everything thoroughly for a few minutes.
- Add the soy sauce and sugar to the pan and continue to stir frequently until well done (approx. 5 minutes), then remove from the heat.
- .
- Place a leaf of romaine lettuce and some sliced cucumber on each plate and then add the contents of the pan onto each plate.
- Garnish with coriander.
- Note: one can sub chicken for the pork or other fish or seafood for the shrimp
- Tip: If desired, fry one egg for each serving and place on each plate and season the egg with black pepper.

286. Mushroom Chili Fry Recipe

Serving: 4 | Prep: | Cook: 20mins | Ready in:

Ingredients

- 300gms mushrooms, cut into quarters
- 8-10 dry red chilies
- 6 flakes garlic, sliced
- 2 onions, sliced thinly
- 3 cardamoms
- 3 cloves
- 1 stick cinnamon
- 2-inch piece ginger, finely sliced
- 1/2 tsp. turmeric powder
- 1 1/2 tbsps coriander seeds
- 1 cup sour curd
- 2 tsps lemon juice
- 1/4 cup coriander leaves, chopped
- 3 tbsps oil
- salt to taste

Direction

- 1. Heat 1 tsp. of oil on the tava and roast the chilies till dark in colour. Fry the coriander seeds, garlic and ginger in the same way, using little oil. When cool, blend into fine powder.

- 2. In a saucepan heat the remaining oil and fry the onions till golden brown and crisp. Drain and keep aside.
- 3. Add the cloves, cinnamon and cardamom to the oil and fry for a minute. Then add the mushrooms, turmeric and salt and fry till mushrooms are half cooked.
- 4. Add the curd, ground powder and cook till done. Add the lemon juice and fried onions just before serving.
- 5. Garnish with chopped coriander and serve hot with any pulao or naans.

287. Not Really Fried Potatoes Recipe

Serving: 5 | Prep: | Cook: 12mins | Ready in:

Ingredients

- 6-8 medium size potatoes, scrubbed, skin on, large -but thin -diced (thick pieces take longer to cook).
- 1 small white onion, diced
- 2 T chopped garlic
- 1 red or greem pepper, diced (optional)
- 2 pads butter or margarine
- seasoned Salt
- garlic pepper
- parmesan cheese - sprinkle
- EVOO

Direction

- Scrub and dice potatoes into bowl of cold water, skin on
- Drain, and transfer to microwavable dish, with lid (preferably vented lid)
- Add onion, peppers, garlic, seasoned salt and pepper
- Stir together
- Top with butter pads
- Lightly drizzle EVOO across top
- Lightly sprinkle parmesan cheese over top
- Cover with lid and pop open vent, OR partially cover with lid
- Microwave approximately 12 minutes. Rotating halfway through if no turntable
- Check for doneness, cook longer if needed
- Careful - steam beneath lid will burn you - learned that the hard way!
- Do not know the wattage, but, I have a high powered microwave. May take 15-16 minutes for lower wattage.

288. OVEN BAKED COTTAGE FRIES Recipe

Serving: 4 | Prep: | Cook: 5mins | Ready in:

Ingredients

- 2 lg. baking potatoes (about 8 oz. each), scrubbed
- 1 tbsp. butter
- 1 sm. clove garlic, crushed
- 1 tbsp. freshly grated parmesan cheese
- 1/4 tsp. paprika
- pepper (freshly ground) to taste

Direction

- Heat oven to 425 degrees. Pour 1/4 cup water into jelly-roll pan.
- Cut unpeeled potatoes into 1/4 inch slices; arrange in single layer in pan. In small saucepan, over low heat, stir butter with garlic to melt.
- Brush flavored butter over potatoes; bake 20 minutes.
- Meanwhile, in small bowl, combine Parmesan, paprika, and pepper.
- Remove potatoes from oven; heat broiler.
- Sprinkle cheese mixture over potatoes; broil 2 to 3 minutes until light golden brown.
- Serve immediately.

289. Oil Boiled Potato Planks Recipe

Serving: 4 | Prep: | Cook: 25mins | Ready in:

Ingredients

- 3 lbs medium or large russet potatoes
- 6 cups oil for frying
- Seasoning:
- 1 t salt
- 1 t garlic salt
- 1 t paprika
- ½ t pepper

Direction

- Leave skins on or off, your choice. I like them on. Cut potatoes in half lengthwise then lengthwise again to make quarters then lengthwise again to make eights. These planks are on the (country) large side but will cook up wonderfully. If you like thinner fries, be my guest to cut them more.
- Place cold oil and fries in a Dutch oven. Turn burner on high and boil for 20 minutes, stirring after 10 minutes. Timer starts as soon as you turn the burner on.
- Drain and season fries. Seasoning is enough for several batches. Add your favourite condiment or even some shredded cheese.
- This method uses less oil than country fried potatoes or even French fries.

290. Okie Fried Okra Recipe

Serving: 4 | Prep: | Cook: 4mins | Ready in:

Ingredients

- Okies Crispy fried okra
- 1 tes ea. Johnny's seasoning, pepper, garlic
- ½ cup corn starch
- 1/2 cup all-purpose flour
- 1/2 cup corn meal
- 1 teaspoon baking powder
- 1 pound okra pods, trimmed, and cut into rounds
- 1 cup cooking oil or Deep frier with oil

Direction

- Mix the flours, baking powder together. Stir to mix well, then drop the okra pods in and stir again.
- Heat oil in a wok or frying pan over medium heat or Deep fryer. Test by adding a drop of batter; when it puffs up immediately, the oil is ready. Remove pods from the batter one at a time and add to the wok, taking care not to crowd. Fry until lightly brown. Drain and keep warm until all the pods are cooked.

291. Okra With Onions And Tomatoes Fried Bhindi Recipe

Serving: 8 | Prep: | Cook: 35mins | Ready in:

Ingredients

- 1/4 cup oil
- 250 gm. onion,thinly sliced
- 1 tbsp cumin seeds
- 1 kg. okra/ladyfinger
- 2 tbsp crushed red chilies
- 2 tbsp. coriander seeds
- 1 tbsp salt or to taste
- 500 gm. tomatoes,finely chopped
- Optional:
- 1 green/raw mango(about 125 gm.),peeled & grated
- OR
- tamarind paste,according to taste

Direction

- Wash the okra and pat dry with absorbent paper (it should be dry to cut).
- Discard top and end, slice okra crosswise into 1/2 inch thickness.

- Heat oil in a wok over medium heat and fry onions till soft.
- Add the okra, cumin seeds and stirring gently, continue frying for another 5 minutes (The okra should be a bright green colour after this).
- Add remaining ingredients and cook, uncovered, on low heat till tender (Do not add water and don't stir too much otherwise it will breakup).
- When the sticky texture disappears and it leaves oil, it's done.
- Serve with chapati/Naan.

292. Oriental Veggie TVP Fried Rice Recipe

Serving: 1 | Prep: | Cook: 10mins | Ready in:

Ingredients

- 0.25 c dried TVP granules
- 0.25 c water
- 1 tsp soy sauce (reduced sodium)
- 0.25 tsp sesame oil
- cooking spray
- 1 tsp minced garlic
- 1 c frozen oriental mix vegetables (or any other mix, you may also use any combination of fresh veggies)
- 0.5 c cooked (leftover) rice (half brown, half white, or whatever)
- 0.5 tsp garlic powder (optional)
- 0.5 Tbsp vegetarian oyster sauce
- 1 tsp soy sauce (reduced sodium)
- 1 Tbsp water
- 1/8 tsp concentrated chili sauce (optional)

Direction

- The first four ingredients are for reconstituting the TVP
- Pour the water, soy sauce & sesame oil over the dry TVP in a microwaveable bowl
- Microwave for 4 minutes (you may want to stop after 2 minutes and stir it up a little). Then set it aside.
- Take a skillet, lightly coat it with cooking spray and let it heat up
- Sprinkle water on the surface to see if it is hot enough. If the water sizzles away, it's ready.
- Brown the minced garlic
- Add the vegetables, add some water to create some steam, stir for about 2 minutes.
- Add the rice and continue stirring.
- Now add the reconstituted TVP.
- Throw on some garlic powder for extra garlicky flavour!
- Add the sauce (the last four ingredients, and mix this up before hand).
- Continue stirring till everything is evenly coated with the sauce.
- Serve it hot & steaming!

293. Outbacks Aussie Fries And Dip Recipe

Serving: 6 | Prep: | Cook: 20mins | Ready in:

Ingredients

- Dip:
- 1 cup sour cream
- 2 tablespoon prepared horseradish
- cayenne pepper, to taste
- salt and pepper, to taste
- Fries:
- 1-2 pound bag frozen french fries
- 1 cup colby-Jack Shredded cheese
- 6 pieces of bacon, cooked and drained
- garlic powder, salt and pepper, optional
- peanut oil for frying

Direction

- In a bowl, mix well all ingredients for dip. Cover and refrigerate until fries are done.

- In a Dutch oven, heat peanut oil until 350°. If you don't have a thermometer, just test with one fry. It should start to cook as soon as it hits the oil.
- Fry the French fries in small batches. Drain on paper towel and season with salt. (I also season the fries with garlic powder and some pepper, but they don't.)
- Put fries on oven-safe platter.
- Preheat oven to 350°.
- Sprinkle cheese and bacon on fries and put in oven until cheese just begins to melt. You don't want it like Cheez Whiz!
- Serve with dipping sauce.

294. Pad Thai Fried Noodles Recipe

Serving: 4 | Prep: | Cook: 10mins | Ready in:

Ingredients

- 1 pkg. rice noodles (if using glass noodles, soak 5 minutes in cold water before using)
- 1 c. pork/chicken/seafood
- 3 tbsp. oil
- 4 tbsp Chinese chive or spring onion
- 1 tbsp. sugar
- 2 tbsp. fish sauce
- 2 tbsp. oyster sauce
- 1 egg, beaten
- handful bean sprout or cabbage
- 3 tbsp. chopped garlic
- 1 c. chopped yellow tofu
- 1/2 c. water

Direction

- Put oil in wok with chopped garlic and fry until golden.
- Add meat, tofu and stir until meat is cooked.
- Add beaten egg.
- Add noodles, water (to make the noodles soft).
- Add fish sauce, oyster sauce, sugar.
- Add bean spout and Chinese chives
- Turn off the heat
- Stir in fresh vegetables (cabbage, bean sprout, spring onion)
- Garnish with ground chillies and limes, to taste

295. Pan Fried Cabbage Recipe

Serving: 6 | Prep: | Cook: 12mins | Ready in:

Ingredients

- 1 head cabbage(cut into slices)
- 1 large onion,sliced
- 1 cup celery, chopped
- 1 cup sliced smoked sausage(you can also use bacon or ham if you prefer!)
- 6 tablespoons butter
- 3 tablespoons(more if needed) olive oil(you could sub vegetable oil)]
- 1/4 cup soy sauce
- 1 teaspoon cracked black pepper
- salt to taste

Direction

- Heat oil in large skillet. Add sausage (or other meat), onions, and celery and cook until sausage is lightly browned.
- Add cabbage and stir well.
- Continue cooking on med/high heat for 3 to 4 minutes, stirring often to prevent sticking.
- Add butter, sour sauce, and black pepper, cover, lower heat to low/med.
- Cook for 2 to 3 minutes.
- Taste, add salt if needed.

296. Pan Fried Tofu With Yoghurt Sauce And Soy Puffs Recipe

Serving: 4 | Prep: | Cook: 5mins | Ready in:

Ingredients

- 1 block extra firm tofu
- garam masala powder
- salt
- pepper
- olive or sesame oil or vegetable oil
- Soy Batter and Puffs:
- 2 eggs
- 1 cup soy protein powder (or may use flour)
- Sauce:
- 1/2 cup thick plain yoghurt (we always use Greek style)
- 1 large garlic clove minced
- 1 tbs fresh chopped parsley or cilantro
- garam masala powder to taste
- salt to taste
- pepper to taste
- oil to fry

Direction

- Drain tofu well
- Cut into 8 equal slices
- Pat dry gently
- Place slices in a flat dish
- Sprinkle evenly with the garam masala powder, salt and pepper to taste
- Note that tofu is quite bland so don't be afraid to season liberally.
- Drizzle over the oil and turn to coat.
- Make the batter
- Fork beat the eggs in one dish
- Add the soy protein (or flour) in another dish.
- Heat oil (few tabs) in skillet over medium high heat
- Dip tofu in egg, then coat in the soy powder
- Fry in the pan golden, turning once on each side
- If necessary wipe out pan with a paper towel between fresh batches and add oil and fry remaining tofu.
- Make sauce (multiply as needed) add spice, salt, pepper, garlic and parsley to yogurt and mix well
- Puffs: with the excess batter, mix egg and powder, season to taste and stir to combine.
- Add some water and stir to make a pancake type of batter
- Drop by spoonfuls in hot pan and fry golden, these go very quickly)
- Serve with tofu and sauce

297. Panisses Chickpea Flour Fries Recipe

Serving: 6 | Prep: | Cook: 7mins | Ready in:

Ingredients

- olive oil
- 2 1/2 cups chickpea flour
- 4 Cups *COLD* salted water
- Salt and freshly ground black pepper
- olive oil/vegetable oil for frying

Direction

- Brush six saucers with olive oil and set aside.
- Pour chickpea flour in a steady stream into 4 cups cold salted water in a large, heavy saucepan, whisking as you pour to prevent lumps.
- Cook over medium heat, whisking vigorously, until mixture thickens, about 5 minutes.
- Remove from heat, still whisking, and pour batter into saucers.
- Fill the saucers up to the rims, about 1/2" thick.
- Cool at least 30 minutes, then gently slide batter off saucers and cut into "steak-fry" shapes, about 3/4" x 3" long.
- Heat 1" olive oil/vegetable oil in a heavy skillet over high heat.

- Fry in batches without crowding, turning often, until golden brown, about 5–7 minutes.
- Drain, season with salt and pepper.

298. Paula Deens Fried Onion Rings With Chili Sauce Recipe

Serving: 4 | Prep: | Cook: 10mins | Ready in:

Ingredients

- chili sauce
- 1 cup mayonnaise
- 3 tablespoons chili sauce
- 1 teaspoon chili powder
- 1/8 teaspoon cayenne pepper
- Onion Rings
- vegetable oil to fry (I used Canola)
- 2 medium white or yellow onions(I used sweet onions)
- 1 teaspoon seasoned salt
- 2 cups all-purpose flour
- salt

Direction

- Preheat oil in a deep-fryer or Dutch oven to 360
- Chili sauce
- Combine mayonnaise, chili sauce, chili powder, and cayenne in mixing bowl and stir well
- Cover and chill until serving time
- Onion Rings
- Slice onions into very thin rings and separate rings
- On baking sheet, spread out and sprinkle with seasoned salt
- Put flour in resealable plastic bag
- Put the onion rings in the bag in batches, close tightly, and shake until coated
- Fry onion rings in batches for 3- 4 minutes, until they are brown and crispy (Only took me 2-3 minutes)
- Remove with tongs and drain on paper towels
- Taste and season with salt, if necessary

299. Portobello Fries Recipe

Serving: 4 | Prep: | Cook: 10mins | Ready in:

Ingredients

- vegetable oil to fry
- 8 portobello mushrooms, stems and gills removed
- 1 3/4 cups all-purpose flour, plus more for dredging
- 2 cups club soda, or beer
- 2 large eggs
- 1 teaspoon coarse salt
- sea salt

Direction

- Cut mushrooms crosswise into 3/8-inch thick slices.
- Lightly dust them with 2 tablespoons flour, set aside.
- In a medium bowl, whisk together flour, club soda, eggs and coarse salt to form batter.
- Dip Portobello fries into batter
- Fry in hot oil in heavy duty pot or skillet till golden
- Drain on a paper towel-lined baking sheet.
- Season with sea salt and serve immediately

300. Quick And Easy Fried Rice Recipe

Serving: 4 | Prep: | Cook: 6mins | Ready in:

Ingredients

- 1 Tablespoon canola oil

- 1 package confetti vegetable mix from Walmart (chopped broccoli, cauliflower, radish & cabbage)
- 1 package Uncle Ben's 2 minute long grain rice
- Quick & Easy Asian Sauce (separate recipe)

Direction

- Heat canola oil on medium heat until clear
- Add confetti vegetable mix and cook on medium heat until begins to soften (1-2 minutes)
- Add package Uncle Ben's 2 minute Long grain rice
- Add Quick & Easy Asian Sauce and cook another 4 minutes (stirring somewhat often) until everything is heated thoroughly and veggies are at desired tenderness.

301. Quick Vegie Stir Fry With Hokkien Noodles Recipe

Serving: 2 | Prep: | Cook: 10mins | Ready in:

Ingredients

- 1 carrot, peeled and thinly sliced
- 1 teaspoon chilli powder
- 1 stem of broccoli or 1 bunch broccolini, chopped into even chunks
- 1/2 cup beans, halved
- 1 red capsicum, chopped into even chunks
- 1/2 cup mushrooms, thickly sliced
- 1/2 bunch baby bok choy
- 1/2 cup bean sprouts
- 1 tablespoon reduced-salt soy sauce
- 1 teaspoon oyster sauce
- 200 g hokkien noodles

Direction

- Chop all the vegetables.
- In a wok, add the carrot, chili and a splash of water, cook for 1 minute or until the carrot becomes tender. Add broccoli and beans and cook for a further 1 minute. Meanwhile, boil the kettle.
- Add all other vegetables, soy and oyster sauce to the wok and stir. Put hokkien noodles in a heat-proof bowl and cover with boiling water, cover and stand for 2 minutes.
- Drain water and add noodles to the wok. Stir until the noodles are coated with the sauce and vegetables are cooked.
- Notes: You can substitute any vegetables.

302. Raw Broccoli And Sprout Stir Fry Recipe

Serving: 2 | Prep: | Cook: 180mins | Ready in:

Ingredients

- broccoli - 2 heads, cut into bite-sized pieces
- mung bean sprouts - 1 large handful
- cabbage - 1 cup, shredded
- garlic - 2 cloves, finely sliced
- apple cider vinegar - 1/2 cup, as needed
- soy sauce - 1/4 cup
- ginger - to taste (optional)
- black pepper - to taste (optional)
- curry powder - to taste (optional)
- red pepper flakes - to taste (optional)

Direction

- Mix the first four ingredients (broccoli, sprouts, cabbage, and garlic) together in a large bowl.
- Mix the apple cider vinegar, soy sauce, and as many spices as you'd like together.
- Pour the sauce over the veggies.
- Let marinade for at least a couple of hours; up to a couple of days is fine.
- Siphon off any excess liquid and serve!

303. Rosemary Roasted Oven Fries Recipe

Serving: 4 | Prep: | Cook: 45mins | Ready in:

Ingredients

- No-Stick cooking spray
- 3 large baking potatoes
- 1/4 cup vegetable oil
- 2 teaspoons dried rosemary leaves
- 1 teaspoon salt
- 1/8 teaspoon pepper
- 1/4 cup grated parmesan cheese
- Ranch or blue cheese dressing (optional), for dipping

Direction

- Heat oven to 450°F.
- Spray baking sheet with no-stick cooking spray.
- Slice potatoes into 1/2-inch wedges.
- Rinse with cold water and pat dry.
- In a medium bowl whisk together oil, rosemary, salt and pepper. Add potato wedges.
- Toss to coat.
- Place on prepared baking sheet.
- Bake 45 minutes, turning every 15 minutes.
- Remove from oven.
- Sprinkle with Parmesan cheese.
- Serve immediately with your choice of dressing for dipping.

304. SO CAL FRIED CORN Recipe

Serving: 6 | Prep: | Cook: 10mins | Ready in:

Ingredients

- 2 LBS corn
- flour
- 1 bell pepper DICED
- 1 LARGE jalapeno CHOPPED
- TABASCO TO TASTE
- black pepper
- CHOPPED onion
- garlic DICED TO TASTE
- cooking oil

Direction

- Mix flour/green pepper/jalapeno/tabasco/black pepper/onion/garlic together
- Coat corn in flour mixture
- Heat oil to 350
- Add corn to covered skillet and fry until lightly browned, stirring often
- Eat

305. Savory Fried Polenta Recipe

Serving: 12 | Prep: | Cook: 50mins | Ready in:

Ingredients

- 1/2 lb bacon, 1/2" dice
- 8 cups low sodium chicken broth
- 3 cups cornmeal (polenta)
- 1 15oz can cream style corn
- 1/4 cup freeze dried chives
- salt, to taste
- fresh cracked pepper, to taste
- Coarse grind garlic, to taste

Direction

- Fry the bacon in a small stockpot until crisp and brown; scoop bacon out onto a plate and reserve. Pour the chicken broth into the pot and bring to just below the boiling point; set the pot off the burner. Very gradually add polenta to the broth, stirring constantly.
- Combine bacon, corn and chives with the polenta; place back on the burner and cook over low heat

- Adjust seasonings; when the mixture is smooth and does not taste raw, usually after cooking for 20 to 30 minutes, it is ready and can be spooned onto a plate for serving.
- The mixture can also be dropped by small scoopfuls into very hot fat and fried like hushpuppies.
- It can also be poured into a flat baking pan to cool and firm. This mixture can be baked in the oven for 20 minutes, or sliced and fried.

306. Scrambled Egg And Potato Fry Recipe

Serving: 6 | Prep: | Cook: 20mins | Ready in:

Ingredients

- 1/4 cup corn oil
- 3/4 cup chopped white onion
- 1 teaspoon ground turmeric
- 1 pound potatoes cut into cubes
- 4 eggs beaten
- 1/2 teaspoon salt
- 1/4 teaspoon freshly ground black pepper
- 10 leaves fresh coriander for garnish

Direction

- Heat oil in large skillet then add onion and stir fry over moderate heat until golden.
- Add turmeric and stir 1 minute then add potato cubes and stir continuously for 5 minutes.
- Cover pan for 1 minute to ensure the potatoes are softened then uncover.
- Push potatoes to one edge of the pan then pour eggs into open space and let them set 30 seconds.
- Mix potatoes into the eggs and add the salt and pepper.
- Scramble mixture over low heat for another 5 minutes so that potatoes and eggs are light brown.
- Serve warm garnished with the coriander leaves.

307. Sesame Asparagus And Carrots Stir Fry Recipe

Serving: 6 | Prep: | Cook: 10mins | Ready in:

Ingredients

- 24 asparagus stalks
- 6 large carrots
- 1/4 cup water
- 1 Tbsp. grated fresh ginger
- 1 Tbsp. reduced-sodium soy sauce
- 1 1/2 tsp. sesame oil
- 1 Tbsp. sesame seeds, toasted

Direction

- Cut the asparagus into 1/2-inch thick slices. Cut the carrots into 1/4-inch thick slices.
- Coat a nonstick Wok or a large frying pan with nonstick cooking spray and place over high heat. Add the carrots and stir-fry for 4 minutes.
- Add the asparagus and water. Stir and toss to combine. Cover and cook until the vegetables are barely tender, about 2 minutes.
- Uncover and add the ginger. Stir-fry until any remaining water evaporates, 1 to 2 minutes.
- Add the soy sauce, sesame oil and sesame seeds. Stir-fry to coat the vegetables evenly.
- To serve, divide among individual plates.

308. Sesame Tofu Stir Fry Recipe

Serving: 4 | Prep: | Cook: 15mins | Ready in:

Ingredients

- 8 oz. firm tofu, drained and patted dry
- 3 T teriyaki sauce
- 1 small head bok choy
- 2 T sesame seeds
- 5 oz. mushrooms, each cut into quarters
- 2 T olive oil, divided
- 1 clove garlic, finely chopped
- 2 carrots, cut into slices
- 1 small onion, cut into 1/4" wedges
- 1 3-oz. pkg mixed bean sprouts

Direction

- Cut tofu into 1/2" thick slices
- Cut slices diagonally in half.
- Marinate tofu in teriyaki sauce for 15 minutes
- Meanwhile, cut Bok choy stems into 1" pieces and leaves into strips
- Set aside
- In large skillet, over high heat, toast sesame seeds until golden about 3-4 minutes
- Remove seeds, set aside
- Heat 1 T oil in skillet
- Drain tofu and reserve teriyaki sauce
- In oil in skillet sauté tofu 5-6 minutes until golden
- Set aside
- In remaining oil sauté garlic 1 minute
- Add carrots, onion, mushrooms and bok choy stems and sauté 8 minutes
- Add bean sprouts and bock choy leaves and cook 1 minute longer
- Return tofu and teriyaki sauce to skillet
- Simmer 1 minute
- Arrange ingredients on platter
- Sprinkle with sesame seeds

309. Shanghai Pan Fried Noodles With Cabbage And Pork Recipe

Serving: 4 | Prep: | Cook: 10mins | Ready in:

Ingredients

- 500g (1 pkg of fresh Shanghai noodles)
- 1/2 head of savory cabbage or Taiwanese cabbage, chopped
- 1/2 stalk of carrots, juliened
- 1/2 onion chopped
- 1 large clove of garlic, minced
- 60 g prawns
- 100 g pork butt, sliced across the grain
- 1 tbsp vegatable oil
- 2 tbsp dark soy sauce
- 2 tbsp light soy sauce
- 1 tsp sugar
- 1 tsp sesame oil
- 1 tsp salt

Direction

- Heat oil in wok, add carrot, cabbage, onion, garlic, pork and stir-fry. Add prawns. Add dark soy sauce, light soy sauce, sugar and paste and stir-fry. Add Shanghai noodle, stir-fry for about 3 minutes, and add sesame oil and salt.

310. Southern Fried Corn Recipe

Serving: 4 | Prep: | Cook: 10mins | Ready in:

Ingredients

- 2 pounds whole kernel corn
- 1/2 cup all purpose flour
- 1 bell pepper, seeded and diced
- 1 tps. salt
- 1/2 tps. black pepper
- 1/4 tps onion powder
- 1/4 tps. garlic powder
- 1/2 cup cooking oil

Direction

- Combine flour, bell pepper, salt, onion, and garlic powder in a bowl. Coat room temperature corn in the mixture. Heat cooking oil over medium high heat until hot. Add coated corn to skillet and fry covered until corn is done and flour is lightly browned. Stir frequently. Taste corn to confirm doneness to your satisfaction.

311. Southern Fried Cream And Butter Corn Recipe

Serving: 6 | Prep: | Cook: 7mins | Ready in:

Ingredients

- 3 cups fresh corn niblets removed from the cob (6-8 ears)
- 1 stick unsalted butter
- 1 tablespoon minced bell pepper (green) Optional
- salt and freshly ground pepper to taste
- 16 ounces half-and-half

Direction

- Melt butter in a 12-inch skillet
- Add corn, bell pepper (if using), salt, and pepper
- Stir and cook for 5 minutes
- Do not overcook
- Add half-and-half and reduce heat to simmer
- When cream has cooked away, about 7-10 minutes, serve hot

312. Southern Fried Okra Recipe

Serving: 5 | Prep: | Cook: 4mins | Ready in:

Ingredients

- 1 pound fresh okra, cut into 1/2 inch thick slices (discard the tips and stem ends)
- 2 cups buttermilk
- 1 cup self-rising cornmeal
- 1 cup self-rising flour
- 3/4 teaspoon salt
- 1/4 teaspoon ground red pepper
- Crisco for frying
- 1/4 cup bacon drippings

Direction

- In bowl, place okra, stirring in buttermilk gently
- Cover, chill for about 40 minutes
- In large bowl, combine cornmeal, flour, salt and pepper, whisk
- Remove okra from buttermilk with slotted spoon, discarding buttermilk
- Dredge okra in batches in the cornmeal mixture
- Spoon Crisco into a Dutch oven or a cast iron skillet (when melted it needs to be about 2 inches depth)
- Add bacon drippings
- Heat on med high or until about 375 degrees
- Fry okra in batches for about 4 minutes or until golden
- Drain on paper towels

313. Southwestern Fried Corn Recipe

Serving: 6 | Prep: | Cook: 8mins | Ready in:

Ingredients

- 1/4 pound mesquite-smoked or regular bacon, cut into small pieces
- 1/4 cup green onions, sliced
- 1/4 cup red bell pepper chopped
- 2 can (11-ounces) super sweet yellow and white corn, drained
- 1/4 cup purchased ranch salad dressing
- 1 teaspoon fresh lime juice
- 1/2 teaspoon cumin
- 1/4 teaspoon crushed red pepper flakes

- 1 Tablespoon fresh cilantro, chopped
- 2 lime slices (garnish)
- 2 fresh cilantro sprigs (garnish)

Direction

- Cook bacon until crisp
- Drain on paper towels and discard bacon drippings.
- In same skillet, add cooked bacon, onions, bell pepper and corn.
- Reduce heat to low and cook for 5 minutes or until thoroughly heated.
- Stir occasionally.
- In small bowl, add the salad dressing, lime juice, cumin and red pepper flakes.
- Mix well.
- Add dressing mixture to corn mixture and mix well.
- Remove skillet from heat.
- Stir in chopped cilantro.
- Garnish with lime slices and cilantro sprigs.

314. SoyaBean Fry Recipe

Serving: 8 | Prep: | Cook: 20mins | Ready in:

Ingredients

- Soya bean chunks - 500 gm
- ginger garlic paste - 1tsp
- Chilly powder - 1 1/2 tsp
- coriander powder -2 tsp
- turmeric powder - a pinch
- salt as per requirement
- cumin seeds - 1/2tsp
- onions 2 nos finely chopped
- curry leaves - 4 stalk
- Green Chillies - 2
- oil for frying
- water for boiling

Direction

- Add soya chunks in boiled water, and soak for about fifteen minutes. Then squeeze out the water and keep the chunks aside.
- Now, heat oil in a skillet, and add onions and sauté until translucent. Now add the ginger garlic paste. Wait for the raw smell to go and then add the red chilli powder, coriander powder, turmeric powder and salt to taste. Now, add the soya chunks kept aside and mix well. If required, you can also add some more oil for binding all the soya chunks together.
- Once this is completely dry, add the curry leaves and slit the green chillies. This can be served hot with rice or rotis; or just take some in a bowl and eat it as a mid-day snack.

315. Spiced Fried Potatoes Recipe

Serving: 4 | Prep: | Cook: 35mins | Ready in:

Ingredients

- 4 large potatoes (cubed)
- 1 bunch spring onion (chopped)
- 2 medium sized tomatoes (chopped)
- 1 green chilli (chopped)
- 3 garlic cloves (chopped)
- 1/4 cup olive oil
- salt per taste
- 1/2 tsp red chilli powder
- 1/2 tsp red chilli flakes
- 1/3 tsp turmeric powder
- 1 tsp cumin seeds
- 1/2 tsp garam masala
- chopped cilantro and mint for garnishing.

Direction

- Heat oil in a wok, add potatoes and cook for about 8 minutes.
- Add garlic and cook for 5 minutes, till garlic is soft and translucent.
- Add tomatoes and cook further 3-4 minutes. Then add all the spices and mix well.

- Add onions and green chilli. Cover and cook on low flame for about 10-15 minutes or till potatoes are tender.
- Garnish with cilantro and mint leaves. Can be served with raita, pita, warm/fried tortilla bread, paratha, naan and steamed rice.
- Cooking time can be minimized if you are using boiled potatoes. But raw potatoes taste better in the end.

316. Spicy Fried Green Tomatoes Recipe

Serving: 4 | Prep: | Cook: 6mins | Ready in:

Ingredients

- 3-4 large green tomatoes
- 1 cup yellow or white cornmeal
- 1 cup all purpose flour
- 1 teaspoon salt-or to taste
- 1 teaspoon black pepper-or to taste
- 1 teaspoon garlic powder
- 1 teaspoon cayenne pepper-or to taste
- 1 1/2 cup buttermilk
- vegetable oil

Direction

- Slice tomatoes to desired thickness (I usually slice them about 1/4").
- In a medium bowl combine cornmeal, flour, salt, black pepper, cayenne peppermint garlic powder.
- Pour buttermilk into another bowl.
- Dip tomato slices into buttermilk the dredge in cornmeal mixture.
- Repeat unto all slices are coated.
- Pour 1/4" to 1/2" of oil into a cast iron skillet. Heat over medium high heat to 350 degrees.
- Fry tomato slices for 2-3 minutes per side or until golden brown.
- Drain on paper towels.
- Serve hot.

317. Spicy Fried Spinach Recipe

Serving: 4 | Prep: | Cook: 30mins | Ready in:

Ingredients

- 1 or 2 bunches spinach
- 2 tablespoons ghee
- 2 tablespoons oil
- 2 large onions, finely sliced
- 2 cloves garlic, finely chopped
- 1 teaspoon finely grated fresh ginger
- 1 teaspoon cumin seed
- 1/2 teaspoon black cumin seeds, optional
- 1/2 teaspoon ground cumin
- 1/2 teaspoon ground coriander
- 1/2 teaspoon ground turmeric
- 1 teaspoon chili powder, optional
- 1 teaspoon salt, or to taste

Direction

- Wash spinach well in several changes of water and remove tough stalks. Heat ghee and oil in a large saucepan and fry the onion until golden, then add garlic and ginger and fry, stirring, for a further minute or two. Add seeds, ground spices and salt and mix well, then turn in the spinach with only the water that remains on the leaves after washing. Toss in the spicy mixture, then turn heat very low and cook uncovered, stirring frequently, until spinach is cooked. It may be necessary to add a little more water to prevent spinach sticking to pan. Serve with rice, chapatis or other Indian breads.

318. Spicy Stir Fried Eggplant Recipe

Serving: 2 | Prep: | Cook: 10mins | Ready in:

Ingredients

- 1 medium eggplant, peeled and cut into 1 in. dice
- 1 tsp. garlic, finely chopped
- 1 tbls. cornstarch mixed with 2 tbls. water to make a paste
- oil for deep frying
- Sauce
- 2 tbls. oyster sauce
- 2 tbls. soy sauce
- 2 tbls. water
- 1 tbls. white vinegar
- 1 tbls. sugar
- 1 tsp. chili paste
- 1/2 tsp. bean sauce
- 1/2 tsp. sesame oil

Direction

- Mix all sauce ingredients together and set aside.
- Put enough oil in wok to deep-fry eggplant.
- Heat to 350.
- Fry eggplant for 1 minute.
- Remove and drain on paper towel.
- Remove all but 1 tsp. oil from wok.
- Stir-fry garlic for 5 seconds then add sauce.
- Reduce heat and simmer for 20 seconds.
- Add eggplant and simmer for 10 seconds.
- Stir in cornstarch paste slowly until desired consistency.

319. Stir Fried Asparagus Recipe

Serving: 4 | Prep: | Cook: 2mins | Ready in:

Ingredients

- 3 tbsp margarine
- 1 tsp chicken bouillon granules
- 1/8 tsp celery salt
- 1/8 tsp pepper
- 1 ½ pounds asparagus trimmed and cut into 2 inch slices (about 4 C)
- 1 tsp soy sauce

Direction

- In large skillet melt butter
- Add bouillon celery salt and pepper. Mix well.
- Add asparagus and toss to coat.
- Cover and cook for 2 minutes over high medium heat.
- Stir in soy sauce.
- Serve immediately

320. Stir Fried Asparagus With Ginger Garlic And Basil Recipe

Serving: 4 | Prep: | Cook: 5mins | Ready in:

Ingredients

- 2 tablespoons soy sauce
- 1 tablespoon dry sherry
- 1 tablespoon chicken stock
- 1 tablespoon canola oil
- 1-1/2 pounds fresh asparagus ends snapped and cut into small pieces
- 2 teaspoons minced garlic
- 2 teaspoons minced fresh ginger
- 1/2 cup minced fresh basil
- 1 tablespoon chopped scallions
- 1/2 teaspoon granulated sugar

Direction

- Combine soy sauce, sherry and broth then set aside.
- Place a large skillet over high heat for 4 minutes.
- Add 2 teaspoons canola oil and heat for 1 minute then add the asparagus and stir-fry for 2 minutes.

- Clear the center of the pan then add the garlic, ginger and remaining oil then sauté for 10 seconds.
- Remove pan from heat and stir the ingredients to combine.
- Place pan back on heat then stir in the soy sauce mixture and cook for 30 seconds.
- Add basil, scallions and sugar.
- Cook and stir 30 seconds longer.

321. Stir Fried Asparagus With Sesame Seeds Recipe

Serving: 4 | Prep: | Cook: 6mins | Ready in:

Ingredients

- 1 tsp sesame seeds
- 1 tsp olive oil
- 1 lb asparagus
- 1 tbsp soya sauce
- 2 tsp sesame oil
- 1/2 tsp sugar

Direction

- Trim the asparagus.
- Cut them into 1 inch pieces.
- Heat your frying pan up and put the sesame seeds in it.
- Stir them constantly until they are toasted.
- Remove them from the pan and set them aside.
- Heat the oil in the pan.
- Add the asparagus and cook, stirring constantly, about 3 minutes.
- If you happen to have a green onion, add it at the same time.
- Add the soy sauce, sesame oil, and sugar and stir.
- Cover and cook another 2-3 minutes, until the asparagus is tender.
- Sprinkle with the sesame seeds before serving.

322. Stir Fried Broccoli Red Onion And Red Pepper Recipe

Serving: 4 | Prep: | Cook: 10mins | Ready in:

Ingredients

- 3 tablespoons olive oil
- 1 tablespoon butter
- 1 head broccoli cut into florets
- 1/2 red onion thinly sliced
- 1 red bell pepper sliced
- 2 tablespoons fresh basil
- 1 tablespoon fresh oregano

Direction

- In large skillet over medium high heat, add oil and butter.
- Add broccoli and toss to coat with oil and butter then cook 8 minutes.
- Add onion slices then cook tossing with broccoli for 5 minutes.
- Add red pepper and continue cooking 2 minutes.
- Toss basil and oregano with broccoli, onion and red pepper then serve immediately.

323. Stir Fried Cabbage Recipe

Serving: 6 | Prep: | Cook: 20mins | Ready in:

Ingredients

- 1 Head cabbage, Chopped
- 2 beef bouillon cubes
- A little vegetable oil
- 4 Slices bacon
- salt/pepper
- Chopped onion
- ¾ Cup water

Direction

- Chop cabbage into bite size pieces.
- Add water to a large pot. It will be a large amount of cabbage, but the cabbage will cook down. Add bacon, onion, vegetable oil, beef bouillon cubes, and salt/pepper. Bring to a boil and turn down to low – medium heat and simmer for 20 minutes till tender but still crisp.

324. Stir Fried Carrots With Cumin And Lime Recipe

Serving: 4 | Prep: | Cook: 20mins | Ready in:

Ingredients

- 2-1/2 tablespoons canola oil
- 2 teaspoons black mustard seeds
- 1 inch fresh ginger peeled and cut into a fine julienne
- 1/2 fresh hot green chile minced
- 3 whole dried red chilies
- 1 teaspoon cumin seeds
- 8 fresh curry leaves torn into pieces
- 1-1/2 pounds carrots peeled and grated on the large holes of a grater
- 3/4 teaspoon salt
- juice of 1/2 lime or lemon

Direction

- Combine oil and mustard seeds in a large wok, kadai or frying pan over medium heat.
- Cook stirring until mustard seeds crackle.
- Add ginger, fresh and dried chilies, cumin and curry leaves and cook 2 minutes.
- Add carrots and cook stirring until warmed through.
- Stir in the salt and the lime or lemon juice.
- Taste for salt and serve hot or cold.

325. Stir Fried Green Beans With Coconut Recipe

Serving: 4 | Prep: | Cook: 20mins | Ready in:

Ingredients

- Stir Fried green beans with coconut
- 4 tablespoons butter
- 1 teaspoon black mustard seeds
- 3 ounces onion finely chopped
- 1 teaspoon freshly grated ginger
- 1 teaspoon salt
- 1 teaspoon freshly ground black pepper
- 1 pound fresh green beans thinly sliced on the diagonal
- 1/4 teaspoon paprika
- 1 ounce unsweetened shredded coconut
- 2 tablespoons freshly chopped coriander
- 2 tablespoons lemon juice

Direction

- Heat butter in a large frying pan or wok over moderate heat.
- Add mustard seeds and fry for 30 seconds.
- Stir in the onions, ginger, salt and pepper and mix well.
- Add green beans and paprika and stir fry 5 minutes.
- Add coconut and coriander then reduce heat to low.
- Cover and cook 10 minutes stirring from time to time until beans are tender.
- Sprinkle with lemon juice and serve immediately.

326. Stir Fried Rice Recipe

Serving: 8 | Prep: | Cook: 40mins | Ready in:

Ingredients

- 3 cups rice
- 6 cups water

- ½ tsp salt
- ¼ cup oil
- ½ cup green onions
- 2 cloves garlic pressed, through garlic press
- ½ cup soy sauce
- ½ cup frozen peas and carrots
- 3 eggs, beaten well

Direction

- Place rice, water and salt in rice cooker or large pot with a tight fitting lid. If using rice cooker, allow to cook normally. If using a large pot, bring to a rapid boil, stir once, put lid on and cook over low heat for 20 minutes.
- Allow rice to cool completely.
- Heat oil in large frying pan. Stir fry green onions and garlic, being careful not to burn the garlic.
- Add rice (break it up with your hands as you add it to the frying pan) and stir rice until it has all had a chance to cook in the hot oil.
- Add the soy sauce and frozen peas and carrots (this is my preference, you can use any type of vegetable or cooked meat that you like).
- Stir well, reduce heat, put a lid on it and cook, stirring a couple times, about 10 minutes.
- Pour egg into hot rice. I like to drizzle it all through it, allow to cook one or two minutes, and stir once more before removing from heat and serving. Some prefer to make a well in the middle of the rice, let the egg cook and then stir into the rice.

327. Stir Fried Sesame Asparagus Recipe

Serving: 4 | Prep: | Cook: 10mins | Ready in:

Ingredients

- 2 Tbs. soy sauce
- 2 tsp. sugar
- 1 Tbs. sesame oil (use less if you don't like this or use olive oil)
- 2 cloves garlic - minced
- 2 pounds asparagus
- 4 tsp. sesame seeds

Direction

- Stir soy sauce and sugar until dissolved.
- Heat oil in large skillet over medium heat and add garlic. Cook for 15 seconds.
- Add asparagus and stir fry until crisp-tender.
- Add soy sauce mix and simmer - tossing to coat.
- Season with salt and pepper.
- Remove and sprinkle with sesame seeds.

328. Stir Fry Garlic Spinach With Anchovies Recipe

Serving: 2 | Prep: | Cook: 10mins | Ready in:

Ingredients

- 200g spinach leaves (stems removed)
- 2 tbsp chopped garlic
- 3 stalks spring onion, cut to 2-inch lengths
- 1/2 carrot, sliced
- 1/4 cup deep fried anchovies aka ikan billis
- 2 tbsp olive oil
- 1 tbsp light soy sauce
- 1 tsp sesame oil
- 1/2 tbsp chinese cooking oil

Direction

- Heat oil in wok and stir fry garlic till golden brown.
- Add spring onions, carrot, anchovies, light soy sauce, sesame oil & Chinese cooking oil. Stir fry for 3 minutes.
- Add the spinach and stir fry briefly. Spinach cooks quickly so off the fire as soon as the leaves have softened/wilted.
- Garnish with fried shallots and served.

329. Stir Fryed Cabbage With Italian Sausage Recipe

Serving: 6 | Prep: | Cook: 75mins | Ready in:

Ingredients

- 1 large cabbage head or 2 sm head of cabbage
- 4 carrots (add 1 more if using 2 sm head of cabbage)
- 3 celery stalk
- 1 pkg mild Italian sausage or hot if you like the hot italian sausage
- 1 T of Minced garlic (add a little more if using 2 heads)
- 1 T onion flakes or small onion (add a little more if 2 heads)
- soy sauce
- Sprinkle of seasoning salt
- Optional: 1/2 cup of red pepper chopped up

Direction

- Wash celery and chop them up.
- Wash carrots, peel and chop.
- If adding peppers, chop them now also.
- Turn the Wok on to about 300.
- Take the Italian Sausage and peel off the skin and break sausage into small pieces. Do this to all of the sausage. But make sure you are stirring them as you as skinning and breaking the sausage so it will not burn. After sausage has brown.
- Add the carrots, celery and peppers. While they are slow cooking, cut the cabbage up. Cut out the core at the top of cabbage and throw away. After cabbage is cut up, add to wok. All the remaining ingredients - onion flakes or small cut up onion, garlic, sprinkle of seasoning salt, soy sauce sprinkle about 8 drops. Add more if it looks like you need to add more.
- Turn wok up to 325 or 350.
- Cover and let it cook.
- Keep an eye on the cabbage and keep stirred until steam builds up on the cover of lid. (Do not add any water. You will take away all of your flavoring which the Italian sausage is going to give your cabbage).
- When steam has built up on lid, you can let it cook and occasionally come and stir cabbage to make sure it does not burn. When cabbage is nice and soft by taste testing, it is done. The time limit is an estimate. I do not like overcooked cabbage. So cook according to your taste buds and how you like it.

330. Stir Fry Chive Recipe

Serving: 4 | Prep: | Cook: 10mins | Ready in:

Ingredients

- 1 teaspoon sugar
- 1 clove garlic, chopped
- 1/2 teaspoon of black pepper
- 1 1/2 tablespoons fish sauce
- 1 1/2 tablespoons of oyster sauce
- 1 tablespoon of thick soy sauce *NOTE* only add if pork or beef are use
- 3/4 lb Chinese chive , Cut into 1 1/2 inch long

Direction

- Heat a wok or a pan on high heat. Add a tablespoon of oil and chopped garlic and stir. When the garlic starts to brown, stir in the meat, if using. Cook until meat are done. Add the chive flowers and stir to cook them. Add fish sauce, thick soy sauce, black pepper and sugar. The chive shouldn't take long to cook. You want it just right, but not overcook.
- IF YOU LIKE IT HOT, you may use dried red pepper (hole).

331. Stir Fry Broccoli Florets With Garlic And Roasted Red Peppers Recipe

Serving: 6 | Prep: | Cook: 2mins | Ready in:

Ingredients

- 4 cups of fresh broccoli florets quickly blanched (frozen are ok but it's not the same)
- 2 cloves garlic diced
- lemon pepper or salt to taste
- fresh ground black pepper to taste
- 3 tbl extra virgin olive oil
- 1/2 roasted red pepper julienned (if using jarred roasted red pepper take 1 tbl of the olive oil for the recipe

Direction

- Heat oil in a skillet till just about smoking
- Add broccoli and cook 30 seconds stirring
- Add red pepper cook 30 seconds stirring
- Add minced garlic (and red pepper juice if using jarred roasted red pepper)
- Cook 1 minute stirring so things don't burn (don't forget to stir!)
- Add salt or lemon pepper and fresh ground black pepper to taste
- Remove from heat when florets are consistency you want (they should be somewhat crunchy)
- That's it!

332. Stir Fried Tofu In Black Bean Sauce Recipe

Serving: 2 | Prep: | Cook: 15mins | Ready in:

Ingredients

- 2 gloved crushed
- 3 tbsp. oil
- 2 tbsp blck bean sauce
- 1 tbsp of sugar
- pinch of salt (be careful on salt, black bean sauce usual come saltly)
- 1 cup of firm tofu diced medium size
- 5 green onion long sliced
- half of onion medium size sliced
- 2 tbsp of oyster sauce

Direction

- In a large skillet, add oil garlic and black bean sauce, cook for about 3-5 minutes on low heat.
- Add onion, oyster sauce and stir for another 2 minutes or until soft.
- Add tofu and green onion, cook for another 5-6 minutes. Stir occasionally.
- Best serve with Jasmine rice....ENJOY!

333. Stir Fried Bok Choy Recipe

Serving: 4 | Prep: | Cook: 10mins | Ready in:

Ingredients

- 1 lb bok choy (washed and cut into individual stalks)
- 1 Tbs. peanut oil (or vegetable oil)
- 1 small onion (or shallot) minced
- 2 garlic cloves, minced (more if you like)
- 2 jalapeno chilies, minced, or 2 tsp. dried red pepper flakes (optional)
- 1 Tbs. grated fresh ginger
- 3/4 cup roasted cashews (or peanuts)
- 3 Tbs. hoisin sauce (optional)
- 2 tsp. Asian dark sesame oil
- Soya Sauce to taste

Direction

- Cut the stems off the bok choy (white part only).
- Separate the bok choy branches and cut away.
- Wash the stems and leaves and dry them.

- Heat the oil in a wide skillet or wok over medium heat and stir in the onion, garlic, and chilies or pepper flakes.
- Stir for 5 minutes or until the onion starts to turn translucent.
- Stir in the ginger and the cashews, turn the heat up to high, and add the bok choy stems.
- Stir or toss over high heat for 5 minutes.
- Stir in the hoisin sauce (optional), sesame oil, and soy sauce and cook for 1 minute more.
- Note: If the bok choy is swimming around in a lot of liquid this sometimes happens if your stove isn't hot enough to quickly boil down the liquids to a glaze- take the bok choy out of the pan with a slotted spoon and boil down the liquids in the pan until there are only about 2 Tbsp. of thick glaze remaining. Put the bok choy back in the pan, stir for a minute to coat it, serve immediately. Goes well with plain white rice.

334. Stir Fried Broccoli Raab Recipe Broccoli Rapa Strascinati Recipe

Serving: 6 | Prep: | Cook: 20mins | Ready in:

Ingredients

- Ingredients:
- 2 1/4 pounds cleaned broccoli raab (wash well, trim roots, and coarsely chop leaves)
- 1/2 cup olive oil
- 2 cloves garlic, crushed
- salt
- hot pepper, if you like it
- 2 anchovies, boned and minced (optional)

Direction

- Preparation:
- Drain the broccoli well and cook them until half done in lightly salted boiling water (3-5 minutes from when the water resumes boiling after you add them to the pot).
- Drain them well, and squeeze them to force out the bitter juices.
- Sauté the garlic in the oil, and when it is golden, add the broccoli. Cook over a brisk flame, stirring constantly, for about 10 minutes. Season with the hot pepper, if you are using it, half way through the cooking, and the anchovies, if you are using them, at the end.
- Before serving check seasoning.

335. Stir Fried Cabbage Recipe

Serving: 4 | Prep: | Cook: 15mins | Ready in:

Ingredients

- 1 tablespoon vegetable oil
- 2 cloves garlic, minced
- 3 cups sliced green cabbage (1/2 small head)
- 3 cups sliced red cabbage (1/2 small head)
- 2 small carrots, sliced (about 1 cup)
- 1 medium yellow onion, sliced (about 1 cup)
- 2 medium red or yellow bell peppers, julienned (about 2 cups)
- 1/4 cup reduced-sodium soy sauce
- 2 teaspoons ground ginger
- 1/4 cup water
- 2 tablespoons cornstarch

Direction

- In a wok or large nonstick skillet, heat oil over medium heat.
- Add garlic and cook, stirring constantly, for I minute.
- Stir in green cabbage, red cabbage, carrots, onion, bell peppers, soy sauce, and ginger. Cover and cook, stirring occasionally, until vegetables are crisp-tender, about 10 minutes.
- In a small bowl, combine water and cornstarch. Mix well. Add cornstarch mixture to wok, stirring until sauce thickens, about I minute. Serve immediately.

- VARIATION
- Use leftover cooked chicken to make a tasty main dish. Add I cup chicken to the wok in Step 3. Proceed as recipe directs.

336. Stir Fried Eggplant Recipe

Serving: 2 | Prep: | Cook: 10mins | Ready in:

Ingredients

- 6 cloves garlic, minced
- 1-3 red chillies (including seeds), depending on how spicy you like it
- 1 Chinese (large, with dark purple skin) eggplant, or 2 (thinner, with light purple skin) Japanese eggplants
- 1/4 cup water
- 2-3 Tbsp. oil
- roughly 1/2 cup (or more) fresh basil
- SAUCE:
- 1 Tbsp. fish sauce
- 2 Tbsp. soy sauce
- 2 Tbsp. oyster sauce (or vegetarian oyster sauce)
- 1 tsp. brown sugar
- 1 tsp. cornstarch mixed with 2 Tbsp. water (mix until cornstarch is dissolved)
- 1 tablespoon of sasemi seed (optional)

Direction

- Mix cornstarch and water in a separate cup or bowl. Set both aside.
- Chop the eggplant up into bite-size pieces (be sure to leave the peel on - this is where most of the nutrients are).
- In a large frying pan or wok, over medium-high heat. Add the garlic, chili, and eggplant. Stir-fry for 5 minutes. When the wok or frying pan becomes dry, add a little of the water (a few Tbsp. at a time).
- Add all sauces and continue stir-frying for 5 more minutes, or until the eggplant is soft.
- Add the cornstarch/water mixture. Stir well so that the sauce thickens uniformly.
- In a serving platter, sprinkle basil leaves and sesame seed over top. Serve over rice.

337. Stir Fried Rice And Dal Recipe

Serving: 8 | Prep: | Cook: 40mins | Ready in:

Ingredients

- 4 cups cooked and cooled basmati rice
- 1/2 cup chana dal(split chickpeas), rinsed well
- 4 cups water
- 1/2 tsp turmeric
- 2-3 thin slices fresh ginger
- 1/4 cup vegetable oil
- 2 cups thinly sliced onions
- 1/4 tsp each fenugreek, cumin seeds, black mustard seeds and fennel seeds
- 1 tsp minced garlic
- 1 cup minced onion
- 1 tsp red chili flakes
- 1/4 tsp garam masala
- 1/4 tsp turmeric
- salt to taste
- 1/4 cup fresh chopped dill or cilantro(cilantro is traditional, but dill is very nice too)

Direction

- Place dal, water, 1/2 tsp turmeric and fresh ginger in a pot and bring to a boil. Reduce heat and simmer until tender, about 25 minutes. Set aside.
- While dal is simmering, heat vegetable oil in a large wok over medium-high heat. Sauté onion slices, stirring frequently 15-20 minutes until caramelized and brown. Remove onions with a slotted spoon, pausing over wok to allow excess oil to drip back into wok, drain onions in a paper towel lined bowl.
- Return wok to heat and add seeded spice mixture, stir-fry until mustard seeds pop.

Lower heat to medium-low and add minced onion, garlic and chili flakes. Stir-fry until onions are very soft, about 8 minutes. Add remaining spices and stir to mix. Add rice, return heat to medium-high and stir-fry to coat with spice mixture. Add the dal and any remaining liquid in the pot to the rice in the wok. Stir-fry all of this, stirring well until dal cooking liquid is absorbed by the rice. Add the chopped fresh dill or cilantro and season to taste with salt. Add the caramelized onions and stir in. Serve immediately with lime wedges.

338. Stir Fry Bean Spout Recipe

Serving: 2 | Prep: | Cook: 20mins | Ready in:

Ingredients

- 1 cup green onion, long 1/2 inch sliced
- 2 cup bean sprouts
- 3 garlic cloves, minced
- 1 tsp. sugar
- 1 tsp. cornstarch
- 3/4 cup water
- 2 tsp. fish sauce
- 1/2 cups of diced tofu (optional)
- 2 tsp. oyster sauce
- pinch of black pepper
- 1/2 cups of cooked pork blood (optional)
- This dish also good with crispy pork...but optional
- *(check out stir-fry sauce for this dish)

Direction

- Heat oil in a frying pan and add the garlic and stir fry about 2 minutes. Add tofu and remaining vegetables and cook and stir for several minutes.
- When the vegetables are half way done, add sugar, black pepper and fish sauce, mix well

- Add cornstarch into the water. When the vegetables are crisp-tender, make a space in the center and add the sauce. Allow to bubble until it begins to thicken and then quickly stir to coat the vegetables.
- Serve over rice.

339. Sugar Snap Peas And Salami Stir Fry Recipe

Serving: 4 | Prep: | Cook: 10mins | Ready in:

Ingredients

- 2 1/2 Tbs soy sauce
- 2 Tbs oyster sauce
- 2 tsp. cornstarch
- 1 tsp honey
- 2 bunches scallion, cut in 1" pieces
- 1/4c finely chooped fresh ginger (about 1 oz.)
- 2 cloves garlic, thin sliced
- 1 lb. sugar snap peas
- 6 oz. salami, cut in strips

Direction

- In med. bowl, whisk together soy sauce, oyster sauce, cornstarch and honey; whisk in 1 cup water.
- In large skillet, cook salami over med. heat till crisp, about 4 mins. Stir in scallions, ginger and garlic and cook 1 min more
- Whisk liquid ingredients again, add to skillet along with sugar snap peas. Increase heat to high and cook, stirring, till sauce thickens, 2 to 3 mins.

340. Summer Stir Fry Recipe

Serving: 1 | Prep: | Cook: 30mins | Ready in:

Ingredients

- 3/4 cup salted water
- 1/3 cup dry bulgur wheat
- black pepper
- 1 cup shredded savoy cabbage
- 2 cloves garlic, chopped
- 3-4 florets each broccoli and cauliflower, chopped
- 1 1-cm slice vidalia onion, diced
- 3 white mushrooms, sliced fairly thin
- Good pinch of red pepper flakes
- about 2 tsp garlic powder
- 1 plum tomato, chopped
- 1/4 cup or so low-sodium teriyaki sauce
- Few dashes worcestershire sauce

Direction

- Bring salted water to boil in a small pot. Add bulgur wheat and a few cracks of black pepper.
- Reduce heat and simmer 5 minutes. Cover pot, remove from heat and let stand 20 minutes.
- Meanwhile, steam cabbage, garlic, broccoli and cauliflower 6 minutes.
- Heat a large frying pan over high heat, spray with cooking spray.
- Add onion and sauté until golden.
- Add mushrooms, red pepper flakes and garlic powder and cook, stirring, until everything begins to brown and become very fragrant, about 2-3 minutes.
- Add tomato and cook another 1-2 minutes.
- Add steamed veggies and toss together.
- Pour in teriyaki sauce and Worcestershire, toss through to coat veggies.
- Add cooked bulgur and stir to combine everything and slightly reduce sauce, 3-4 minutes.
- Serve immediately.

341. Sweet And Sour Stir Fry Vegetables Recipe

Serving: 4 | Prep: | Cook: 15mins | Ready in:

Ingredients

- 3 tablespoons oil
- 3 cloves of garlic, crushed
- 1 onion, sliced
- 1/2 of broccoli, cut into bite sized pieces
- 1 medium carrot, peeled and cut into strips
- 8 small baby corn
- 2 tomatoes cut into 4 wedges
- 2 long green bean cut into 1/2 inch long
- 1 cucumber medium size sliced
- 1/2 cup pineapple cubes/chunks in natural juice (leave juice)
- 1 big red and green bell pepper, discard seed medium size sliced
- 1-2 tablespoons lime juice (rughly the juice of one plump lime)
- 3 level tablespoons sugar
- 2 tablespoon fish sauce
- 2 tablespoon oyster sauce
- 2 tablespoon soy sauce
- 3 tablespoons tomato ketchup
- 2-3 tablespoons remaining pineapple juice
- 1/2 cup of spring onion long sliced
- 1 tablespoon of cornstarch mix well in water for thickness

Direction

- In a frying wok, add garlic until golden, add the onion and stir-fry for 2 minutes.
- Add all the vegetables accept, pineapple and spring onion, stir for about 3-4 minutes.
- Add the tomato ketchup and continue to stir until the vegetables are cooked.
- Add the pineapple, spring onion and remaining sauce, stir to combine.
- Add cornstarch for thickness of sauce.
- When done, place on serving plate and it's ready to serve. Best with Jasmine rice.

342. TWISTED STIR FRY Recipe

Serving: 6 | Prep: | Cook: 12mins | Ready in:

Ingredients

- 4 stalks of cleaned asparagus
- 1/2 cut up cucumber
- 1 rib of red bell pepper
- 1/4 of a rib of yellow pepper (mostly for color)
- 1/2 rib of green bell pepper
- 1/2 chopped tomato
- pepper
- olive oil
- 1 table spoon of Italian dressing if desired
- 1/4 grated Jack cheese
- small amount of grated cheddar cheese
- 1/2 cup of thinly sliced pepperoni

Direction

- Prepare all veggies and pepperoni.
- Heat olive oil and add vegetables and pepperoni to hot oil.
- Cook as you would any regular stir fry dish.
- Add the cheese and heat until just barely melted.
- Serve hot.
- Pepper to taste (only if desired).

343. Teriyaki Vegtable Fried Rice Recipe

Serving: 4 | Prep: | Cook: 20mins | Ready in:

Ingredients

- 1.5-2 Cups fresh or frozen, diced/sliced/jullianed vegetables (suggestions: bell peppers, onion, mushrooms, carrots, peas, water chestnuts, bamboo shoots, broccoli, celery)
- 1/4 Cup teriyaki sauce
- 2 teaspoons Seasame Seed oil
- 2 Cups Cooked and cooled white rice
- 4 teaspoons soy sauce
- 1 package Morningstar Farms® Meal Starters™ Chik'n Strips (optinal, could probably also use real chicken or tofu)
- 1/4 Cup peanuts or cashews (optinal)
- chow mein noodles (optinal)

Direction

- Add vegetables to skillet or wok. Pour teriyaki over vegetables. Cook on medium heat until teriyaki is mostly gone stirring frequently. (If adding Chicken you can tear the strips to bite sized pieces and put a little soy sauce on them. Then microwave or heat the Chicken in a separate skillet. Add heated Chicken either to the vegetables before the rice, or at the same time as the peanuts.)
- Push vegetables to the side. Put Sesame Seed oil on open side of skillet. Add rice and pour soy sauce over rice. Stir just rice/soy sauce until heated and mixed completely.
- Sprinkle peanuts on top and mix everything together.
- Serve with chow Mein noodles and extra soy sauce if desired.

344. Tofu Cashew Stir Fry Recipe

Serving: 2 | Prep: | Cook: 12mins | Ready in:

Ingredients

- 2 T oil
- 1 large onion, finely chopped
- 3 cloves garlic, crushed
- 1 dash red chili sauce
- 1 tsp grated ginger
- 1 block firm organic tofu
- half a head of broccoli florets
- 1/3 c. cashews
- 4 T soy sauce
- 2 T toasted sesame oil for garnish

Direction

- Heat the oil in a frying pan or wok.
- Add the onion, garlic; stir for two minutes. Don't let the garlic burn.
- Add the tofu and broccoli (or substitute/add bok choy or any other greens you have on hand)
- Mix in the fresh ginger, chili sauce, and soy sauce.
- Heat ingredients well until the broccoli is tender-crisp.
- Throw in the cashews and stir until heated through, about one minute.
- Remove from heat and garnish with the sesame oil. Hint: sesame oil's flavor is best as a garnish for a dish - don't cook it.

345. Tofu Veggie And Almond Stir Fry Recipe

Serving: 24 | Prep: | Cook: 15mins | Ready in:

Ingredients

- 1/2 block of firm tofu (can substitute chicken) cubed
- 2 tbsp almonds
- 1 large onion (sliced)
- 1-2 carrots (sliced)
- frozen green beans
- frozen peas
- 2 cloves chopped garlic
- 1 tbsp chopped ginger
- 1 tbsp Chilli powder (suit to taste)
- 2 eggs
- soy sauce
- cooked rice

Direction

- Heat skillet to medium heat and thaw frozen green beans and peas for a couple minutes; take out into bowl.
- Add oil to pan; add fry cubed tofu until fried on all sides; take out into bowl.
- Add more oil if needed; fry carrots, 2 minutes.
- Add onions; once slightly golden, add slivered almonds.
- Add ginger.
- Add garlic.
- Add green beans and tofu.
- Add chili powder.
- Add 2 eggs and stir into mix.
- Add soy sauce to suit taste.

346. Tofu Veggie Stir Fry Recipe

Serving: 2 | Prep: | Cook: 15mins | Ready in:

Ingredients

- 4 or 5 small pieces of cauliflower
- 4 o5 small pieces of broccoli
- 5 or 6 baby carrots
- 1/5 package of firm tofu
- 1/2 tbsp.Ceasar salad dressing(optional)
- 1/2 tsp. butter or margarine

Direction

- Cut up your veggies to a reasonable size to fry them. Slice the carrots into small round slivers, slice the broccolis in half, etc.
- Cut about a fifth off of the end of your firm tofu. Wrap up the rest and refrigerate. Cut the tofu into small, bite-size cubes.
- Take a medium to large sized frying pan and turn your element on to 8, or between the maximum and medium.
- Put about half a teaspoon of butter on the pan. When the butter starts to sizzle and melt, slide it around so it covers the entire pan.
- Put the veggies and tofu into the pan. Make sure to spread them out a bit. Cover with a lid.
- Let them fry for about 3 or 4 minutes. When the underside of them is a darkish-brown, flip them around and cover again. Continue doing

this every few minutes until veggies/tofu are cooked to your desire.
- Turn off the element, scoop the veggies on a plate, and drizzle the Caesar dressing over the veggies. Mix them around to so most of them have some on them. Grab a fork and enjoy!

347. Toor Dal Fry Recipe

Serving: 3 | Prep: | Cook: 25mins | Ready in:

Ingredients

- 1 cup Toor Dal
- 3/4 tsp mustard seeds
- 1/4 tsp cumin seeds
- 1 sprig curry leaves
- 2 tbsp ghee
- 1 medium tomato (Diced)
- 1 small onion (Chop)
- A pinch of turmeric
- salt to taste
- A pinch of hing
- 2 red chilis
- coriander leaves

Direction

- Wash toor dal and Pressure cook dal for 12-15 mins and keep aside for cooling.
- Heat ghee in a pan on low flame, add mustard seeds and hing let it splutter.
- Add the cumin and curry leaves and leave that for a few seconds.
- Add the onion and chillies and fry till it onion is brown and then add the tomato pieces and fry that till tender.
- Add turmeric powder and fry for a few more seconds. When done, add the dal salt.
- Add a little water as required and leave it for some time on simmer. Garnish with coriander leaves.
- Serve with Hot Rice or Chapati

348. Turkish Style Fried Mussels Midye Tava Recipe

Serving: 5 | Prep: | Cook: 5mins | Ready in:

Ingredients

- Midye Tava - Fried mussels
- 5 Servings
- 1 1/2 cups salad oil
- 1 cup beer
- 1 cup trator sauce
- 1 egg lightly beaten
- 1/2 cup flour
- 20 mussels
- salt
- ½ tea spoon black pepper
- ½ tea spoon baking soda

Direction

- Open the 20mussels by inserting a knife along the flat side and running it along to the other side.
- Remove them from their shell.
- Wash and dry mussels, flour (stir flour with black pepper and baking soda) each one separately.
- Dip them first into beer, then into the beaten egg.
- Fry in hot oil until golden brown on all sides.
- Sprinkle with salt and serve immediately with a bowl of tarator sauce.

349. Tyler Florences Fried Green Tomatoes Recipe

Serving: 4 | Prep: | Cook: 10mins | Ready in:

Ingredients

- 1 cup cornmeal
- 1 cup all-purpose flour

- 1 Tbl garlic powder
- large pinch of cayenne
- 1 1/2 cup buttermilk
- kosher salt and course ground black pepper
- 4 large, unripe tomatoes, cut into 1/2-inch thick slices
- 1/4 cup vegetable oil
- 1 Tbl butter

Direction

- In a large bowl, combine the cornmeal, flour, garlic powder, and cayenne pepper. Pour the buttermilk into a separate bowl and season with salt and pepper. Dip the tomatoes in the buttermilk and ten dredge them in the cornmeal mixture, coating both sides well.
- Please a large skillet over medium heat and coat with oil. When the oil is hot, pan-fry the tomatoes until golden brown and crispy on both sides. Carefully remove the tomatoes and drain. Serve with hot pepper sauce.
- Personal note: These are delicious with sunny-side eggs and biscuits.

350. Ultimate Comfort Food Fried Potatoes With Eggs Recipe

Serving: 1 | Prep: | Cook: 15mins | Ready in:

Ingredients

- Basic math is 1 egg and 1 large or 2 medium potatoes for each generous serving
- coarse salt and freshly ground black pepper to taste
- fresh dill weed, chopped semi-coarsely
- cooking oil
- butter
- Several "gawkers" below mentioned onions. By all means, add some! I'd toss them in at the same time as the potatoes, so that they caramelize well. Yum yum.

Direction

- Peel and julienne potatoes. I slice them 4 times lengthwise, and then cut across to get a "French fry" cut.
- Beat the eggs and set aside
- Heat about 4 tbsp. cooking oil in a deep skillet. If you like crispier fries, use just oil, if you like them softer, add some butter to it.
- Toss the potatoes in the oil and fry, shaking or stirring occasionally for about 10 minutes.
- Add salt, pepper and dill weed
- Cook another 5 minutes or so until potatoes are almost done.
- Pour the eggs over the potatoes and stir well once
- Cover and cook for another couple of minutes until eggs are firm enough to eat. I like them slightly runny, but it's totally up to you.

351. Vegetable Fried Rice Recipe

Serving: 6 | Prep: | Cook: 15mins | Ready in:

Ingredients

- vegetable Fried rice
- 1-tbspn sesame oil
- 2-tspn bottled minced garlic
- 2-tspn fresh minced ginger
- 1-cup jarred red peppers, chopped
- 1 green bell pepper, chopped
- 1-onion chopped
- 1 small can sliced mushrooms, drained
- 1-cup baby carrots, sliced lengthwise three times each carrot
- 1 head of bok choy coarsely chopped
- 3=cups cooked brown rice, cooled
- 1 green onion, snipped tops and bottom

Direction

- Cook garlic and ginger in oil for 1 ½-minutes.

- Add mixed vegetables and bok choy and cook for 8 minutes.
- Stir occasionally.
- Add rice and soy sauce and cook and stir for about 5 minutes. Sprinkle with green onions and serve.

352. Vegetable Mushroom Fried Rice Recipe

Serving: 45 | Prep: | Cook: 30mins | Ready in:

Ingredients

- 2 cups brown rice (cooked – follow the package instruction)
- 1 medium carrot cut into cubes
- 1 cup chopped broccoli
- 1 cup chopped cauliflower
- 1 cup chopped beans
- 1 small red onion, chopped
- 1 can mushroom in oil
- 2 teaspoons olive or vegetable oil
- salt and pepper

Direction

- 1. Heat 1 inch water to boiling in skillet. Add carrots, broccoli, cauliflower and beans. Heat to boiling; reduce heat to medium. Cook until crisp-tender; drain.
- 2. Mixed Vegetables: Heat oil in skillet over medium heat. Cook onion in oil, stirring occasionally, until tender. Stir in brown rice, carrots, broccoli, cauliflower, beans and mushroom. Add salt and pepper to taste. Cook 1 minute, stirring occasionally. Remove mixture from heat; keep warm.
- 2. Mushroom: Heat mushroom in oil in skillet over medium heat. Add onion, stirring occasionally, until tender. Stir in brown rice, add salt and pepper to taste. Cook 1 minute, stirring occasionally. Remove mixture from heat; keep warm.
- Serve warm.

353. Vegetable Stir Fry Recipe

Serving: 4 | Prep: | Cook: 10mins | Ready in:

Ingredients

- 3 tablespoons chopped garlic
- 2 tablespoons olive oil
- 5 cups raw vegetables, cut into strips or small pieces - I use a mixture for color and flavour
- 1/2 cup soy sauce
- 1 tablespoon balsamic vinegar
- 2 tablespoons honey
- 2 teaspoons sesame oil
- 2 tablespoons cornstarch
- cooked rice or soba noodles

Direction

- In a large non-stick frying pan or wok, heat olive oil and add garlic.
- Cook 2-3 minutes then add raw vegetables.
- Stir fry vegetables until tender-crisp.
- Add soy sauce, vinegar and honey, stirring to coat vegetables.
- Drizzle sesame oil over vegetables and stir just before the end of cooking.
- Mix cornstarch with a little water and stir in to thicken sauce to cling to vegetables.
- Serve over hot rice or noodles.

354. Vegetables Stir Fry Vegetarian Recipe

Serving: 4 | Prep: | Cook: 5mins | Ready in:

Ingredients

- 1/4 cup honey
- 1/4 cup prepared stir fry sauce

- 1/4 tsp. crushed red pepper flakes (1/4 to 1/2 tsp.)
- 4 tsps. peanut oil or vegetable oil
- 2 cups small broccoli florets
- 2 cups small mushrooms
- 1 small onion, cut into wedges and separated into 1-inch strips
- 1 medium carrot, cut diagonally into 1/3 inch slices

Direction

- Combine honey, stir-fry sauce and pepper flakes in small bowl; set aside.
- In wok or large skillet, heat oil over medium-high heat.
- Add vegetables and toss while cooking, about 2-3 minutes.
- Add honey sauce, stir until all vegetables are glazed and sauce is bubbly hot, about 1 minute.
- Serve as a vegetable side dish or over steamed rice or noodles for a main dish.

355. Vegetables Stir Fry Recipe

Serving: 4 | Prep: | Cook: 20mins | Ready in:

Ingredients

- 1 carrots, cut into julienne strips
- 1/2 cup shiitake mushrooms, stems discarded, thinly sliced
- 2 bundle brocolli
- 2 large garlic cloves, minced
- 1/2 onion, sliced
- 3 tablespoons vegetable broth
- 2 tablespoons chinese rice wine
- 1 teaspoon sugar
- 1 teaspoon cornstarch
- 1 teaspoon salt
- 2 tablespoons vegetable oil
- 1/4 teaspoon sesame oil

Direction

- In a small bowl stir together broth, rice wine, sugar, cornstarch, and salt until smooth. Set aside.
- Heat a wok over high heat until hot. Add vegetable and sesame oil and heat until it just begins to smoke.
- Stir-fry carrots 3 minutes. Add mushrooms, cabbage, garlic, and ginger and stir-fry 2 minutes, or until carrots are crisp-tender.
- Add broth mixture to vegetables.
- Stir-fry vegetables an additional minute to coat. Add scallions and stir to combine. Serve immediately.

356. Vegetarian Fried Rice Recipe

Serving: 4 | Prep: | Cook: 15mins | Ready in:

Ingredients

- 5 eggs, beaten
- 1 T cooking oil
- oil as needed
- 1 medium onion, chopped
- 1 clove garlic, minced
- 2 stalks celery, thinly bias-sliced
- 4 oz fresh mushrooms, sliced
- 1 medium green sweet pepper, chopped
- 4 c cold cooked rice
- 1 - 8 oz can bamboo shoots, drained (optional)
- 2 medium carrots, shredded
- 3/4 c frozen peas, thawed
- 3 T soy sauce or more to taste
- 3 green onions, sliced

Direction

- The stir-fry secret is a hot pan.
- Gather all ingredients, utensils and serving bowl before you start, this is a quick process.
- Make sure pan is hot before each stir-fry.
- Add oil to pan after each stir-fry.

- Mix veggies after each addition to serving bowl.
- In a small bowl break eggs and add 1 tablespoon water, set aside.
- Put 1 tablespoon cooking oil into a wok or heavy skillet.
- Preheat over high heat.
- Stir-fry chopped onion and garlic in hot oil about 2 minutes or until, onion is wilted; remove to serving bowl.
- Add egg mixture to wok and scramble until set; remove eggs from the wok to serving bowl. Chop up large pieces of egg.
- Stir-fry celery in hot oil for 1 minute; remove to serving bowl.
- Add mushrooms and sweet pepper to wok; stir-fry for 1 to 2 minutes more or until vegetables are crisp-tender. You may want to rinse your pan, dry and add more before adding the rice.
- Add cooked rice, bamboo shoots, carrots, and peas to wok.
- Cook and stir until heated.
- Make a well in center of pan and put 3 tablespoons soy sauce in the center.
- When the soy sauce foams, start blending in the rice mixture to pick up the flavor (this prevents the rice from being wet with the sauce; repeat if more sauce if needed).
- Add to serving bowl and add green onions and mix well.
- Serve immediately.
- Garnish with lemon slices and tomatoes, if desired.

357. Vegetarian Rice Vermicelly Stir Fry Recipe

Serving: 2 | Prep: | Cook: 15mins | Ready in:

Ingredients

- 400 grams of soaked rice vermicelly
- 100 grams of firm toufu
- 100 grams of shitake mushrooms
- 50 grams of carrot, juliened
- 1 small onion or spring onion, finely sliced
- 1 bell pepper, finely sliced
- salt and pepper to taste
- 1 tsp minced garlic
- 1 tsp minced ginger (optional)
- 1 tbs of soy sauce
- 2 tbs of vegetarian "oyster" sauce
- 1/2 tsp of sugar
- 2 tbs of olive oil mixed with 1 tsp of sesame oil
- 1/2 cup of water or vegetable broth

Direction

- Cut tofu into small strips, pan seared until golden brown, do the same with the shitake mushrooms. Tofu and mushrooms will be the "meat" in this recipe
- In medium low heat sauté onion with oil until fragrant
- Add bell pepper, and carrots until soft
- Add mushrooms, vermicelli, turn the fire into medium high at this moment
- Add tofu, add the rest of the ingredients, stir until everything is well mixed, serve hot

358. Veggie Fried Rice Recipe

Serving: 2 | Prep: | Cook: 10mins | Ready in:

Ingredients

- 2 tbps peanut oil or any oil you have on hand
- green beans cut to bite sized pieces
- sliced mushrooms
- 3 cloves of garlic finely chopped
- 1 onion finely chopped
- broccoli cut to bite sized pieces
- 2 eggs
- 2 cups of pre-cooked rice (brown or white) (room temp, crumble w/ fork, set aside)
- 1/4 cup oyster sauce or soy sauce
- salt and pepper to taste
- 1 tsp sriracha hot sauce (optional)

Direction

- In a hot skillet, fry two eggs over medium or to your liking then set aside.
- Add oil to skillet and fry onions and garlic till onions are transparent
- Then add green beans, mushrooms, broccoli or other vegetables to the oil and stir fry till Broccoli is a bit tender.
- Add the rice first and mix thoroughly with veggies then add oyster sauce and stir till rice is coated well and browned.
- Continue to stir fry on high and add salt, pepper and hot sauce to taste.
- Serve immediately with egg on top
- Enjoy!

359. Veggie Sun Fry Recipe

Serving: 24 | Prep: | Cook: 1mins | Ready in:

Ingredients

- One cup mung bean sprouts
- One quarter cup finely chopped leek or other onion
- One tomato sliced in thin slices
- One red or any color bell pepper cubed
- One bunch bok choy or lettuce cut into thin strips
- One eggplant thinly sliced and dipped in olive oil, both sides
- Two portobello mushrooms thinly sliced and dipped in olive oil

Direction

- Put each veggie out on a plate in the sun, under plastic wrap. You can optionally add a little olive oil and/or water to help all the veggies sun fry. Let sit for half an hour to an hour.
- Mix together in a bowl and add a diced avocado.
- Season with paprika or other spices, olive oil or lemon, and Celtic sea salt if desired
- Serves 2 hungry raw vegans

360. Chinese Deep Fried Green Beans Recipe

Serving: 2 | Prep: | Cook: 10mins | Ready in:

Ingredients

- 1/2 lb green beans, topped, tailed, cut into 2" sections
- 3 cups peanut oil
- 2 cloves garlic, finely chopped
- hefty pinch of sugar
- 1/2 - 1 tsp good quality soy sauce

Direction

- Rinse and drain the green beans
- Heat the oil until very hot and add all the beans
- Fry, turning often until they are soft and browned a bit (about 5 - 7 minutes)
- Drain the beans well then toss with the garlic, sugar, and soy
- Serve it forth

361. Fried Pies Recipe

Serving: 0 | Prep: | Cook: 15mins | Ready in:

Ingredients

- Your favorite biscuit recipe.(sweetend)
- fruit filling (any) or cooked meat
- lard amount varies
- 1 egg
- 1 tbls melted butter
- !/4 cup brown sugar

Direction

- Roll out dough to double hand size. In middle of dough place filling (any).Fold over and seal edge. Brush butter and egg mixture along edge to seal. Lay each side down in plate of sugar and place in hot grease. Brown each side remove and let set. Serve or wrap each pie to go.

362. Maori Fried Bread Recipe

Serving: 1 | Prep: | Cook: 30mins | Ready in:

Ingredients

- self rasing flour salt warm water cooking oil

Direction

- We will number these for you! Just hit 'enter' after every step.

363. Pan Fried Green Beans Recipe

Serving: 4 | Prep: | Cook: 10mins | Ready in:

Ingredients

- 1 pound fresh greenbeans
- 3tablespoons light soy sauce
- 1 tablespoon balsamic vinegar
- 1 teaspoon white sugar
- 2 tablespoons sesame oil
- 2 teaspoons minced garlic

Direction

- Place beans in pot and bring to boil
- Cover and cook 5 minutes
- In small bowl mix soy sauce, vinegar, and sugar
- Heat oil in skillet
- Add garlic and cook until brown
- Add beans and stir to coat with the oil and garlic
- Stir in soy sauce mixture and simmer for about 2-3 minutes uncovered to reduce the sauce
- Transfer to serving dish
- ENJOY!!!

364. Sweet Fried Chicken Recipe

Serving: 4 | Prep: | Cook: 15mins | Ready in:

Ingredients

- boneless chicken - 1/2 kg (cut into 1 inch pieces)
- corn flour - 3 tbsp
- turmeric powder - 1 tsp
- red chilly powder - 3 tsp
- ginger garlic paste - 1 1/2 tsp
- soya sauce - 1 1/2 tsp
- egg - 1
- olive oil (for frying)
- salt (to taste)
- honey - 1 tbsp
- celery (for garnishing)
- spring onion (for garnishing)
- roasted & chopped cashew nuts (optional)

Direction

- Marinate chicken pieces with corn flour, turmeric powder, red chili powder, ginger garlic paste, soya sauce, egg and salt.
- Refrigerate it for 3-4 hours.
- Deep fry in olive oil.
- Strain.
- Pour some honey over the hot fried chicken.
- Garnish with chopped celery, spring onion and cashew nuts.
- Serve hot

365. Vegetarian Fried Rice Recipe

Serving: 6 | Prep: | Cook: 15mins | Ready in:

Ingredients

- 6 tablespoons vegetable oil
- 2 eggs
- 1 teaspoon salt
- 1 onion, chopped
- 3 cups vegetarian chicken chunks
- 4 cups cold, cooked rice
- 1/2 cup cooked peas
- 1/4 cup canned diced bamboo shoots (optional)
- 2 tablespoons soy sauce

Direction

- Heat two tablespoons cooking oil. Beat eggs with 1/2 teaspoon salt and scramble in oil until firm, breaking into small pieces. Remove and reserve.
- Heat remaining oil. Add chicken chunks and remaining salt. Cook until browned. Break up lumps of cold cooked rice and add to the frying pan. Stir until rice is heated and the grains of rice are separated.
- Add all the rest of the ingredients except soy sauce. Stir until thoroughly heated and mixed. Sprinkle soy sauce over rice and mix evenly through. Cook until the rice is just beginning to brown, then remove.

Index

A

Ale 32

Almond 6,7,112,146

Anchovies 7,138

Apple 3,4,5,6,10,31,57,69,86,87,118

Artichoke 5,87,88

Asparagus 4,5,6,7,58,61,73,88,108,114,115,130,135,136,138

Avocado 3,6,17,103

B

Bacon 3,4,5,6,18,41,59,60,65,70,87,91,117

Banana 4,5,6,46,89,99,112

Basil 7,135

Beans 4,5,6,7,59,64,96,112,137,152,153

Beef 84

Beer 4,61

Bran 50

Bread 3,6,7,20,107,153

Broccoli 4,7,58,63,128,136,140,141,152

Burger 3,32

Butter 4,5,6,7,41,45,63,64,74,99,106,108,115,132

C

Cabbage 5,6,7,72,82,90,91,108,125,131,136,139,141

Carrot 3,4,7,18,34,47,130,137

Cashew 7,145

Catfish 5,91

Cauliflower 3,4,5,35,63,66,83,91

Cheddar 4,6,60,75,113,117

Cheese 3,4,5,18,21,23,32,34,62,70,75,114

Chicken 3,4,5,6,7,11,12,36,66,69,74,82,110,115,116,145,153

Chickpea 6,117,126

Chilli 32,133,146

Chipotle 3,17,22

Chips 3,4,15,19,32,50

Chocolate 5,92

Cider 6,113,114

Coconut 5,7,68,137

Coleslaw 113

Coriander 3,17

Cottage cheese 17

Crab 6,97

Cream 5,6,7,70,116,132

Crumble 104

Cucumber 6,106

Cumin 3,4,5,7,26,39,72,137

Curd 113

D

Dal 5,7,72,73,142,147

Dijon mustard 23,113

Dill 5,94

E

Egg 3,4,5,6,7,17,23,24,32,35,62,71,74,84,110,115,130,134,142,148

F

Fat 5,15,17,30,74,83,108,117

Fish 5,91,95,96

Flour 6,17,40,74,115,126

French beans 17

French bread 23,85,102,103

G

Garlic

3,4,5,6,7,18,28,29,36,39,45,46,54,74,91,97,108,109,135,138,140

Gin 3,6,7,12,109,135

Grapes 46

Gravy 6,113,114,116

H

Ham 3,23

Hoisin sauce 102

Honey 9

Horseradish 5,9,89

J

Jam 15

Jus 19,76,153

K

Ketchup 3,4,5,26,46,72

L

Lard 84

Lemon 3,6,19,98,117

Lime 7,11,12,137

M

Mayonnaise 5,91

Milk 115

Mince 55,139

Molasses 14

Mushroom 4,6,7,58,121,149

Mussels 7,147

Mustard 9,113

N

Noodles 4,6,7,57,125,128,131

Nut 15,25,26,65

O

Oil 6,31,39,54,74,103,104,107,113,123

Okra 5,6,7,65,73,75,99,105,123,132

Olive 31,39,113

Onion 3,4,5,6,7,22,25,26,34,37,38,57,61,67,83,86,91,102,112,116,120,123,127,136

Oyster 5,76

P

Parmesan 3,4,20,23,27,28,36,37,40,41,49,61,122,129

Parsley 39,54

Peas 7,143

Peel 9,13,14,15,19,20,21,28,32,42,45,47,48,50,51,62,70,71,81,82,83,84,89,100,103,111,112,115,118,148

Pepper 4,5,6,7,17,38,40,66,70,74,79,89,109,136,140,145

Pickle 5,6,94,100,102

Pie 7,115,152

Pizza 4,41

Plain flour 74

Plantain 6,100

Polenta 7,129

Pork 7,113,131

Port 5,7,80,127

Potato 3,4,5,6,7,9,10,11,13,14,15,16,19,20,24,26,30,31,32,35,37,39,42,43,44,45,46,47,49,50,51,53,55,57,62,66,67,69,83,85,100,101,102,104,108,111,113,122,123,130,133,148

Pumpkin 3,15

R

Red onion 16

Rice 4,5,6,7,58,60,66,68,77,79,109,119,121,124,127,137,142,145,147,148,149,150,151,154

Rosemary 3,4,7,24,43,129

Rum 4,43

S

Sage 6,114,115

Salad 6,101,114

Salami 7,143

Salt 5,17,39,40,45,70,72,74,81,85,105,108,114,122,126

Sausage 5,7,66,94,139

Savory 3,7,13,129

Seasoning 24,36,54,56,123

Seeds 3,7,17,136

Shin 120

Soup 115

Spinach 5,6,7,78,103,134,138

Squash 6,105,115

Squid 6,103

Steak 3,4,6,17,29,44,113

Sugar 7,15,30,70,114,143

T

Tabasco 46

Taco 3,5,6,21,56,96,107

Taro 19

Teriyaki 6,7,110,145

Tofu 5,6,7,77,92,104,126,130,140,145,146,151

Tomato 3,5,6,7,26,36,73,97,98,118,123,134,147

Truffle 4,55

Turnip 4,47

V

Vegan 3,12

Vegetables 3,4,5,7,10,30,40,47,57,76,144,149,150

Vegetarian 5,7,82,149,150,151,154

W

Waxy potato 120

Wine 5,80,91

Worcestershire sauce 90

Y

Yam 3,4,10,16,20,49

Yoghurt 6,126

Conclusion

Thank you again for downloading this book!

I hope you enjoyed reading about my book!

If you enjoyed this book, please take the time to share your thoughts and post a review on Amazon. It'd be greatly appreciated!

Write me an honest review about the book – I truly value your opinion and thoughts and I will incorporate them into my next book, which is already underway.

Thank you!

If you have any questions, **feel free to contact at:** _author@fetarecipes.com_

Mary Correa

fetarecipes.com

Made in the USA
Columbia, SC
01 December 2023